HEMINGWAY, STYLE, AN[illegible] OF EMOTION

In *Hemingway, Style, and the Art of Emotion*, David Wyatt shows that the work of Ernest Hemingway is marked more by vulnerability and deep feeling than by the stoic composure and ironic remove for which it is widely known. This major reassessment of the shape of Hemingway's career recovers the soul of the author's work, revealing him as an experimenting writer rather than a static icon. Wyatt claims that Hemingway's famous early style does not embrace emotional reticence but works instead to measure the cost of keeping thoughts and feelings under the surface. By the early 1930s, Hemingway also turned away from the art of "the omitted" and began to develop a vision and style more accommodating of the awkwardnesses and embarrassments of everyday life. Relying on a thorough knowledge of the vast archive Hemingway left behind at his death, this book reveals Hemingway as a complex and ever-evolving figure.

David Wyatt is Professor of English at the University of Maryland, College Park, where he has been named a Distinguished Scholar-Teacher. His books include *The Fall into Eden: Landscape and Imagination in California* (Cambridge University Press, 1986), *Out of the Sixties: Storytelling and the Vietnam Generation* (Cambridge University Press, 1993), *Secret Histories: Reading Twentieth-Century American Literature*, and *When America Turned: Reckoning with 1968*. Wyatt's essays have appeared in *American Literature*, *The Kenyon Review*, *The Hopkins Review*, and *South Atlantic Quarterly*.

HEMINGWAY, STYLE, AND THE ART OF EMOTION

DAVID WYATT

The University of Maryland, College Park

CAMBRIDGE
UNIVERSITY PRESS

CAMBRIDGE
UNIVERSITY PRESS

University Printing House, Cambridge CB2 8BS, United Kingdom

One Liberty Plaza, 20th Floor, New York, NY 10006, USA

477 Williamstown Road, Port Melbourne, VIC 3207, Australia

4843/24, 2nd Floor, Ansari Road, Daryaganj, Delhi - 110002, India

79 Anson Road, #06-04/06, Singapore 079906

Cambridge University Press is part of the University of Cambridge.

It furthers the University's mission by disseminating knowledge in the pursuit of education, learning and research at the highest international levels of excellence.

www.cambridge.org
Information on this title: www.cambridge.org/9781107525290

First published 2015
First paperback edition 2017

A catalogue record for this publication is available from the British Library

Library of Congress Cataloging in Publication data
Wyatt, David, 1948–
Hemingway, style, and the art of emotion / David Wyatt.
pages cm
ISBN 978-1-107-10982-7 (hardback)
Includes bibliographical references and index.
1. Hemingway, Ernest, 1899–1961 – Criticism and interpretation. 2. Hemingway, Ernest, 1899–1961 – Literary style. 3. Emotions in literature. I. Title.
PS3515.E37Z97 2015
813′.52–dc23 2015011159

ISBN 978-1-107-10982-7 Hardback
ISBN 978-1-107-52529-0 Paperback

For Howard and Jane

A book is the product of a different *self* than the self we manifest in our habits, in our social life, in our vices. If we would try to understand that particular self, it is by searching deep within us and trying to reconstruct it there, that we may arrive at it. Nothing can exempt us from this effort of the heart.

–Marcel Proust, *By way of Sainte-Beuve*

Contents

Acknowledgments *page* ix

Introduction: Hemingway Unbound 1

PART I ANXIETY

1 At the Beginning: "Indian Camp" 13

2 A Second Will: *In Our Time* and *in our time* 27

3 The End of Pleasure: *The Sun Also Rises* 47

4 False Surmise: *A Farewell to Arms* 63

5 Making a Wound: *A Farewell to Arms* and "Now I Lay Me" 81

PART II EMBARRASSMENT

6 Awkwardness and Appreciation: *Death in the Afternoon* 99

7 Hunting Shame: *Green Hills of Africa* 117

8 Empathy and Candor: "The Short Happy Life of Francis Macomber" 133

PART III FORGIVENESS

9 Taking Time: *For Whom the Bell Tolls* 147

10 Forgiveness: *For Whom the Bell Tolls* 162

11 Befriending: *The Old Man and the Sea* 179

PART IV REMORSE

12 Replacement and Remorse: *The Garden of Eden* and *A Moveable Feast* 197

13 How to End It: *The Garden of Eden* and *A Moveable Feast* 212

Scattered Papers 233
Notes 235
Works Cited 259
Index 267

Acknowledgments

I am happy to dedicate this book to Howard Norman and Jane Shore, who provide me, each week during the school year, with a clean, well-lighted place in which to stay.

I am indebted to John Irwin, who published my first essay on Hemingway almost forty years ago and who has remained a generous supporter of my work.

Two old friends helped with the difficulties of setting out: Donald Sheehy smoothed out some bumps in the Introduction, and Leslie Gossage gave Chapters 1 and 2 the benefit of her jeweler's eye. My sister Meleesa Wyatt also went over the early chapters with her usual tact and care.

Robert Levine helped me settle on a publisher, and, at Cambridge I am indebted to Ray Ryan and his no-nonsense oversight, Caitlin Gallagher and Elizabeth Shand for assisting with production, and Joann Woy for her superb copyediting.

Susan Beegel, while shepherding Chapter 6 through publication in *The Hemingway Review*, revised it in exemplary fashion. Permission to reprint "Awkwardness and Appreciation" is here gratefully acknowledged.

At the Kennedy Library, Susan Wrynn, Stacey Chandler, and Maryrose Grossman offered me their hospitality and assistance.

I have my students at the University of Maryland to thank for continuing to open their hearts to a writer against whom so many hearts have been preemptively closed.

Finally, I look forward to returning with my wife Ann to our beloved Friuli and to slipping across the border to Kobarid for another plate of that lovely seafood risotto.

Introduction
Hemingway Unbound

In mid-summer of 1961, a shrimp boat left Havana harbor and headed for Tampa. The boxes in its hold contained handwritten and typed manuscripts, galleys, letters, postcards, photographs – even a few stray bullfight tickets. After arriving in Florida, the boxes eventually made their way to a storage facility in Waltham, Massachusetts, and, in 1980, to the John F. Kennedy Library in Boston. The contents of those boxes were to effect a sea change in our understanding of the achievement of one of America's greatest writers.

Fidel Castro had come to power in Cuba a few years earlier, in 1959. While Ernest and Mary Hemingway were on good terms with Castro – he won a fishing contest sponsored by Hemingway in 1960 – they quickly saw that life in a revolutionary Cuba might become untenable. They began to make plans for a permanent relocation from their home in the hills above Havana, the Finca Vigía, a move interrupted by Hemingway's suicide on July 2, 1961, in Ketchum, Idaho.

The United States had attempted to invade Cuba at the Bay of Pigs three months before Hemingway took his own life. At this extreme low point in Cuban-American relations, Mary Hemingway was faced with the challenge of re-entering Cuba in order to recover her husband's belongings. Her friend William Walton had strong ties to the Kennedy family; Walton spoke to President Kennedy, passage was quickly arranged, and Mary and her assistants returned to the Finca in late July.

The Cuban government had already informed Mary that it intended to appropriate the Finca Vigía and convert it into a museum. It was agreed that Mary could remove papers and personal effects from the Finca and from a Havana bank vault. In a steel file in the library, she found an envelope on which was typed: "IMPORTANT To Be Opened in Case of My Death Ernest Hemingway May 24, 1958." The letter inside directed his executors not to publish any "letters written by me during my lifetime." But the hoard of paper argued otherwise, testifying to a concern for posterity, and the instructions were disregarded. Mary and her team attempted to separate "the worthy from the worthless," consigning bank books, check stubs, old magazines and newspapers, and unanswered correspondence to a bonfire below the tennis courts.

As a result of the haste imposed upon Mary's rescue mission, virtually all of Hemingway's library of 9,000 volumes and a significant number of letters and manuscripts had to be left behind. Among the most valuable items later discovered in the basement of the Finca was a pencil draft of an epilogue to *For Whom the Bell Tolls.*

In April 1962, Mary was invited to a White House party for Nobel Prize winners; a photograph of the occasion shows her beaming up at an elegantly dressed president. Two years later, she offered the Hemingway papers to the Kennedy Library. A 1968 exchange of letters between Mary and Jacqueline Kennedy sealed the deal, and, in 1972, the papers began arriving at the library's temporary storage facility in Waltham, Massachusetts. The papers were first opened to general research in 1975 and found their permanent home in Boston when the library building was dedicated in 1980.

When school is on and I am teaching at the University of Maryland, I spend Tuesday and Wednesday nights with Howard Norman and Jane Shore in their home in Chevy Chase. Howard's insomnia has made him especially susceptible to Elizabeth Bishop's daunting admonition, "Read ALL of somebody." On any given morning Howard greets me with a cup of coffee and the fruits of his nocturnal reading, a line from Max Frisch, an anecdote from Conrad, a letter by Siegfried Sassoon.

One morning early in the fall of 2011, Howard adverted to my recent summer reading project. At the age of sixty-two, and finding myself between books, I had cast about for something to do and had decided to work my way through the thirty-eight plays in *The Norton Shakespeare.* "OK – you like these big reading projects," Howard said. "Why not spend a summer reading Hemingway?" He likes to give me these assignments as much as I like to fulfill them, and, since I had been writing about and teaching Hemingway's work for more than forty years, I decided to give it a go.

By the end of my summer of reading, I had come to believe that the Hemingway reader must inevitably fare forward, as I had, under the sway of three emotional states: anxiety, embarrassment, and remorse. One is anxious about what will happen to a character; one is embarrassed by how a character behaves; or one is remorseful for what a character has done or become. These emotions are not easily separated and can often coexist – they could, indeed, be said to comprise a "Hemingway-complex." By virtue of emphasis and consistency, however, they are experienced as sequential and belong successively to the early, the middle, and the late career. Catherine Barkley's "I see me dead in it" gives way, in the early thirties, to Robert Wilson's feeling "very embarrassed," which is then supplanted in *The Garden of Eden* by an aging writer's looking back on the story of his early life with feelings of "terrible remorse."

For Whom the Bell Tolls stands apart from this pattern as the one work in which Hemingway summoned each of these feelings in order to greet them with a motion toward forgiveness. Admiring this novel as I do, and acknowledging that it marks only the end of the middle of the journey, I would like to believe of it, and of the man who wrote it, something written on a "manuscript fragment" from the novel in Hemingway's hand: "People are not as they end up (finish) but as they are in the finest point they ever reach." The novel he is now writing, Hemingway ventures, can be likened to an "altimeter which registers the ultimate height that is reached." In this lovely fantasy, the finest thing a man does along the way matters more than how he might "end up."

What I had discovered in my reading is that Hemingway's writing engages in a career-long struggle with emotional vulnerability. Given the obvious resistance to expressed emotion in the early work, the claim may seem counterintuitive. But, even during the period when Hemingway appeared to be most devoted to not talking about thoughts and feelings, his "theory" of "the omitted" worked, as he himself argues, to make people "feel more." The early style does not embrace emotional reticence but sets out, instead, to measure the cost of it. As Hemingway's characters build defenses – their necessary fictions – in order to protect themselves, Hemingway the author remains at once empathetic toward and critical of these strategies.

My book, therefore, challenges a number of long-held beliefs about the structure of Hemingway's career. I argue, in brief, that, as a writer, Hemingway changed; that his attempt to work through the "Hemingway-complex" required a shift away from his early art of omission and toward an art of inclusion; and that this development was, in many ways, a change for the better.

The veneration of the iceberg principle has worked to obscure the outlines of this development and has encouraged an overinvestment in the features of Hemingway's early style. But Hemingway's ongoing act of self-revision requires us to give equal weight to the nonfictional experiments of the 1930s, to the often-undervalued *For Whom the Bell Tolls*, and to the late, unfinished projects, *The Garden of Eden* and *A Moveable Feast*. *Revision* itself becomes a major subject and feature of the career, with Hemingway's continual rewritings and eventual not-finishings becoming a big part of the story.

By the time I finished re-reading Hemingway, the count of his published works had risen to thirty-five. Although he has been dead for more than fifty years, books by Hemingway continue to appear, with the latest additions to the canon being the Hemingway Library Edition of *A Farewell to Arms* (2012), the second volume of the Cambridge edition of *The Letters of Ernest Hemingway* (2103), and the Hemingway Library Edition of *The Sun Also Rises* (2014). Eighteen of Hemingway's thirty-five published works have in fact been issued posthumously, including such beloved books as *A Moveable Feast* (1964) and obscurities like *Dateline Toronto: The Complete "Toronto Star" Dispatches, 1920–1924* (1985).

Once I had assembled my stack of books, I read straight through the list in the order of publication. Of course, the order of publication does not reflect the order of composition, not, at least, with the books published after the Second World War. Up through *For Whom the Bell Tolls* (1940), Hemingway wrote a book and then published it. During the twenty-one years of life left to him after 1940, however, only four books by Hemingway were published – *Men at War* (1942), *Across the River and into the Trees* (1950), *The Old Man and the Sea* (1952), and *The Short Stories of Ernest Hemingway* (1954) – and the two novels on this list were themselves quarried from an ongoing and unfinished work. Books brought to market out of the manuscripts Hemingway left behind have appeared and will appear, it perhaps goes without saying, with no regard to when they may have been composed.

To re-enter Hemingway's vast achievement was then to find myself carried back to my early fascination with how things end and begin. My 1977 essay "Hemingway's Uncanny Beginnings" had opened with the following sentences:

> Hemingway had a hard time imagining beginnings but an easy time inventing ends. Middles challenge him most of all. His works constantly anticipate, when they do not prematurely achieve, the sense of an ending.

While the deficiencies of such unqualified assertions may announce themselves all too obviously, the operative terms – beginnings, ends, middles – continue to govern my sense of the Hemingway project. Despite my tone of youthful certainty, the claims made then still appear to me to be more or less accurate. There is no need to turn upon an earlier formulation, however much I might now put it differently. One of the central arguments of the present book is that a writer's achievement acquires its meaning and force in respect to prior work he refigures but does not renounce. The meaning of such an achievement, as Robert Penn Warren maintains, is not to be found in any one writing event but in "the motion through the event." Like every ambitious artist, Hemingway wanted to control the shape of this motion, and what made beginnings "hard" and endings "easy" for him – the two adjectives are borrowed from the final exchange in "Indian Camp" – was his acute awareness that how things end was something over which the self has far more say than it does over how they begin.

Given that Hemingway's endings are usually either sad, or bathetic, or downright tragic – and that they are *entailed in his beginnings* – his reader is therefore called upon to fare forward with an almost crushing burden of awareness. Insofar as the word "courage" has its place here, it is to the reading experience that it should be applied. The kind of courage Hemingway demands of his reader is, however, no more and no less than the kind of courage anyone must summon in order to live in a world where, as he wrote in *Death in the Afternoon*, "all stories, if continued far enough, end in death."

That so many of Hemingway's books have been published posthumously has become one of the most arresting and ambiguous features of his story. The two initial gifts to readers from beyond the grave, *A Moveable Feast* and *Islands in the Stream*, issued in 1964 and in 1970, did not, however, draw particular attention to this fact. But with the opening of the Hemingway Papers to research in 1975, a new Hemingway began to loom into view. The archive revealed a post-Second World War productivity giving the lie to any sense of Hemingway as a late-life burnt-out case. As these papers were then edited into books by various hands and brought into print, the obvious obsession with endings *in* the work became the central question *about* the work. When could Hemingway's writing be said to have actually ended?

In *A Second Flowering*, Malcolm Cowley argues that it ended with *For Whom the Bell Tolls* and that Hemingway lacked the capacity for "growth after middle age." Rose Marie Burwell has written the most compelling rebuttal to Cowley's claim. In *Hemingway: The Postwar Years and the Posthumous Novels* (1996), she recovers fifteen years of imaginative work from the neglect to which it can all too easily be consigned. It is not true, Burwell's research shows, that Hemingway stopped growing after the war. What he did do was to stop publishing. As early as 1931, he wrote in a letter to a bibliographer: "The first right that a man writing has is the choice of what he will publish."

During "The Final Years," as Michael Reynolds calls them, Hemingway became a master of looking back. By 1944, according to Reynolds, "Hemingway's life was becoming his story." Not in the obvious sense that a man's writing forms a sort of spilt autobiography. The "life" that was becoming the "story" was Hemingway's prewar life, and Hemingway returned upon it not so much in order to renarrate it as to judge it. The "sizable component of melancholy" Earl Rovit and Gerry Brenner locate in the postwar writing arises from this ongoing ordeal. When Hemingway decided against the publication of his postwar findings, he did so in order to protect both himself and the people he loved from the harsher consequences of his ongoing act of last judgment.

In deciding not to bring to market the vast and interconnected writing projects of the postwar years, Hemingway left behind a work steeped in "the most terrible nostalgia anyone has ever had." It is Marita who says to David Bourne "you write with the most terrible nostalgia anyone has ever had," and she says this to him in the manuscript of *The Garden of Eden*, on page four in Folder 21, Box 34. Only someone who has read through the full manuscript of the novel, one abridged and published as *The Garden of Eden* in 1986, will have seen these words. The existence of this manuscript, along with the many others donated by Mary Hemingway to the Kennedy Library, has converted the Hemingway Room on the fifth floor of the black-and-white building overlooking Boston Harbor into a site of pilgrimage. Early on in my researches for the present book, I knew I would have to go to Boston and to spend some time in that room.

On the first Thursday in July 2012, I parked my car in front of the Kennedy Library and walked across the sizzling parking lot. Once inside, I was taken to an elevator where a guard punched the button for the floor marked "Research." After signing in, I was then ushered upstairs to the Hemingway Room. The room is kept locked, so whenever I exited or entered it, I had to be accompanied by a librarian.

The room is triangular in shape, with a wall of windows overlooking the harbor forming the hypotenuse. A researcher works at one of the three cherry tables that run alongside the windows. In the middle of the room lies the skin of the lion Mary shot on safari in 1953. Next to a couch are two armchairs, and, between the chairs, on a small table, sit two glasses filled with fake ice cubes and an empty bottle of Pernod.

In this quaint and cozy room of only five hundred square feet, what really matters are the contents of the two interior walls. These walls contain 3,000 linear feet of shelf space. On one wall is gathered a collection of the books published by and about Hemingway. On the other wall sit more than one hundred green boxes. The Ernest Hemingway Personal Papers contain forty-five boxes labeled "Manuscripts" and thirty-four boxes labeled "Correspondence." The remaining boxes contain newspaper clippings and "other material," copies of material still being held at the Finca Vigía, and incoming correspondence.

Once admitted, a researcher need only reach for any box he wishes to examine. The boxes contain photocopies of all the Hemingway manuscripts held by the library; the originals are held in "the vault." To open a box is to find a letter, a handwritten draft, a typescript, galleys, notes written by Hemingway to himself, and, on the front and the back and in the corners of many pages, the scribbled sums of figures – usually of accumulating word counts – Hemingway was in the habit of adding up. Each manuscript is given an identification number, with items varying in length from one page to a complete draft of a novel.

The contents of the boxes destabilize virtually everything bound in covers on the facing shelves: Hemingway Bound faces Hemingway Unbound. The boxes reveal a canon unbound in two important ways: first, because the books published during Hemingway's lifetime were heavily revised by the author himself and so exist in a multiplicity of forms; and second, because the thousands of pages left unbound at Hemingway's death continue to solicit the attentions of editors who continue to gather them between covers. Given the riches contained in the boxes, then, there appears to be no foreseeable end to the process of processing Hemingway.

Two examples may suffice. *A Farewell to Arms* was published in 1929 and became justly famous for its ending, in which Catherine Barkley dies in childbirth and Frederic Henry walks home alone in the rain. By the mid-1970s, as the Hemingway papers became widely available to scholars, it was then discovered that this ending was by no means the original one. Hemingway worked toward it by trying out and rejecting more than forty variant endings, and, as Bernard Oldsey and Michael Reynolds drew attention to this effort, the alternatives considered and rejected became the seven-eighths of the iceberg shadowing the meaning of the published ending. It was perhaps inevitable that Hemingway's grandson would bring out in 2012 *A Farewell to Arms: The Hemingway Library Edition*, a volume containing forty-seven "alternative endings." The question of which edition of the novel to read or to assign to students suddenly became an open one.

When I speak of the work Hemingway left behind as "unfinished," I mean to refer to the writing he did not choose to submit to publication. Burwell numbers the unfinished works at four. At the time of her writing, in the mid-1990s, three of these works had been published, *A Moveable Feast, Islands in the Stream*, and *The Garden of Eden*. "Half of the fourth work, the African book," Burwell writes, "was excerpted in magazines; but it remains unedited, and there seem to be no plans for book publication." Three years after the appearance of her study, the African book was published, as *True at First Light*.

Then, in 2005, the African book was published again.

The two scholars who brought out *Under Kilimanjaro* did so with the intention of providing "a complete reading text of Ernest Hemingway's manuscript based on his second East African safari." Describing *True at First Light* as "an abridged version of the work," they attempted to come "as close as we could come to what we think its author might have hoped to publish." Seán Hemingway's 2009 "Restored Edition" of *A Moveable Feast* attempts much the same thing. But the ongoing publication of books never finally edited by their author argues rather for the possibility of an unending series of *re*-editings, as Hemingway relatives and scholars vie to impose upon the career their preferred version of "closure." A respect for what an author might have hoped to publish appears to have its limits, however, since neither edition of the African book chooses to end with the ending Hemingway actually wrote, a sentence stopping with a preposition: "'That's too bad,' I said, and I remembered the old days and how you looked forward to the one one beyond all price in."

"One one," Hemingway writes. Surely, in revising, he would have separated these two words with a comma and have found a way to end his sentence and his story. But he did not do so. The unfinished sentence at the end of the African manuscript serves as a reminder that none of the endings of Hemingway's posthumously published books was supplied by Hemingway himself.

In *The Sun Also Rises*, as Jake Barnes instructs Brett Ashley in how to watch a bullfight, she comes to see it as "something that was going on with a definite end, and less of a spectacle with unexplained horrors." Hemingway liked to give his stories a definite end. His endings have about them the sense of an expectation fulfilled. Such endings helped to compensate for the uncertainties of setting out and for the unexplainable horrors encountered along the way.

The editors who have attempted to supply endings for the books Hemingway did not manage to finish have, for the most part, produced works of considerable beauty and power. Taken together, their achievements have supplied a new ending to the Hemingway story. Far from closing that story down, however, these posthumous editions have only succeeded in opening it up. Hemingway's devoted readers are now required to return, as the dying writer Harry Walden does in "The Snows of Kilimanjaro," to "*the start of all he was to do.*" To return to the start of Hemingway's career and to read forward in the full knowledge of how it ended is to honor what has already been learned in reading any one of Hemingway's extended fictions: that any sense of any ending is to be understood as the earned consequence of how it all began. So, I begin where Hemingway as a writer himself began, with the first sentence in the first story in his first strong book: "At the lake shore there was another rowboat drawn up."

PART I

Anxiety

CHAPTER I

At the Beginning
"Indian Camp"

A young boy finds himself crossing a lake in the dark. He sits with a father's arm around him. By the end of the story, fewer than five pages later, he will recross the lake, now sitting alone. In the meantime, the boy has been asked to bear witness to a beginning and to an ending. His experience of witness involves a looking away from a violent and bloody birth and a good view of a quiet, off-stage death. This premature initiation becomes his unique inheritance, both a wound and a promise.

But to note all of this is to accomplish the very thing Nick Adams wishes for but cannot do – it is to jump ahead. Wanting to see and to know and to control what lies "ahead" may be the deepest wish engendered by a story in which both character and reader find themselves continually falling "further" behind. "Indian Camp" begins, after all, with a world already filled with objects; there is a sense of having arrived too late. No attempt is made to explain where we are or who we are with or why we are there. One of the imperatives thereby conveyed is the necessity to fare forward in the face of uncertainty, to keep rowing and reading *ahead*.

The first edition of *In Our Time*, published in 1925, begins with "Indian Camp" and opens with the following sentences:

> At the lake shore there was another rowboat drawn up. The two Indians stood waiting.
>
> Nick and his father got in the stern of the boat and the Indians shoved it off and one of them got in to row. Uncle George sat in the stern of the camp rowboat. The young Indian shoved the camp boat off and got in to row Uncle George.
>
> The two boats started off in the dark. Nick heard the oar-locks of the other boat quite a way ahead of them in the mist. The Indians rowed with quick choppy strokes. Nick lay back with his father's arm around him. It was cold on the water. The Indian who was rowing them was working very hard, but the other boat moved further ahead in the mist all the time.
>
> "Where are we going, Dad?" Nick asked.

Another rowboat? Why mention another rowboat, when there has been no reference to a first one? And why introduce the two Indians with the definite article "the," a word implying some sort of knowledge of them that the reader does not possess? In these inaugural sentences, we are being addressed as if the unfamiliar were familiar. Why might the narrator of the story elect to speak to us in this way? And why does he give us so little while sounding as if he had already given us so much? Here, we are introduced to a central Hemingway effect, a sense of the world as at once mysterious and homelike.

Nick begins as a lost son – and this despite the fact that he is with his father. By the time he asks "Where are we going, Dad?" the question may have become the reader's as well. Nick's father supplies a kind of answer:

> "Over to the Indian camp. There is an Indian lady very sick."
> "Oh," said Nick.

Nick *begins* here, for the Hemingway reader; "Indian Camp" is the first story in which Nick Adams appears. The acute sense of setting out also quickly reveals itself as a journey back, into American origins. Hemingway inaugurates his career by choosing to return to a site connected to the prehistory of his country, as well as to the night on which the Hemingway character is born.

Sentence sound and structure are carefully deployed to engender the unsettled mood. It is a prose of "quick choppy strokes" except where it is a prose of sentences extending themselves through "and's": "Nick *and* his father got in the stern of the boat *and* the Indians shoved it off *and* one of them got in to row." In an interview given in the 1950s, Hemingway spoke of using "the word 'and' consciously over and over the way Johann Sebastian Bach used a note in music when he was emitting counterpoint." The paratactic "and's" provide a counterpoint to the short, uncompounded sentences. Whereas the short sentences bespeak control, those governed by "andness" surrender instead to the unsubordinated arrival of the next thing. So, an opposition is set up between sentences that chop the world into arresting and shapely bits and sentences that attempt to register the experience of being in a series of which we do not know the extremes. The very sound and shape of these sentences address the matter of having or surrendering control.

Hemingway puts us with Nick, asks us to come along for the ride. As he explained in a letter to his father in March 1925, he wanted to write "so that when you have read something by me you actually experience the thing." Owen Wister later described the Hemingway reader as "a participating witness." The phrase nicely captures the complexity of any reader's stance toward the story, since, while he begins by sharing an extraordinary intimacy with Nick, as the story proceeds, the reader is also invited to stand back and observe Nick as he struggles to take in and fend off all that happens at Indian Camp.

Despite the fact of Nick's being told by his father that the Indian woman's screams are "not important," her act of giving birth receives considerable attention, and each of the four male figures in the story is required to deploy his unique defense against it. Dr. Adams adopts the pose of the cool professional, retreating into technique. Uncle George passes out cigars, gets bitten, and leaves. The Indian husband kills himself. Nick looks away.

As he finds himself thrust into a tight situation, Dr. Adams attempts an explanation:

> "This lady is going to have a baby, Nick," he said.
> "I know," said Nick.

Nick's response not only deflates the pretense to knowing but indicates that, in a moment of difficulty, one useful response is to deny what is really going on. Nick will become skilled at learning to say the opposite of what he actually thinks and feels; for him, the depth of a fear can often be measured by the strength of a denial.

Nick also takes refuge in abstract nouns. He sees his father put "several things" into the hot water and later watches him put "something into the basin." The narrator continues, "Nick didn't look at it." Another sentence, "It all took a long time," provides for a summary exit from a paragraph choosing not to detail what happens once Nick's father begins to operate. Given their capacity to indicate things and feelings without naming them, the words *it* and *something* will become a distinctive feature of the Hemingway vocabulary.

It would be more accurate to say that the narrator rather than Nick takes refuge in abstract nouns, since Nick is not telling this story. "Indian Camp" is nevertheless focalized through Nick, and the words applied to or withheld from his experience seem to express a reticence he shares with the narrator. The reader, however, enjoys no such protection, since a normal guessing curiosity quickly supplies the omitted concretion and translates the word "something" into the word "afterbirth." In performing such a substitution, readers participate in one of the crucial transactions made possible by Hemingway's art of omission. As he writes in *A Moveable Feast*, it is an art in which "you could omit anything if you knew that you omitted and the omitted part would strengthen the story and make people feel something more than they understood."

The birth of Nick's defenses receives considerably more attention in the story than does their object. The Indian woman is the true thing left out here. Nick's emerging sense of things will nevertheless come to depend upon this mysterious and homelike figure. Hemingway's imagination can, however, only allow for such an explicit and sexual scene by way of a woman of color; it is unimaginable in this fictional world that a boy of no more than eleven years would be allowed to act as an "interne" for a caesarean section performed on a white woman's body.

For Nick, the color of the Indian woman will prove, however, incidental to her status as a mother, a body, and a cut thing. What we so casually call "the facts of life" are perhaps the story's deepest subject, and these facts, as Hemingway's word choices so carefully reveal, can only be approached by way of terms that displace and disguise. Euphemism, for instance, is used in order to prevent a full articulation of the scene. Calling the Indian woman "sick," as Dr. Adams does, is a way of indicating that she is pregnant and about to give birth. To talk in this way is to reinforce the cherished adage from *The Sun Also Rises*, "You'll lose it if you talk about it," where "it" remains an umbrella term for that which ought to have remained hidden and secret and yet comes to light. Leslie Fiedler was among the first to recognize that in Hemingway's fiction childbirth "customarily presents itself as the essential catastrophe," and "Indian Camp" is the story that, even in its evasions, articulates an abiding anxiety about the nature and consequence of human beginnings.

The anxiety pervades *In Our Time* like a spreading stain. In the chapter immediately following "Indian Camp," we read of "*a woman having a kid with a young girl holding a blanket over her and crying. Scared sick looking at it.*" Mr. and Mrs. Elliott try "very hard to have a baby" and fail. Finally, in the last story in which we see him before he goes off to Big Two-Hearted River in order to put "everything behind," Nick says "There isn't any good in promising" given the "hell" of his wife's pregnancy. When Hemingway added "On the Quai at Smyrna" to the 1930 edition of *In Our Time*, he also added a scene of women "having babies" at the harbor. "They had them all right. Surprising how few of them died. You just covered them over with something and let them go to it."

"The scenes of childbirth in Hemingway's writing," Robert Scholes and Nancy Comley write, "are vivid testimony to his sense of the price women paid in becoming mothers." But, of course, the price being attended to in "Indian Camp" is the one being paid by Nick. The woman's screams – and by extension her pain – are deemed unimportant. Nick's pain takes the form of a complex set of recognitions – a fall into knowledge – immediately offset by carefully marshaled defenses. The knowledge registers itself nevertheless: the male self is thrown into the world in a moment violent and uncontrollable and out of a body unlike his own and after that body has itself been entered and impregnated by another male who cannot "stand" the consequences of his act of engendering. The child born is sentenced to the lifework of trying to return to this site of origin in order to reconfigure the initial and unaccommodating terms. Out of such beginnings is therefore also born the attempt at refinding that we know by the name of "love."

Nick sees something "that ought to have remained hidden and secret, and yet comes to light." I fall back on Freud here and on his 1919 essay "The 'Uncanny'" not in order to privilege his insight above Hemingway's or to make "Indian Camp" a proof-text of the rightness of Freud's theories. The point rather is that, within the space of five years, two original minds each found a unique mode of expressing a shared vision of why human beings might be required to work so hard at converting the world into a home. After much wandering, Nick's story will culminate in a profound act of substitution at Big Two-Hearted River, where he finds himself in his "home where he had made it." Freud articulates why such an act of refinding might be necessary and also offers up the destination term "home" as the most uncanny of words.

The subject of the uncanny, Freud allows, "undoubtedly belongs to all that is terrible – to all that arouses dread and creeping horror." At the outset of the essay, then, the uncanny is defined as the scary Other. Yet, as Freud quickly goes on to assert, a survey of the meaning of the word in the course of its history reveals the uncanny as "that class of the terrifying which leads back to something long known to us, once very familiar." Or, in Hemingway's phrase, a phrase deployed as Nick crawls into the tent he has pitched at Big Two-Hearted River, the uncanny is that which is experienced as at once "mysterious and homelike."

This complementarity of meaning, it turns out, inhabits the German word for the "familiar" or "belonging to the home," the word *heimlich*. Freud makes the point by quoting a dictionary list of definitions of the word, a list in which the word begins to merge with what appears to be its antonym. "*Oh, we call it 'unheimlich'; you call it 'heimlich,'*" one of the later entries reads. After this unsettling example, a shift in the hominess of the term begins, with it now taking on the nature of something "Concealed, kept from sight, so that others do not get to know about it." At this point, the *heimlich* sounds like the sort of secret one family might keep from another, but this is only a stopping point along the way. At the end of his excursion, Freud concludes: "What interests us most in this long extract is to find that among its different shades of meaning the word *heimlich* exhibits one which is identical with its opposite, *unheimlich*."

As a word "which develops toward an ambivalence," *heimlich* nicely captures the complex of feelings and responses Nick experiences at Indian Camp. On the one hand, he claims to "know" what is happening; on the other, he cannot bring himself to take it in. Freud and Hemingway are students of how the mind realizes and hides from itself in words, and Freud's essay has proved congenial to the study of literature because of its reliance on a complex feat of etymology. In listening to his patients, Freud came to see that dreams and speech are filled with puns and slips and other kinds of revealing play, a lesson he had already acquired from reading his beloved Shakespeare. His enduring power as a thinker about experience derives in good part from his willingness to play with words, with the essay on "The 'Uncanny'" reading as if Jorge Luis Borges had attempted to provide one word with its own unique and renegade *OED* entry. It is a venture into the multiplicity of meanings that can accrue to a given word at any one moment and through historical time.

Freud is also pointing to an embarrassment *in* words, to their refusal to simply mean. In Hemingway's early work – and it is a central argument of this book that his vision and style do change over time – the manifest is ghosted by the latent. "Meaning" itself becomes uncanny in the encounter with the early Hemingway text since it can only be fully realized in the off-the-page transaction in the reader's mind as he attempts to respond to the gap between the said and the unsaid. Never fully invited into the words on the page, these meanings, like Hemingway's characters, are not quite at home in the verbal space that pretends to house them. For early Hemingway, the relation of words to meanings is profoundly *ironic*.

The most dramatic example of irony in "Indian Camp" occurs in its closing sentence. "In the early morning on the lake sitting in the stern of the boat with his father rowing, he felt quite sure that he would never die." But for the fact that the sun is coming up over the hills, Nick appears to be whistling in the dark. "Quite sure," the sentence says. Surely, these words indicate a protesting too much, a claim made by a narrator on behalf of a character who appears to be feeling the opposite of what the words say. If we buy the claim, we have chosen to go with Nick's emerging defenses, whereas, if we hear the irony in it, we are learning one way to read Hemingway.

Nick's denial of his mortality expresses a simple wish. It is not difficult to be moved by the wish and possible even to recognize it as a wish that was once one's own. There is something pitiable in the longing being expressed, and the pity felt is more akin to empathy and awe than to disdain. The perception of verbal irony is thereby caught up and diffused into a richly textured complex of emotions. In Hemingway's words, a reader, confronted with "the omitted part" – in this case, a feeling directly expressed – is made to "feel something more."

Hemingway's sense of the inseparability of irony and pity is made explicit in a conversation between Jake Barnes and Bill Gorton in chapter 12 in *The Sun Also Rises*:

> "What's all this irony and pity?"
> "What? Don't you know about Irony and Pity?"
> "No. Who got it up?"
> "Everybody. They're mad about it in New York."

The exchange itself appears to be ironic, since the characters feature their investment in two words by attempting to downplay it. But the attentive reader of Hemingway's first novel will have already noticed how often Jake's attempts to armor himself in irony collapse into moments of searing self-pity, an emotion Hemingway treats with tenderness rather than with scorn. This extension of generosity toward his characters begins with Nick Adams.

Death is on Nick's mind at the end of "Indian Camp" because he has just seen what the Indian father has done to himself. "Nick, standing in the door of the kitchen, had a good view of the upper bunk when his father, the lamp in one hand, tipped the Indian's head back." A reader is told this after having been invited, all unawares, "to have a look at the proud father":

> He pulled back the blanket from the Indian's head. His hand came away wet. He mounted on the edge of the lower bunk with the lamp in one hand and looked in. The Indian lay with his face toward the wall. His throat had been cut from ear to ear. The blood had flowed down into a pool where his body sagged the bunk. The head rested on his left arm. The open razor lay, edge up, in the blankets.

This description is as calm as the language of the birth scene is agitated. "She is the most easy thing to find that I know of," Hemingway wrote in 1954, after surviving a second plane crash in Africa and after being accused in the premature obituaries of having "sought death all my life." His use of the word "easy" echoes Dr. Adams's response to Nick's question about dying being hard. "No, I think it's pretty easy, Nick. It all depends." On the other hand, while Dr. Adams says "No" to Nick's question, "Do ladies always have such a hard time having babies?" the action of the story offers up quite another answer.

In "Indian Camp," looking at death is much easier than is looking at birth, and the paragraph describing the Indian father's self-inflicted wound is a remarkably toneless and even an easeful one. Moreover, the paragraph comes to the reader unmediated by any sense of how Nick may be taking it in and therefore carries with it none of Nick's gathering anxiety about the act of seeing.

Behind the moment of the Indian baby's birth stands the act of conception itself, a primal scene invoked by the Indian father's somehow having managed to cut himself in the foot with an ax "three days before." In doing so, he also places himself precisely where he does not wish and yet somehow deserves to be and therefore undergoes an experience he cannot stand. When Nick asks his father, "Why did he kill himself, Daddy?" his father replies, "I don't know, Nick. He couldn't stand things, I guess."

Just what these "things" are is left, for Nick, mercifully unclear. A reader is nevertheless invited to speculate about what some of these things might be. No great effort of imagination is required to read the Indian man's two acts of self-wounding as a punishment for having implicated himself in fathering a child.

At Indian Camp, Nick confronts a primal scene and a terminal one. It is as hard to look at the one scene as it is easy to look at the other. "I see," Nick says, as he looks away from the birth. Nick has a good view, on the other hand, as he gazes into the upper bunk. For Hemingway's early characters, anticipating endings will remain "easy" and recalling beginnings will remain "hard."

Since the vision of human beginnings in "Indian Camp" is offered up *at the beginning* of Hemingway's writing career, its take on things can easily assume a central place in any reading of that career. Although the story may appear to be making certain claims about "the facts of life," the phrase can have in this instance only an ironic application. Hemingway is not attempting to give an authoritative account of how things are but rather to detail the ways in which an unknowing and unformed imagination, finding itself thrust into an overwhelming situation, might begin to construct a sense of the world. The story possesses a dream-like intensity and Gothic extremity of mood Hemingway never attempted to duplicate or surpass. The very extremity of the fiction calls attention to its status as a fiction about the nature and force of human origins. Nick stands at the center of the story but is not the originator of it. It is Hemingway the writer who originates this vision and who chooses to begin with it, just as it is Hemingway who will, through writing, work to revise the hold of the vision upon his imagination in order to deliver his characters and his readers into a sense of more abundant life.

The crossing of a body of water in the dark, the unnamed conductors, the intrusion of the protagonists into an aboriginal culture, the mixture of banalities like "Damn squaw bitch!" with profundities like "Is dying hard, Daddy?" – all this gives to Hemingway's story the quality of a fairy tale. If we reduce the six major characters to fairy-tale types, they can be named as the following: the Screaming Mother, the Guilty Father, the Unprepared Physician, the Unsympathetic Attendant, the Baby Born, and the Reluctant Interne. Given the preponderance of types hailing from the helping professions, the offered fable might be said to convey the conviction that birth is a catastrophe that cannot be helped.

Of course, there is a seventh figure present here, one often close at hand in Hemingway's work: the Empathetic Reader. Just as five of the characters become elements in a psychomachia experienced by a sixth, so Nick's situation presents itself as in need of interpretation by the empathetic seventh. "Empathy" is the word to apply because Hemingway imposes on Nick and on the reader demands so similar as to make it difficult not to feel with him. The strategy is initiated in the opening paragraphs, where our uncertainly so closely parallels Nick's that, by the time he asks his question, it has become ours as well.

In likening "Indian Camp" to a fairy tale, I mean to argue for it as an invention independent of anything that might have actually happened to Hemingway. The writer attempted to guide his readers toward such an awareness in the original ending to "Big Two-Hearted River," on pages given the title "On Writing" in Philip Young's edition of *The Nick Adams Stories.*

As the passage opens, Nick has one good trout. It turns out he will do no more fishing that day. Instead, he begins remembering summers spent with Bill Smith, segues to memories of bullfighting, and ends up thinking about writing:

> *The only writing that was any good was what you made up, what you imagined. That made everything come true. Like when he wrote "My Old Man" he'd never seen a jockey killed and the next week Georges Parfrement was killed at that very*

> *jump and that was the way it looked. Everything good he'd ever written he'd made up. None of it had happened. Other things had happened. Better things, maybe. That was what the family couldn't understand. They thought it was all experience.*

The passage contains two surprises: first, Nick is revealed to be the author of *In Our Time*; and second, Nick writes from imagination, not simply "about" experience. Even though the claims are here displaced onto Nick, the sentences quoted come as close to an Ars Poetica as the young Hemingway ever wrote.

A few sentences further on, in this "mental conversation," as Hemingway later described it, another clear message is sent about his understanding of the relation between an author's life and his work: "*Nick in the stories was never himself. He made him up. Of course he'd never seen an Indian woman having a baby. That was what made it good.*"

"*Never himself,*" Hemingway writes. From its beginnings, however, Hemingway studies has all too often made the assumption that a character invented by Hemingway is *always himself.* The intensity and precision of Hemingway's descriptions have been taken as proof that the man who wrote them must have lived the thing being described. And so, in most casual exchanges about Hemingway, conversations fueled by books like *The Paris Wife*, talk about the work devolves into gossip about the life. Hemingway's books are thereby reduced to transcripts of experience rather than being valued for what they truly are – works of the imagination.

"Indian Camp" appears to be a story about trauma: is not a wound being inflicted? Nick surely undergoes something very painful. Yet, as we have seen, Hemingway chooses to focus less on the wound itself than on Nick's response to it. Nick, like all of Hemingway's characters, is a hero – or a victim – of the imagination, and the deepest subject of his story is the growth of the hero's mind. Despite the defensive character of Nick's mental operations, his is an act of making: he is beginning to create the self with which he will meet the world.

And, of course, the entire trauma at Indian Camp never happened – not, at least, to Nick Adams. It is all a complex experiment with verisimilitude. In writing *In Our Time*, Hemingway invents a character, Nick Adams, who turns out to be a writer who in turn invents for himself a usable but imaginary past.

Hemingway, along with Freud, is above all a student of mind. As the two writers moved ever deeper into their researches, they came to see the self as more active than acted upon. Although Freud never dismissed the shaping power of actual childhood traumas, he did come to place considerable emphasis on what William Blake called "mind-forg'd manacles." Neurosis, it turned out, often originates from a *fantasy* about the past. The elusive goal of achieving mental health therefore comes to depend upon a continuing act of the mind in which what "is done to oneself," as Hemingway writes in *For Whom the Bell Tolls*, must be weighed against how one takes and refigures both the done and the not done. And many of our most significant wounds, Freud and Hemingway came to believe, are those we inflict on ourselves when we treat the conditions of a universal bequest as a unique experience of victimhood. The nature of Hemingway's "wound," then, is not to be sought in the pages of his biographies but in the worlds he chose to imagine. It is what one *makes* of trauma that matters to Hemingway, even and especially when that trauma is imaginary.

The mind Nick Adams begins to make in "Indian Camp" evolves a mode of accommodating experience that resurfaces in the narratives told by Jake Barnes and Frederic Henry. Since Hemingway was a writer rather than a doctor, he sought to contain the psychological concerns and difficulties faced by his characters through the formal means of his art. The mental self-editing Nick and Jake and Frederic feel compelled to impose upon themselves required their author to develop an art of omission. There is a cutting involved: "How good a book is should be judged, by the man who writes it, by the excellence of the material that he eliminates." While Hemingway spoke of eliminating as a "good" thing throughout his writing life, his actual practice eventually swerved away from the strictures of his most famous theory. By the time he came to write *Death in the Afternoon*, he found himself increasingly drawn to an art of inclusion, and, by the time he came to write *A Moveable Feast*, the book in which he gives the clearest formulation of the art of omission, it truly had become for him an "old rule."

To return, however, to that early practice: the fable enacted in "Indian Camp" could be called "The Tale of Three Cuts." These cuts are in some way elective and are initiated by and inflicted on an adult. The first cut is administered by the Indian man to himself with an ax. The Indian woman experiences the second cut, an "incision" in the abdomen. The third cut is administered by the Indian man to his own throat, "cut from ear to ear." Each cut leads, in turn, to another, as the ax gives way to the jack-knife and the jack-knife to the razor.

The three cuts invoke another cut we must all suffer, to the umbilical cord. One of the striking things about "Indian Camp" is that it once existed in a version containing a direct allusion to this primal act of severing.

The allusion occurs in "Three Shots," a title assigned to the first manuscript excerpt in *The Nick Adams Stories*. The pages comprising "Three Shots" were composed as a sort of prologue to "Indian Camp" and describe Nick's state of mind in the days and hours before he is rowed across the lake in the dark. Alone in a tent at night, Nick remembers: "*Just a few weeks before at home, in church, they had sung a hymn, 'Some day the silver cord will break.' While they were singing the hymn Nick had realized that some day he must die. It made him feel quite sick. It was the first time he had ever realized that he himself would have to die sometime.*" Hemingway eventually decided to eliminate these pages, in part because they preempt Nick's much more dramatic realization of the fact of death in the cabin at Indian Camp.

The silver cord breaks when we die. But what of the cord that must be cut in order for us to live? At the end of *A Farewell to Arms*, Frederic Henry is told his son was never alive: "The cord was caught around his neck or something." The silver cord can only break *after* the umbilical cord has been successfully cut: we can only die because we have experienced birth. For Hemingway, the necessary cutting of the first cord was to occasion as much or more anxiety as was the inevitable breaking of the second.

Hemingway was fascinated by what he later called "Caesars form of childbirth," in part because it involved a bypassing of the trauma of a normal birth. When Catherine Barkley is belatedly cut open in *A Farewell to Arms*, Frederic Henry says, "I do not think I could have watched them cut." But he is capable of observing "the wound closed into a high welted ridge with quick skillful-looking stitches like a cobbler's, and was glad." As Michael Reynolds notes, "the paragraph describing Catherine's sutures gets much of its detail in the revision." As he took a second look at the pages of the novel during a final stretch of writing at Key West, Hemingway added words like "thick-edged," "high welted ridge," and "wound."

Cutting not only initiates life as separation from the mother but functions, in many cultures, as a way of marking and differentiating the genders. And cutting is also something an author is often required to impose upon a manuscript. Knowing where and how to cut became for Hemingway the true mark of the professional. "I always cut a lot," Hemingway said in 1947. Even *War and Peace*, he claimed in the Introduction to *Men at War*, "would be greatly improved by cutting."

I count twenty-one usages of the word "cut" in *In Our Time*, where it appears mostly as a verb. In one opportune moment, when Nick cleans the two male trout as he faces the swamp, the participle "slitting" is used instead of the word "cutting." In an earlier and equally telling substitution, Nick's father refers to the "incision" he is now "going to sew up." In an outburst of braggadocio, Dr. Adams says, "That's one for the medical journal, George. . . . Doing a Caesarian with a jack-knife and sewing it up with nine-foot, tapered gut leaders."

Cutting for Hemingway was to remain an image of mastery, whether over the birth of a baby or of a manuscript. But there were abiding anxieties implicit in the activity as well: the threat of loss, the failure to make something truly come alive. Although Hemingway's sense of what to omit and what to include did change over time, he continued to believe in the necessity of stringent self-editing. There is a certain poignancy, then, in the scene with which Tom Jenks, assigned the task of editing the manuscript of *The Garden of Eden* for publication, chose to end the novel. In the final paragraph of Jenks's version, David Bourne magically recovers the sentences of a manuscript his wife has burned in a fire. As the sentences return "to him complete and entire," David is able to put them down, to correct them, and to "cut them as if he were going over proof." In this fantasy of mastery and recovery, all of a writer's lost sentences return to him "intact."

By the time he wrote the pages that would become *The Garden of Eden*, Hemingway had long since discovered that in the process of being brought to market a manuscript never survives intact. An intact manuscript was as unlikely a thing for the world to produce as was an intact person. The writer who seemed capable of generating "one true sentence" after another turns out to have been, in his many work spaces, an inveterate reviser. He also understood the act of composition as a cutting into an ongoing *durée*. A story has to start somewhere, but the successful beginning must be made to feel neither arbitrary nor preordained. In seeking to impose an arrangement on *In Our Time*, Hemingway's solution was to cut in at the beginning so as to align his act of setting out as a writer with his uncanny sense of the way in which we all start.

But how then to continue? In the following chapter, we will see that the making of *In Our Time* involved a complex act of editing in which two volumes composed at distinct intervals were carefully sutured together. The resulting structure can be said to resemble a series of scenes intercut as in "*a cinematograph film*." For the reader of *In Our Time*, the jump cuts between its stories and its vignettes raise the question of whether it might be possible to see the book steadily and to see it whole. For the writer of *In Our Time*, the technical issues involved in shaping its parts into a whole proved inseparable from the existential issues giving rise to the book in the first place. The anxieties sending up the performance could only be given form and meaning, Hemingway discovered, through the incisive power of the storyteller's art.

CHAPTER 2

A Second Will

In Our Time and *in our time*

When Hadley Hemingway packed up her husband's papers and carried them in an overnight bag to the Gare de Lyon in December 1922, she set in motion a process that would have profound implications for the composition of *In Our Time*. After placing her valise in her overnight compartment, Hadley took a walk around the train station. When she returned to her compartment, her luggage was gone. It contained almost all of the work Hemingway had done since moving to Paris a year earlier. What survived the loss were poems already published or in the mail, a chapter of a long fishing story, and some Paris sketches, as well as two short stories, "Up in Michigan" and "My Old Man." Only one of these pieces, the story about a boy and his horse-riding father, would eventually be included in the sequence of stories and sketches that make up *In Our Time*.

Hemingway later made much of this early loss and gave it fictional form in *The Garden of Eden*, where David Bourne also suffers the destruction of his written work through actions taken by a wife. When David sits down to write again, he can at first recover nothing, but, on his second try, in a deeply wish-fulfilling scene, he remembers the burned sentences "as though they were being delivered to him like enlargements of contact prints from negatives he had sent to the photographers."

"Memory is the best critic," Ezra Pound had responded, when Hemingway wrote to him about the lost manuscripts. "The *point* is," Pound went on, "how much of it can you remember?" Unlike David Bourne, Hemingway did not attempt any photographic recovery of the sentences that had been stolen. Instead, he turned to new work.

Within a month or two of Hadley's fateful train trip, Hemingway began writing the "series of short prose sketches" that became the foundation of *in our time*. Each new sketch "was the product of a score of crossed-out beginnings," as Carlos Baker writes. Once six of the sketches were completed Hemingway gave them to Jane Heap for publication in the April 1923 issue of *The Little Review*. In that month, he also wrote "Out of

Season," his first attempt at a full-length story since the loss of the manuscripts. That summer, Robert McAlmon published Hemingway's first book, *Three Stories and Ten Poems*. The volume contained the remnant stories, "Up in Michigan" and "My Old Man," as well as the new "Out of Season."

Hemingway continued work on the prose sketches that would become *in our time* during the summer of 1923. By late August, when he and Hadley departed for Toronto, where their son was to be born, Hemingway had completed eighteen sketches and had given them to Pound for one final editing. Pound had earlier questioned whether "there was any controlling logic to the experiences," and Hemingway had responded, "It has form all right." On April 3, 1924, Shakespeare and Company sold its first copy of *in our time* for thirty francs.

The sketches took violence as their recurring subject. They dealt with potting Germans at forty yards, firing squads, Nick's wounding, bank robberies, bullfights, hangings. On their own, the sketches read as language games, experiments in tone and point of view. Read as part of *In Our Time*, where they would take their rightful place, they become something much more grave and disturbing, the iceberg cruising beneath.

Hemingway could not have known when he sailed for Toronto that the form he had found was to discover its final home as part of a larger form. Although he was later to claim to have written the vignettes of *in our time* as "chapter headings" for the stories in *In Our Time*, the great burst of creativity that began as early as November 1923 and continued on into the following fall was an act of working toward an encompassing form, not from an overall design imposed at the very start.

In this effort, Hemingway devoted considerable attention to how his book should begin and end: as manuscript evidence makes clear, "Indian Camp" and "Big Two-Hearted River" became the key pressure points. With the publication of Philip Young's *The Nick Adams Stories* in 1972, much of this evidence became widely available. Young did not attend, however, to the process of composition itself. Yet, as the papers at the Kennedy Library reveal, an understanding of *how In Our Time* took shape is crucial to any sense of *what* it might mean.

By late January 1924, when Ernest and Hadley returned to Paris from Toronto, it is likely that Hemingway had already begun "Indian Camp" since page nine of the earliest manuscript version of the story is typed on the back of an unfinished and unsent letter dated November 6, 1923. The story was in any case finished by mid-March, when Ford Madox Ford accepted it for publication in the April 1924 issue of *Transatlantic Review*. Hemingway's first paying short story appeared alongside a section from *Finnegans Wake*.

"I am writing some damn good stories," Hemingway told Pound, in the letter informing his friend of Ford's acceptance of "Indian Camp." But "not even in his few moments of hope could he have predicted," Paul Smith writes, "the close to miraculous half-year of writing that started with this story." The writing of "Indian Camp" marked the beginning of an outpouring of eight stories in three months: "Indian Camp," "Cat in the Rain," "The End of Something," "The Three-Day Blow," "The Doctor and the Doctor's Wife," "Soldier's Home," "Mr. and Mrs. Smith" (later "Mr. and Mrs. Elliot"), and "Cross-Country Snow." Still to come was "Big Two-Hearted River," begun in May 1924 and finished in November, as well as the final addition, "The Battler," a story written after Boni and Liveright objected to the explicit sexual content of "Up in Michigan," which contained sentences like, "Oh, it's so big and it hurts so. You can't. Oh, Jim. Jim. Oh." It turned out that Gertrude Stein had been right all along in finding the story "*inaccrochable*" – unhangable.

By August 1924, Hemingway could count twelve completed stories as destined for *In Our Time*. There were the three from his first book, the eight written that spring, and the big fishing story now well under way. Thinking his new book needed to be longer, he began feathering into it the sketches from *in our time*. In the process, "A Very Short Story" and "The Revolutionist" were converted from vignettes into stories. The unity of the emergent book was one to be realized by zooming in and zooming out, Hemingway wrote to Edmund Wilson, "like looking with your eyes at something, say a passing coast line, and then looking at it with 15× binoculars. Or rather, maybe, looking at it and then going in and living in it – and then coming out and looking at it again. . . . I think you would like it, it has a pretty good unity."

"What will I have to cut?" Hemingway asked the friend who cabled him in February 1925 with the news of the Boni and Liveright offer to publish *In Our Time*. One of the things he had to cut was the beginning. Hemingway had long imagined his book as commencing with "Up in Michigan." "All the stories have a certain unity," he wrote Edward J. O'Brien in the fall of 1924. "The first 5 are in Michigan, starting with the Up in Michigan." Even at this late date, Hemingway was conceiving of the unity of his book as grounded in locale rather than in character. But "Up in Michigan" was not a Nick Adams story, and Nick, whether Hemingway quite yet knew it or not, was to provide the book's center of concern.

Once Hemingway wrote "The Battler" as a replacement story for "Up in Michigan," he began calling it "about the best I've ever written." The story was unique in the volume in showing a working couple, despite their being a punch-drunk ex-boxer and his "negro" partner. Bugs manages Ad's dementia with a tender-hearted violence, and the two men offer Nick a unique vision of civility and hospitality. It is hard to imagine any member of another couple in the book saying "I like to be with him," as Bugs does about Ad. With the addition of "The Battler," completed in the winter of 1925, the opening sequence of five Nick Adams stories was now complete, one ending with the striking image of a young man looking back at a fire in the dark.

Although it was a publisher's resistance that forced Hemingway to uncover the true beginning of his book, he quickly recognized the logic of the change and acknowledged as much in a letter to Horace Liveright:

> The new story makes the book a good deal better. It's about the best I've ever written and gives additional unity to the book as a whole.
>
> You are eliminating the second story – Up in Michigan. The next three stories move up one place each and this new story – The ~~Great Little Fighting Machine~~ Battler – takes the place at present occupied by – The Three Day Blow.

By March 1925, when this letter was written, Hemingway had experienced a crucial recognition: whether or not "Up in Michigan" was to remain a part of *In Our Time*, it could not be the first story in the book. That place, he had come to realize, was to be reserved for "Indian Camp," which was to take "its rightful place," in Paul Smith's words, "as the first story in that remarkable collection. For once then, a benighted and overly scrupulous publisher moved a Hemingway story to its perfect position." *In Our Time* now began where Nick himself begins, at the lake shore where there was another rowboat drawn up.

There is an endless revelatory power to a literary archive. One fiction readily set aside after even a casual perusal of the Hemingway papers at the Kennedy Library is the fiction of the "one true sentence." Given the chiseled finish of the published work, it is easy to believe Hemingway's description of his writing process in *A Moveable Feast*, where the older man looks back upon the days of writing *In Our Time*:

> But sometimes when I was starting a new story and I could not get it going, I would sit in front of the fire and squeeze the peel of the little oranges into the edge of the flame and watch the sputter of blue that they made. I would

> stand and look out over the roofs of Paris and think, "Do not worry. You have always written before and you will write now. All you have to do is write one true sentence. Write the truest sentence that you know." So finally I would write one true sentence, and then go on from there.

One of the illusions being entertained here is that true sentences come to Hemingway fully formed. The surviving manuscripts reveal instead a much more searching style and a writing practice devoted to returning upon the already-written in order to revise it. And this pattern obtains from the very beginning, in the opening words of "Indian Camp."

I have made much of the force and effect of the adjective "another" as it appears in the first sentence of the story. It was therefore a considerable shock to discover, on my second visit to the Hemingway papers, that the word "another" does not appear in the earliest surviving version of "Indian Camp." The two sentences leading off the story were originally combined into one. Without the crossings out and the insertions so clearly visible on the manuscript page, that sentence reads as follows: "At the lake shore there was a white rowboat drawn up with two indians standing beside it."

At some point in the revision process, Hemingway came to see that he needed to add a key word and that his flaccid opening sentence needed to be broken up into two true ones. The manuscript records this process:

> At the lake shore there
>
> nother
>
> was a ~~white~~ rowboat drawn up
>
> ~~with~~ x Two indians ~~standing~~ stood
>
> beside it.

(The "x" is Hemingway's mark indicating a period. The word "another" angles up the page after the word "a." The lower case "t" has been revised into a capital "T.") As Hemingway reworked the sentence, the letters "nother" were simply sutured onto the original word "a" and were angled up the page to fit into the space above the word "white." By the time "Indian Camp" appeared in the *Transatlantic Review*, Hemingway had also come to see that the word "another" required the reinforcing addition of the word "The":

> At the lake shore there was another
> row-boat drawn up. The two indians
> stood waiting.

In replacing the words "beside it" with the word "waiting," Hemingway created an air of expectation. More importantly, the first two sentences of *In Our Time* were now virtually intact: all that remained was to drop the hyphen in "row-boat" and to capitalize the word "indians."

That hard-won beginning was itself the result of another cut. Well before Hemingway began wrestling with Liveright over "excisions," he had begun wavering on the question of how "Indian Camp" itself should begin. The dramatic cutting in "At the lake shore" was not, in fact, the original opening of the story. That opening can be found in Item 493 at the Kennedy Library.

Readers of *The Nick Adams Stories* will be familiar with this opening under the title "Three Shots." The eight pages of manuscript written as the original beginning for "Indian Camp" were eventually to be condensed into three and a half pages in Philip Young's 1972 compilation. In the fragment, Nick feels "*ashamed*" about his memory of the previous night. Left alone in a tent by his father and Uncle George, Nick had been revisited by a fear he had felt before. "*He was afraid of dying.*" Unable to subdue his fear, he picks up a rifle and fires a prearranged signal of three shots. When the two men return to the tent, Nick claims to have heard something. The next morning, Dr. Adams finds two trees that rub together in the wind, and he asks Nick if "*that was what it was*?" "*Maybe*," Nick answers. The fragment ends with Nick being told – he has been undressing for bed as he remembers – to put on his clothes so that he can set out across the lake for the Indian Camp.

Whether we view it as an omitting or as a "*deleting*," as Paul Smith calls it, Hemingway's decision to cut his original beginning was one made for fairly obvious reasons. "Three Shots" makes Nick's shame and fear so explicit as to spare the reader the work of having to infer. It also indulges in "mental conversation," a phrase Hemingway applied to the original last nine pages of "Big Two-Hearted River," pages he also eventually cut. That ending was as unnecessary to the project of *In Our Time* as was opening with the scene of Nick in the tent. Both passages show a character thinking, and the life of the mind was an experience Hemingway chose to externalize rather than to represent directly in his early work. So, as Bernard Oldsey notes, Hemingway engaged in his "usual method of arriving at a true beginning by cutting."

But the story of the beginning was not yet over. Anyone picking up a copy of *In Our Time* today will see that the volume begins not with "Indian Camp" but with "On the Quai at Smyrna." In the story, two unnamed narrators describe the consequences of the Turkish drive through Anatolia in 1922. As a structural addition to *In Our Time*, the story reaches forward to connect up with "L'Envoi" on the book's final page, a vignette dealing with the Greek king deposed after his country's defeat in the Greco-Turkish War. The net effect of the addition of "On the Quai at Smyrna" to *In Our Time* is to enclose the book within a circle bounded by a war fought directly *after* the war to end all wars.

"On the Quai at Smyrna" is a publisher's artifact. *In Our Time* was originally published by Boni and Liveright in New York on October 5, 1925. After being wooed by Max Perkins, an editor at Scribner's, Hemingway set out to break his contract with Boni and Liveright by writing *The Torrents of Spring*, a lampoon of Sherwood Anderson, one of B & L's leading authors. Once B & L declined to publish Hemingway's *inaccrochable* parody, he was free to sever his contract with them and to move to Scribner's. In the summer of 1930, as Perkins was making plans to reissue *In Our Time*, he asked Hemingway to provide it with an Introduction. Hemingway begged off the request but did send Perkins a story about the fall of Smyrna, one he had worked on in late 1926 and early 1927. It was offered to Scribner's as an "Introduction by the Author" and was published at the head of the reissued volume under that title. Only in the 1938 collection *The First Forty-Nine* did the story acquire the title it carries to this day, "On the Quai at Smyrna." The copyright page of subsequent editions of *In Our Time* contained the following sentence: "'On the Quai at Smyrna' was first published as the introduction to the 1930 edition of IN OUR TIME." The beginning that has come down to us seems to be saying: here is where we find ourselves, on the quai at Smyrna; now, in "Indian Camp," let me show you how we got there.

Hemingway possessed an affective theory of literary form: the "unity" of a book was an effect resulting from the experience of a carefully structured whole. His recurring use of the words "reading" and "reader" signals his commitment to writing as an act of appeal to the heart and mind of an audience. The gift on offer in Hemingway's early work, as he understood it, was to allow the reader to "feel more," a response usually provoked by his carefully managed art of omission.

The first time we see Nick after "Indian Camp" he is sitting with his back against a tree. He is "reading." One wonders whether Hemingway offers Nick this activity as an adaptive response to the overwhelming scene of instruction in which he has just participated. Reading will in any case perform such a function for Krebs. After returning from the war, he discovers that he has to lie in order to be listened to, gives up talking about the war, and begins "reading a book" about it. "It was the most interesting reading he had ever done. . . . Now he was really learning about the war."

The husband in "Cat in the Rain" spends the entire story reading in bed, and Nick, confronted at the end of the book with the option of fishing the swamp, "wished he had brought something to read." In the final paragraph of "Big Two-Hearted River," Nick climbs the bank and cuts up into the woods toward the high ground. "He was going back to camp." In the manuscript, this sentence reads as follows: "He was going back to camp to read." When the sentence was typed up, the phrase "to read" had been cut.

Through the figure of Krebs, Hemingway anticipates his upcoming program of reading as well, a course of study entered into in order to prepare for the writing of *A Farewell to Arms*. In the case of both character and author, the point worth making has to do with the relationship between experience and afterthought. Learning is only completed when the self returns upon the lived experience by way of "a second Will more wise," in Wordsworth's phrase, in an act of imaginative encounter (reading) or refiguration (writing) that discovers the shape and meaning of what the self has lived through. Through this process, private memories and fantasies are transformed into a shared and usable past. For Hemingway, the shaping and meaning-making process involved in writing was typically subjected to a further correction by a second will, as the words first put down on the page were themselves so often subjected to revision.

Despite Hemingway's claim that in *In Our Time* "everything hangs on everything else," it can prove difficult for a reader of the volume to connect what lies "behind" with what lies "ahead." Hemingway's book asks us to infer, to search for patterns of continuity underlying seemingly disparate episodes. In the end, for one reader at least, as Edmund Wilson wrote in 1941, "the parts held together and produced a definite effect."

One continuity to be discovered while reading *In Our Time* is the life history of a character who feels present even when absent, as in the suite of marriage stories in which Nick Adams does not appear but where the characters stand in for and act out the possibilities of love both in Nick's adulthood and "in our time." Nick's story culminates in "Big Two-Hearted River," where he returns to the landscape of "Indian Camp" in order to restart his story on his own terms. Between the beginning and the return, Nick sees his father humiliated, ends an affair, drinks and talks with a friend, confronts incest and homosexuality, is wounded in war, and then passes through a series of veiled avatars – a numb veteran, a friend of a jailed revolutionary, a partner in three troubled marriages – before re-entering the text as the anxious husband in "Cross-Country Snow" who plucks his mind out while skiing in lieu of confronting the "hell" of his wife's pregnancy.

Nick Adams had such a hold upon his author's imagination that Hemingway continued to write about him for eight more years after the publication of *In Our Time*. Nick appears in five of the stories in the 1927 *Men Without Women*, in five of the stories in the 1933 *Winner Take Nothing*, and again in a number of fragments – including an unfinished novel that Hemingway eventually chose not to publish. In the last completed Nick Adams story, "Fathers and Sons," the boy from "Indian Camp" has become a father himself, one who has learned from his father how not to treat a son. As Hemingway wrote in 1938, "there is a line in all the Nick stories that is continuous."

In his review of *In Our Time*, D. H. Lawrence made the case for Nick as a unifier: "It is a short book: and it does not pretend to be about one man. But it is. It is as much as we need know of the man's life." One might add that by having Nick appear, disappear, and reappear, Hemingway succeeds in intensifying a reader's curiosity about his fate.

In constructing *The Nick Adams Stories*, Philip Young attempted to make Nick's story even more "continuous." Young arranged all the available stories about Nick "chronologically," in the order, that is, of the sequence of events in Nick's life. Since the order of the publication of the stories is read by Young as a "jumbled sequence," Hemingway's development as a writer is thereby subordinated to Nick's development as a character.

In Young's scheme, Nick's story becomes overarranged. Even then, Young appears to have gotten the sequence wrong. "The End of Something" and "The Three-Day Blow" are positioned after "Big Two-Hearted River" in Young's "over-all narrative." But Nick is clearly younger in these stories than he is in "Big Two-Hearted River," at most a boy in his late teens. Marjorie is one of Nick's early loves, and Bill is the confidant who fills out the triangle. "Big Two-Hearted River" is the story of an older man, now married, coming back from the war, although there is no mention of the war in it.

Young's arrangement of the Nick Adams stories pays no attention to a reader's experience of *In Our Time* as he moves through it. Deeply attentive to the logic of sequence, Hemingway created a book in which the reader's attempt to discover sequences would give the experience much of its meaning and its force. While Nick's life is offered up as the through-story, we are diverted from it by his disappearance from the text after his wounding in chapter VI and also by the continual intervening presence of the vignettes.

Yet, however disconcerting a reader might find them, the vignettes are where Hemingway believed they should be. As he wrote to Ernest Walsh in March 1925: "Book is called In Our Time like the little one. Is short stories,

15 of them, with a chapter of In Our Time between each story. That's what I originally wrote them for. It all hooks up." When Max Perkins suggested grouping together all the vignettes for the 1930 reissue, Hemingway responded: "Max *please believe* me that those chapters are where they belong." Despite Hemingway's claim, it is not always possible to discern a clear connection between a vignette and the story it precedes or follows. The last vignette written for *in our time* did, however, find a place in *In Our Time* that is both necessary and overdetermined. How that vignette got written also reveals much about Hemingway's use of revision to give form to the overall structure of a book.

Ernest and Hadley Hemingway met Ezra Pound within a few months of their arrival in Paris in December 1921. By the period in which Hemingway was finishing up *in our time*, Pound had become a fast friend and a frequent correspondent: of the 247 letters published in the second volume of the Cambridge edition of *The Letters of Ernest Hemingway*, thirty-two are addressed to Pound. In a letter written in early August of 1923, Hemingway responded to Pound's critique of the vignette sequence. One change made involved shifting the death of Maera (chapter XIV in *In Our Time*) from a hospital room to the bullring. But the biggest change was the addition of a final vignette based on a story Hemingway had shared with Pound about the hanging of a Chicago gangster in 1921. Pound had liked the story and urged Hemingway to work it up into one more of his "frozen moments."

Hemingway's letter to Pound about the emerging form of *in our time* reveals both his willingness to revise and his abiding concern with reconciling the way things "start" with how they "finish off":

> Dear Ezra,
>
> I will do the hanging. Have redone the death of Maera altogether different and fixed the others. The new death is good. Don't know about Gobar.
>
> They should each one be headed Chapter 1, Chapter 2 etc. When they are read together they all hook up. It seems funny but they do. The bulls start. then reappear and then finish off. The war starts clear and noble just like it did, Mons etc., gets close and blurred and finished with the feller who goes home and gets clap. The refugees leave thrace, due to the Greek ministers, who are shot. The whole thing closes with the talk with the King of Greece and his Queen in their garden (just written), which shows the king all right. The last sentence in it is - - - Like all Greeks what he really wanted was to get to America. ––– My pal Shorty, movie operator with me in Thrace, just brings the dope on the King. Edifying.
>
> The radicals start noble in the young Magyar story and get bitched. America appears in the cops shooting the guys who robbed the cigar store. It has form all right.

The king closes it in swell shape. Oh that king.

I will commence hanging. Then I think she rides. Will try and drop in on you tomorrow a.m.

Immer
Hem.

The story of the hanging of Sam Cardinella was needed, then, in order to make the thing ride. Two years later, as Hemingway began interpolating the vignettes from *in our time* between his new short stories, the question became: where would the hanging take its place in the long structure of *In Our Time*?

Not, at first, in the place it finally assumed. Item 97A in the Kennedy Library contains a Cablogramme with a handwritten table of contents of "Chapters from In Our Time." It lists a chapter, as the vignettes were to be called, and then a story. At the end of the list, the story "My Old Man" is followed by "Chapter Fourteen," the Sam Cardinella vignette. Then Hemingway has listed "Big Two-Hearted River." The last long story was to be printed without an intervening vignette.

Having given the matter a second thought, Hemingway then drew an arrow down the page, one pointing from "Chapter Fourteen" to the space between Part One and Part Two of "Big Two-Hearted River." The revised list looks like this:

Chapter Fourteen x (They hanged

Sam Cardinella at six o'clock in the

Morning in the corridor of the county jail"

Big Two Hearted River

Part one

Insert chapter–Hanging–

Part two

In looking over the book's overall design, Hemingway came to see that the hanging belonged between the two parts of the final story, where it would become chapter XV.

"*They hanged Sam Cardinella at six o'clock in the morning in the corridor of the county jail.*" The condemned man has to be carried to the place of execution. He is attended by a priest who says, "*Be a man, my son.*" In his fear, Sam Cardinella loses "*control of his sphincter muscle.*" The disgusted guards strap him into a chair, and the priest skips back from the scaffolding just before the drop falls.

The difficulty of sustaining the performance of being male, of operating within what Thomas Strychacz calls "Hemingway's Theaters of Masculinity," is here given its most efficient treatment. Told to "*be a man*," a man shames himself in the most abject and public way. In his reading of *In Our Time*, Strychacz draws a sharp contrast between Sam Cardinella and Nick Adams. Sam's "humiliation is intensified by his inability to control the theatricalization of his last moments"; a scaffold, after all, is also a stage. Nick, on the other hand, "postulates the existence of a self-possessed and nontheatrical masculinity, fashioned without an empowering audience. In this respect, Cardinella's heroic opposite must be said to be the Nick Adams of 'Big Two-Hearted River.'"

It is more accurate to say that Sam is Nick's dark familiar. The considered positioning of the Sam Cardinella vignette, coming as it does between the two parts of "Big Two-Hearted River," itself makes this case. Part I ends with Nick pitching camp, eating dinner, remembering Hopkins, crawling into his tent, executing a mosquito, and going "to sleep." On the facing and the following page is positioned the Sam Cardinella vignette. The reader reads the vignette, turns the page, and finds the first sentence of "Big Two-Hearted River: Part II": "In the morning the sun was up and the tent was starting to get hot."

What happens to Sam Cardinella happens while Nick is asleep. We recognize the concerns of the vignette as Nick's concerns; he is less the heroic opposite of the condemned man than simply another character struggling to understand what it might mean to "be a man." Of course, these are thoughts Nick attempts not to think: "He felt he had left everything behind, the need for thinking, the need to write, other needs." "*He was not thinking*," Hemingway wrote about Nick, in the concluding pages eventually cut from "Big Two-Hearted River." "*He was holding something in his head.*" The last sentence of "On Writing," as Philip Young chooses to title these pages, repeats the claim: "*He was holding something in his head.*" Sam's story is what fills Nick's head when he is not awake; Sam, that is, is Nick's nightmare.

Nick's nightmare of Sam Cardinella reverberates backward through the reading experience of *In Our Time* in the same way that the word "another" in the first sentence of "Indian Camp" anticipates what is to come. The linking of the vignette to Nick's inner life thus makes possible the following claim: in *In Our Time*, the vignettes are the dreams haunting the minds of the characters met in the stories.

In Our Time offers a reader an experience of two kinds of material, what might be called its manifest and its latent content. The book contains testimony about waking life as well as an account of the dream work arising in the nights that fall between the book's "plenty of days." In taking up the challenge of seeing how "it all hooks up," the reader is placed in a position of great difficulty and great dignity, since the role being assigned to him resembles nothing so much as that of the dedicated analyst. As Hemingway issues his call for an act of listening, one testifying to his trust in the capacity of his audience to confront "things" from which Nick himself will often turn away, Nick's unfinished education becomes an occasion for a reader's painful and potentially liberating effort of understanding.

The richest subject for analysis provided by *In Our Time* is the book's ending. Just as "Big Two-Hearted River" has two parts, so it can be read as having two endings: the scene in which Nick pitches his tent and the scene in which Nick confronts the swamp. Twoness can be said to be the subject here, as Hemingway's book refuses to end in just one way. Nick's behavior on his return to the landscapes of his youth is so layered and so complex as to have solicited an unending outpouring of critical speculation.

At the beginning of the story, Nick arrives at a place where "even the surface had been burned off the ground." Yet this return to his own personal waste land contains within it the possibility of a resurfacing. For Nick, the resurfacing takes two forms: given the utter effacement of the town he once knew, it remains for him to reinscribe with meaning the landscape he moves through. At the same time, he works hard to prevent certain kinds of thoughts and feelings from coming to the surface, works hard, as D. H. Lawrence has it, to keep himself "loose."

"Big Two-Hearted River" opens with a third-person narrator describing Nick's return: "The train went on up the track out of sight, around one of the hills of burnt timber. Nick sat down on the bundle of canvas and bedding the baggage man had pitched out of the door of the baggage car." It is striking to discover the original manuscript of "Big Two-Hearted River" beginning quite differently: "We got off the train at Seney. There was no station." The "We" would later be changed to a "They." These attempts at a beginning contain two quite unimaginable outcomes: Nick as not alone but accompanied, part of a "They"; and Nick as the first-person narrator of the story he is in, part of a "We." In the end, Hemingway realized that the story had to be focalized through Nick but not narrated by him and that Nick had to be alone.

"The story was about coming back from the war but there was no mention of the war in it." This sentence about the meaning of "Big Two-Hearted River" can be found in chapter 8 of *A Moveable Feast.*

Since the claim was made more than thirty years after the story was written, it has the status of after-wisdom. Hemingway's insight into what goes unmentioned was itself the result of second thought; the sentence about coming back from the war cannot be found in the manuscript version of the passage about writing "Big Two-Hearted River." The sentence was added quite late to a typescript of "Hunger Was Good Discipline" (JK/EH 150, 8) and is interpolated in Hemingway's big, looping hand.

Nick's obsessively tidy mental and physical habits can certainly be read as a response to shell shock. His walk toward the campsite at the river is carefully calibrated. "He did not need to get his map out. He knew where he was from the position of the river." The landscape he walks through figures forth a concern with limits and boundaries: "Sharp at the edge of this extension of the forest floor commenced the sweet fern." Here, the vegetable world appears to create a neat pattern as if in response to a command issued by Nick's edginess. The alliterative "s's" and "t's" and "f's" also give an edge to the very sound of the sentence itself.

It was perhaps during the writing of "Big Two-Hearted River" that Hemingway came to realize that the mind needs a landscape, a set of physical contours through which to realize itself and to think things out, and so thinking becomes like a walk through an ever-materializing past, where the rememberer bumps up against his unavoidable spots of time. Later, in "A Way You'll Never Be," when Nick remembers the low house painted yellow by the canal, he knows that the scene means something to him, however much Hemingway's prose refuses to spell out those meanings. "That house meant more than anything," Nick thinks to himself. Not what the lay of the land means but *that* it means and continues to acquire meaning by way of Nick's repeated night thoughts – this is the crucial insight.

While Nick's war experience surely conditions much of his behavior in "Big Two-Hearted River," the first culmination provided by the story, the scene in which Nick pitches his tent, makes much more sense when read as his response to the awkwardness of beginnings as they are imagined in "Indian Camp." For Nick, I am arguing, the original traumatic event is not the Wound of War but the uncanny fact of having been originated – and even that trauma is one entirely mediated by how Nick chooses to take it.

Nick levels a piece of ground, smoothes out the sandy soil, unpacks his tent, pegs the sides taut, and then crawls in:

> Inside the tent the light came through the brown canvas. It smelled pleasantly of canvas. Already there was something mysterious and homelike. Nick was happy as he crawled inside the tent. He had not been unhappy all

day. This was different though. Now things were done. There had been this to do. Now it was done. It had been a hard trip. He was very tired. That was done. He had made his camp. He was settled. Nothing could touch him. It was a good place to camp. He was there, in the good place. He was in his home where he had made it. Now he was hungry.

He came out, crawling under the cheesecloth. It was quite dark outside. It was lighter in the tent.

The short four- and five-word sentences and the repeated sounding of the word "done" here lend to Hemingway's prose and the psyche being notated by way of it a quality of running in place. Nick has reached a kind of end, even perhaps the possibility of rest, and yet the overly insistent tone takes on, as so often with Nick, a sense of protesting too much. Sartre's description of the Hemingway style hits home here: "Each sentence refuses to exploit the momentum accumulated by preceding ones. Each is a new beginning." While the phrase "new beginning" may sound promising, such an effect is the opposite of what Nick is trying to achieve – a resolved ending. The rhythm of the prose here conveys a sense that Nick's actions are still compelled rather than free and that the many efficient motions being made are unintegrated.

Three words in the passage capture what Nick has lost – or never had – and is hoping to refind: "the good place." Just as every bull has its "*querencia*," its "preferred locality" in the ring, so Hemingway characters will continue to seek and to find and, more often than not, to lose again the good place. "This place is pretty good," Nick says in "Now I Lay Me," about the room where he lies and hears the silkworms eating. "It seemed like a good place," Frederic Henry thinks about the barn where he takes refuge during the retreat from Caporetto. "There were still good places to go," Hemingway tells himself, near the end of *Green Hills of Africa*. And, in *Islands in the Stream*, Johnny Goodner says to Thomas Hudson about Bimini, "It's a good place."

However homelike it may feel, the good place is also experienced as "the strange country." "The Strange Country" is the title given to a fragment of a novel Hemingway worked on in the late 1940s and early 1950s. In it, an older man has an affair with a younger woman; he calls her "daughter" and refers to himself as "father." When Roger and the girl make love for the first time "in the dark he went into the strange country and it was very strange indeed, hard to enter." Hard to enter perhaps because, given the incestuous dimensions of the affair, the girl's strange country stands in for the good place the male originates from and is thereafter forbidden to re-enter. "This *unheimlich* place, however," as Freud maintains, "is the entrance to the former *heim* (home) of all human beings, to the place where everyone dwelt once upon a time and in the beginning."

Nick creates a space, crawls into it, feels hungry, crawls out again. The desire to control beginnings here fulfills itself as Nick restages his birth on his own terms. But, of course, Nick's tent is sterile, empty except for his "things." Something crucial to any lasting recovery has been left out: the female body. Nick here indulges in a fantasy of autogenesis that attempts to supplant sexual genesis. The striving to fulfill such a fantasy can, for the male imagination, sometimes result in the making of art. Yet any enduring possibility of success in that kind of making, Hemingway comes to believe, depends upon taking the risk of creating a good place with an actual woman.

By the time of his culminating appearance in the Hemingway canon, Nick Adams appears to have worked things out. In "Fathers and Sons," published in 1933, Nick makes peace with his beginnings by remembering his father as both caring and limited, by acknowledging and celebrating his sexual history, and by instructing his son with a tact and protectiveness never shown him when he was young. Somehow, in the eight years between the writing of "Big Two-Hearted River" and the writing of "Fathers and Sons," Hemingway has been able to imagine Nick's growing up. That Nick has only begun to do so on his fishing trip at the end of *In Our Time* is indicated by the phrase still haunting his erection of the tent. For all his belief that things can be "smoothed out," the good place he has attempted to create remains, also, "mysterious and homelike."

Part II of "Big Two-Hearted River" ends with the even more suggestive set piece of the swamp. No single passage in the Hemingway canon has occasioned so many symbolic readings. "It's a symbol," Bill says to Nick in "The Three-Day Blow," as they discuss the meaning of the sword in *Forest Lovers*. "'Sure' said Nick, 'but it isn't practical.'" Symbolic readings of Hemingway's early work prove impractical largely because of that work's resistance to the notion that one thing can be compared to something else: it is a prose noticeably absent of metaphor. Hemingway's early avoidance of figurative language has the curious effect, however, of endowing everything noticed as somehow significant. Since so few details are elevated by figuration above any others, the entire field of experience comes to feel suffused with meaning and value. Every little detail can speak with what Richard Hovey calls "hallucinated urgency." Or, as Hemingway himself put it, in *Death in the Afternoon*, his work aims to provide "the sequence of motion and fact which made the emotion." In moving through a story like "Big Two-Hearted River," then, a reader can feel a continuous pressure to interpret its every fact and motion as somehow expressive of how Nick is feeling.

The swamp occupies, however, a different order of importance than the grasshoppers that have turned black after the fire or the fact that Nick likes to open cans. It occupies the place of an ending. And it is easy enough to see why *In Our Time* would come to rest here: not only does the swamp contrast with the tent in such a way as to indicate that Nick's work is not yet done, but it also conjures up, in its darkness and its wetness and its interweavings and in the motions required of those brave enough to move through it – "You would have to keep almost level with the ground to move at all" – the uncanny place that is the home of every one of us, once upon a time and in the beginning.

Whatever the swamp may be taken to be, a more pressing question is left open at the end: will Nick fish the swamp? As he considers whether or not to do so, Nick kills and cleans two male trout. "All the insides clean and compact, coming out all together." The cleanness and compactness of these "insides" evoke Nick's tent and contrast with the imbrications of the swamp. Nick's act of cutting and cleaning gives a kind of answer to the looming question; he, in any case, stands up, climbs the bank, and begins to return to camp. "He looked back. The river just showed through the trees. There were plenty of days coming when he could fish the swamp." With these sentences, the story ends.

The phrase "plenty of days coming" sounds forward across more than thirty years of writing to find its echo in Hemingway's memory, one recorded in *A Moveable Feast,* of sitting in the Closerie des Lilas and writing "Big Two-Hearted River":

> When I stopped writing I did not want to leave the river where I could see the trout in the pool, its surface pushing and swelling smooth against the resistance of the log-driven piles of the bridge. The story was about coming back from the war but there was no mention of the war in it.
>
> But in the morning the river would be there and I must make it and the country and all that would happen. There were days ahead to be doing that each day.

Hemingway's story and the memory of it turn upon the repetition of a single word. "There were days ahead to be doing that each day," he writes, later, about how he felt then. "Ahead the river narrowed and went into a swamp," he wrote then, about what Nick finds himself facing at the end. In the story, Nick is smoking and watching the river when this sentence abrupts into view. While it is often difficult to see ahead and fearful to move ahead in *In Our Time*, it is nevertheless the direction in which Nick and the reader are asked to go. In the passage from *A Moveable Feast*, Hemingway accomplishes a revision of the force of the word "ahead," converting it from a source of anxiety into a sense of promise. What lies ahead is the possibility of writing more stories that express fears and apprehensions but that also allow for an experience of working through. Of course, as Hemingway remembers the promise of days ahead in his memoir, he is actually looking back at a work already accomplished and so assures himself that the promise made was a promise kept.

In this reading, the swamp does not symbolize the female body, or mature sexuality, or the unconscious, or the stream of consciousness, or a regression to origins. It is, quite simply, the *ahead*. And the meaning given in *A Moveable Feast* to what lies ahead, something the young Hemingway clearly apprehended as he wrote his story in 1924, was the promise of a career.

But will that career achieve a reconciliation between Hemingway's anxiety about the uncontrollability of beginnings and his obsession with trying to control endings such that a character might be allowed the experience of life, of a true middle? The beginning of an answer can be found in an ending considered and rejected for "Big Two-Hearted River."

In August of 1924 Hemingway wrote the editor of *The Little Review* about his having "finished a swell story of 100 pages." These were handwritten pages, and my count of the pages in the manuscript of "Big Two-Hearted River" held at the Kennedy Library puts the number at 113. It was a long story, and, at some point in the next few months, Hemingway realized that it had to be cut.

In the story, as Hemingway wrote to Gertrude Stein and Alice B. Toklas, he had been "trying to do the country like Cezanne." He even said so in the story itself. "*He, Nick, wanted to write about the country so it would be there like Cezanne had done it in painting.*" This sentence can be found in the "On Writing" section of *The Nick Adams Stories*.

The pages printed by Philip Young mark a striking departure from Hemingway's chosen practice. Previously, whenever Nick's mind has begun "starting to work," Hemingway has chosen to "choke it" with various stylistic and narrative strategies. Now, as he nears the end, Hemingway allows Nick's mind to range freely in both memory and thought. Nick thinks about "*writing that was any good*," and then makes the connection to Cezanne, a painter who "*started with all the tricks*" and who then "*broke the whole thing down and built the real thing.*"

When shown these pages of "meditations," as Gertrude Stein was to describe them, she responded by saying, "Hemingway, remarks are not literature." Stein's own remark may have prompted Hemingway to cut his meditations; by November of 1924 he was in any case writing Donald Ogden Stewart "that the last eleven pages of the last story I got you are crap" and that Stewart was to "detach" them and to "substitute the five pages enclosed." Stewart had been circulating the manuscript of *In Our Time* to publishers in New York, and it was therefore imperative that the substitution be made quickly. "Wouldn't it be funny," Hemingway had written another friend a few days earlier, "if some publisher had accepted it because of the stuff that had to be cut?"

So, a long passage of "mental conversation" was replaced by "just the straight fishing." The material had to be cut because it violated a contract made with the reader involving the maintenance of a certain kind of dignity. "The dignity of the movement of an ice-berg," like the dignity of Hemingway's early style, "is due to only one-eighth of it being above water." As he wrote in *Death in the Afternoon*,

> If a writer of prose knows enough about what he is writing about he may omit things that he knows and the reader, if the writer is writing truly enough, will have a feeling of those things as strongly as though the writer had stated them. The dignity of the movement of an ice-berg is due to only one-eighth of it being above water. A writer who omits things because he does not know them only makes hollow places in his writing.

This passage, along with the sentences in *A Moveable Feast* describing "my new theory" of the "omitted," constitute Hemingway's most cogent defense of the purposes of his early style. Realizing that the final pages of "Big Two-Hearted River" had violated those purposes by giving his reader direct access to the motion of Nick's mind, Hemingway decided to cut them.

The decision not to include Nick's mental conversation has more to do with form than with content. What Nick thinks about is less striking – and disruptive of the Hemingway project – than is the fact that the reader is allowed to see a man thinking. To be able to go into the mind and to represent a character as feeling at home there is, at this point in the career, the undiscovered country. Hemingway will, however, eventually find the courage to explore it and, with a change of style, comes a change of subject. This, too, is anticipated in the closing paragraphs of "On Writing."

It happens when Nick stops thinking about how "*Cezanne would do the stretch of river and the swamp*" and decides to begin "*moving in the picture*" he has been imagining. At this point in the passage, Nick does two things. He reaches for the one trout still in his sack, finds "*the old boy was alive,*" and lets him go. He then begins to walk back to camp. On the way, he runs into another animal, also alive. "On Writing" concludes with these sentences:

> *Ahead of him he saw a rabbit, flat out on the trail. He stopped, grudging. The rabbit was barely breathing. There were two ticks on the rabbit's head, one behind each ear. They were gray, tight with blood, as big as grapes. Nick pulled them off, their heads tiny and hard, with moving feet. He stepped on them on the trail.*
>
> *Nick picked up the rabbit, limp, with dull button eyes, and put it under a sweet fern bush beside the trail. He felt its heart beating as he laid it down. The rabbit lay quiet under the bush. It might come to, Nick thought. Probably the ticks had attached themselves to it as it crouched in the grass. Maybe after it had been dancing in the open. He did not know.*
>
> *He went on up the trail to the camp. He was holding something in his head.*

Letting a seemingly doomed animal live will become for Hemingway an increasingly attractive thing. Near the end of *Across the River and into the Trees*, Bobby the bird dog returns with "a mallard drake in his jaws. The gray white neck and the green head were swaying up and down as a snake's might move. It was a movement without hope." Despite the summary judgment, Colonel Cantwell realizes the drake is only wing-tipped and therefore decides to spare his life. "We'll keep him for a caller or to turn loose in the Spring."

What Hemingway was clearly holding in his head as he tried out and discarded the scenes with the trout and the rabbit was a new sense of an ending. The animal most in need of a reprieve, it would turn out, was the human animal. The motion apprehended as possible but not yet accepted as plausible was to imagine life as more than a movement without hope. The ending, like the beginning, could not change: "There is no end except death and birth is the only beginning." But perhaps a heart could nevertheless be left "beating" at the end. This will be the gift offered to Robert Jordan in the final sentence of *For Whom the Bell Tolls*. In the fifteen years between the sparing of the rabbit and the writing of that sentence, the hard facts surrounding beginnings and endings would not change. But Hemingway's attitude toward beginnings and endings did change, and in that changing what was felt about love, and time, and life itself changed as well.

CHAPTER 3

The End of Pleasure

The Sun Also Rises

It is "against time" that characters in Hemingway's early fiction must make their difficult way. How long things last and that things end are among their overriding concerns, and Hemingway comes to their assistance by deploying the narrative devices of digression, repetition, and deferral. Immersion – whether in a meal, a landscape, or a bullfight – is also frequently on offer. Each of these fictional strategies serves an implicit demand, "the demand," as Reynolds Price writes, "to survive the end of pleasure."

The fishing trip Jake Barnes and Bill Gorton share in Burguete is a case in point. The trip interposes a little ease, a relief after the numbing routines of Paris, and a breather before entering the overwhelming "hum" of the fiesta in Pamplona. Hemingway was to become a master of turning aside from the momentum of a narrative headed for an unhappy ending, and nowhere is his art of digression on better display than in chapters XI, XII, and XIII of *The Sun Also Rises*.

"We all got in the car and it started up the white dusty road into Spain." Having arrived in Pamplona, Jake and Bill catch a bus for Burguete. Riding on the top in the sun, they share a wineskin with some Basques going their way. It is cold in the hotel when they arrive, so they order a hot rum punch. A dinner of vegetable soup, stew, and wild strawberries follows. That night Jake hears the wind blowing. "It felt good to be warm and in bed."

Chapter XII is the heart of the interval. Jake wakes early on a clear day, digs for worms, talks with Bill, shares coffee with buttered toast and jam. Then they begin the walk to the Irati River. "It was a long walk and the country was very fine." At the river, Jake offers his friend some worms but Bill opts for flies and heads downstream. Fishing at the foot of a dam, Jake soon has six trout. Bill returns to display his catch, each trout bigger than anything Jake has caught. They share a lunch of chicken and hard-boiled eggs and the wine Jake has kept cool in the water of a spring. They talk about "this Brett business." The day wanes, and they start up

> the road into the woods. It was a long walk home to Burguete, and it was dark when we came down across the fields to the road, and along the road between the houses of the town, their windows lighted, to the inn.
>
> We stayed five days at Burguete and had good fishing.

Chapter XII ends with the paragraph beginning "We stayed five days at Burguete and had good fishing."

It has been a fine trip, and it sounds as if it were over. But the reader is treated to a pleasant surprise on turning the page to chapter XIII: "One morning I went down to breakfast and the Englishman, Harris, was already at the table." We have just met Harris in the previous paragraph, and it had seemed he was a mere detail in Jake's summary of a good time. Instead, we are invited to extend our play by way of a "healthful interlude" in which Harris expresses his "pleasure" in the company of the two Americans and gently attempts to persuade them to stay. Even at the end of the stay in Burguete, there is the promise of repetition. "We'll fish together again," Jake says to Harris, as he and Bill take their leave.

Hemingway's handling of the end of the fishing trip can be contrasted with his management of the end of the fiesta. Romero fights and kills his bull despite having been "badly marked" by the beating Cohn has given him the night before. Then Brett goes off with Romero. Jake admits to feeling "low as hell" and turns to absinthe, pouring "the water directly into it . . . instead of letting it drip" and thereby violating the protocol of how the drink ought to be made. Jake now wants to hurry his sensations. Bill responds: "Don't drink it fast that way. It will make you sick." Feeling drunk, Jake tries and fails to go to sleep. He rejoins Mike and Bill downstairs "at the table, and it seemed as though about six people were missing." Book II ends with these words, and, on the following page, instead of delivering a reprieve, Hemingway writes: "In the morning it was all over."

Hemingway knew that a pleasure cannot be a pleasure unless it ends. Time and pleasure are locked in a lovely dance of death, with the unrepeatable forward movement of the one partner to the dance at once defining and delimiting the duration of the other. An epigram considered for *The Sun Also Rises* was lifted from Andrew Marvell's "To His Coy Mistress." "Had we but world enough and time," the poem begins, but we have enough of neither, and a challenge is thereby taken up by Hemingway's imagination: to become, as Vladimir Nabokov called him, "an epicure of duration."

The fishing trip reveals what pleasure so often is in Hemingway: walking, looking, eating, drinking, fishing, talking. Of course, loving is the great pleasure imagined by Jake and denied to him. While sex often occurs off the page in Hemingway, this must necessarily be the case for Jake, given the nature of his physical wound, and so the most we can expect from the narrator, as in the scene between Jake and Brett in his room in Paris, is a somewhat cruel ellipsis: "Then later: 'Do you feel better, darling? Is the head any better?'"

Reading can be added to the list of Hemingway's favorite pleasures. Jake loves to read all kinds of newspapers and surrounds himself with a good supply of books. They help him get through the nights. "After supper we went up-stairs and smoked and read in bed to keep warm." Any number of other pleasures could be added to the list, but only two, as Nick Adams admits in "On Writing," give "*the greatest pleasure*" – making and learning about art.

In *The Sun Also Rises*, Hemingway begins to work toward the recognition that the pleasure we take in our many pleasures is indistinguishable from the pleasure we take in narrative itself. And that pleasure is all about a good timing of things. A short story consumed in a single sitting is less likely than is the long form of the novel to develop in the reader a capacity for both patience and expectation. To use Hemingway's own terms, the giving and having of pleasure turns upon the word "wait" and upon the word "again."

"Why don't they start?" Robert Cohn asks before the first bullfight. He finds it difficult to wait. As early as chapter III, Robert displays a "look of eager, deserving expectation." As he complains to Jake, "my life is going so fast and I'm not really living it." Cohn's quarrel with time's rush and its deferrals translates into an "incapacity to enjoy." As a man condemned to only stand and wait, Jake finds Cohn's impatience difficult to take. In Pamplona, it bespeaks a fundamental misunderstanding of the pleasure on offer at any scheduled public performance. The timing of the event is out of one's control, and one must wait for it to begin. Even the matador must do so, as Hemingway writes in *The Dangerous Summer*: "As the bull came he waited until the exact moment when the horns would get him."

In the climactic bullfight scene at the end of Book II, Romero kills "not as he had been forced to by the last bull, but as he wanted to." He kills *recibiéndo*. In *Death in the Afternoon*, Hemingway describes this technique as the "most difficult, dangerous and emotional way to kill bulls." It is difficult because in killing *recibiéndo* the matador kills "the bull from in front awaiting his charge with the sword without moving the feet." It is difficult because the matador has to stand and wait:

> The bull charged and Romero waited for the charge, the muleta held low, sighting along the blade, his feet firm. Then without taking a step forward, he became one with the bull, the sword was in high between the shoulders, the bull had followed the low-slung flannel, that disappeared as Romero lurched clear to the left, and it was over.

In the first draft of this scene, as Frederic Svoboda has shown, the matador kills in the manner of modern bullfighting by going to the bull. "He made the three steps, the one that takes the measure, the one that gets there and then the one that carries the left shoulder forward and drives in the sword." In the revised version of this scene, Svoboda writes, "the narrator's expertise is no longer shown in interpretation" but rather in the simple enactment of the pleasure given by watching the matador awaiting what is to come.

In the work of writing or reading a fictional narrative, a sustainable desire depends upon a mastery of the various disciplines of deferral. The impatient reader turns to the back of the book and reads the ending. But to give away the ending to oneself is to be deprived of the equally edifying experience of the middle. This is where things can happen, where life is lived out.

Fitzgerald was generous in noting Hemingway's commitment to the art of deferral. "Your Englishman on the fishing trip in T. S. A. R.," he wrote in his "Notes" on *A Farewell to Arms*, "contributes to the tautness of waiting for Brett." An interval giving so much pleasure to the reader is experienced, Fitzgerald realized, as the price of having to wait for the arrival of another and equally compelling pleasure. Even for characters who feel "caught by time," the having of pleasure depends upon the taking of the time that should truly be allowed for the doing of a thing. In the case of having a drink, for instance, this means allowing some time to pass before "drinking this, the first one of the day, the finest one there is." What makes this drink in the opening scene of *Green Hills of Africa* so compelling is not only that it is the first one of the day but that Hemingway has waited for it. The sentence had to be waited for as well; it did not exist in the original version of the scene. After being written, that version was crossed out in Hemingway's hand. In it, he had written simply "of drinking the whiskey and water alone in the car with the driver" and of feeling "closer to Africa than I had yet been."

Another pleasure made available by a life in time is the experience of return. Hemingway was skeptical about attempts at return – "Don't go back," he wrote, after revisiting the site of his wounding at Fossalta – but he also understood that much pleasure seeking is driven by a longing to connect again with something once had and lost, something often called "home." For most people, the impossibility of a literal return home in adult life is compensated for by the experience of love. In the character of Jake Barnes, Hemingway created a character cut off from this option. While Jake's war wound may seem to be the origin of the problem, the scene where Jake walks across the town square in Pamplona reveals him as having been cut off from the possibility of return – from homecoming – well before ever going to war. The scene contains the single memory of home Jake is afforded in the novel:

> Walking across the square to the hotel everything looked new and changed . . . I felt as I felt once coming home from an out-of-town football game. . . .They were raking the lawns and burning leaves in the road, and I stopped for a long time and watched. It was all strange. Then I went on, and my feet seemed to be a long way off, and everything seemed to come from a long way off, and I could hear my feet walking a great distance away. I had been kicked in the head early in the game. It was like that crossing the square.

The one time Jake comes "home" in *The Sun Also Rises*, he returns to find it "strange." This primal sense of dispossession, as much as any wound of war, stands behind the novel's profound sense of lovelessness and condemns Jake to waiting for a return that will never occur. For Jake, the most important thing will not happen again. Instead, he is offered the pleasures of dailiness, as an early reviewer of the novel discerned: "it is a mannerism of Hemingway's to recount exactly his characters' physical evolutions, through doors, up and downstairs, in and out of bed, as though establishing alibis." In having Jake attend so closely to these humble repetitions, Hemingway attempts to exonerate him from the crime of killing time.

Deferral and repetition are pleasures of the text. But Jake is in the narrative, not reading about it, and so he can experience the strategies that allow for a reader's pleasure as quite another thing. For him, waiting and repetition mean, mostly, pain. What is deferred – endlessly – is the experience of sexual union with Brett. And what is repeated, except during the interval of the fishing trip, are a series of motions that come to feel like anything but a "good time."

On the evening after the first bullfight, as everyone gathers for supper, Jake has "a feeling of things coming that you could not prevent happening." He feels apprehension about what lies ahead because he so often experiences the "feeling of going through something that has all happened before." This feeling first arises while he is joking with Brett and the Count about their "little friend, Zizi." "I support that boy," the Count says, "but I don't want to have him around." Brett responds: "He is rather hard." Then the Count says, "About his future you can't ever tell."

In French, "zizi" is a slang term for "penis." All the joking in the world cannot undo the fact that Jake's "little friend" has gone missing. What follows the joking is therefore predictable: "'Oh darling,' Brett said, 'I'm so miserable.'" It is after Brett says this that Jake has the feeling of going through something that has happened before. They keep dancing and talking, and the feeling of recurrence recurs. "I had the feeling as in a nightmare of it all being something repeated, something I had been through and that now I must go through again."

Experience here reduces to déjà vu. Just what is being repeated Jake cannot or will not articulate: it is "something." So the recognition of the pattern also involves a familiar anxious hiding behind an abstract noun. Jake certainly has unique and powerful reasons for feeling anxious. On the other hand, the obviousness of his sexual wound does act, and has acted for generations of readers, as a screening mechanism, a sort of ever-ready explanation for why and how Jake behaves and feels as he does. The repetitiveness of his behavior so beautifully captured in the paragraph opening chapter V – "I walked . . . I read . . . I got . . . I walked . . . I passed . . . I stepped . . . I walked . . . I walked" – bespeaks a sense of injury and displacement occurring long before Jake ever went to war.

Hemingway devoted much of his early career to the patient excavation of the "something" being repressed. While *The Sun Also Rises* presents the problem in action, it does not set itself the task of trying to understand it. Instead, the novel gives us Hemingway's most poignant depiction of the many strategies his characters have devised for talking around things. "I just talk around it," Brett says near the end. The upside for the reader is to come to feel more than he understands, a consequence, as Hemingway maintained in a passage in *A Moveable* Feast, of reading through a text in which "you could omit anything if you knew that you omitted and the omitted part would strengthen the story and make people feel something more than they understood."

So, what is it that a reader comes to feel if not fully to understand? That if learning what it is all about proves an unachievable option, then perhaps the best available strategy for minimizing pain in this fictional world is to find a way to be "in it." In chapter XIV, as Jake thinks about all he has "paid" in loving Brett, he appears to renounce any interest in learning as a preparation for experience. "Perhaps as you went along you did learn something. I did not care what it was all about. All I wanted to know was how to live in it. Maybe if you found out how to live in it you learned from that what it was all about." The fiesta becomes the perfect proving ground for Jake's theory of immersive learning: "This hum went on, and we were in it and a part of it."

The theory would seem to reject the belief that an education can be acquired in advance of living out the lessons it is supposed to impart. In this model of experience, the how inevitably precedes the what. As a result, learning arrives too late to spare the self the many forms of self-disgust. Jake wishes Mike would not behave so terribly to Cohn, but he also admits liking "to see him hurt." The realization of his complicity in Cohn's humiliation "made me disgusted at myself. That was morality; things that made you disgusted afterward."

Bullfighting has the appeal of providing Jake with an experience in which it is possible in advance to know what it is "all about." Hemingway underscores the point by repeating the phrase from chapter XIV: "I sat beside Brett and explained to Brett what it was all about." A bullfight can be anticipated and explained because it has a definite end:

> I sat beside Brett and explained to Brett what it was all about. I told her about watching the bull, not the horse, when the bulls charged the picadors, and got her to watching the picador place the point of his pic so that she saw what it was all about, so that it became more something that was going on with a definite end, and less of a spectacle with unexplained horrors.

And Brett gets it; "She saw," Hemingway writes, "She saw," "She saw."

Given its built-in sense of an ending, bullfighting can be taught in the way one teaches a work of art. It provides a contained arena in which attentiveness and the perception and the appreciation of style and pattern can be developed. These capacities can then be applied while living outside of the ring. An analogy with the work of art in which Hemingway's characters find themselves suggests itself: we keep writing and reading and teaching such novels because we have come to trust that they can, in their containments, help us to gain some sense of what life is "all about" before we live it.

There is the making of art and then the explaining of it; the achievement of the artist generates the existence of the critic. Jake meets a bullfight critic on the day after he stages the scene of instruction with Brett. "I like it very much that you like my work," Romero tells the critic. "But you haven't seen it yet. To-morrow, if I get a good bull, I will try and show it to you."

Then comes the response: "I am anxious to see it," the critic says. "I would like to be convinced."

Here, criticism is depicted as a negative activity in which one stands off and is . . . critical. Hemingway offers the critic as a parody of the role Jake has already succeeded in fulfilling in the bullfight scene with Brett. We know he has succeeded as a teacher because Hemingway tells us so. Brett does not just see the things Jake tells her to watch; "she saw why she liked Romero's cape-work and why she did not like the others." The word "why" testifies to Brett's rapid development of a critical faculty in light of Jake's patient act of instruction and so reminds us that criticism is not nay-saying but rather the act of praising something by showing how it works.

The particular artwork being praised is distinguished by its "purity of line." "I've never seen him do an awkward thing," Brett says about Romero's artistry in the ring. In its purity of line, Romero's art might be said to resemble Hemingway's, but, in its lack of awkwardness, it does not. Insofar as *The Sun Also Rises* gives "real emotion," it does so by way of a continual series of awkwardnesses and embarrassments.

The supreme embarrassment arrives when a character can say, as Brett does after falling for Romero, "I've lost my self-respect." Mike, Robert, and Jake also pay for what they do by losing self-respect: Mike, by being unable to pay his own way; Robert, by acting "sentimental"; and Jake, by consenting to "pimp" for the woman he loves. "Don't we pay for all the things we do," Brett says to Jake early on, as if she grasps the dynamic. Payment, however, like so much in the novel, is deferred and is usually experienced by a character as a feeling of being disgusted with himself afterward.

The figure of Montoya becomes the repository of the novel's most complex sense of embarrassment. When Jake first sees the hotel owner on his arrival in Pamplona, Montoya is "smiling in his embarrassed way." At this point, the embarrassment has to do with Montoya's sharing "a very special secret" with Jake, the secret of *aficion*. Each man feels a passion for the bullfights and "it would not do to expose it to people who would not understand." There is a pleasure in this sharing, "the pleasure of discovering what we each felt." But the intensity of the shared feeling also renders each man vulnerable and "a little on the defensive." Hence "there was this same embarrassed putting the hand on the shoulder, or a 'Buen hombre.' But nearly always there was the actual touching."

The nature of Montoya's embarrassment undergoes a radical shift, however, as he watches Jake assist in the seduction of Romero. No longer embarrassed with Jake, Montoya becomes embarrassed for him. And, unlike the characters who cannot seem to protect themselves from having to pay, Montoya sees in advance what is coming. So he comes to Jake's room smiling "his embarrassed smile" and attempts, without making an outright request, to persuade Jake not to carry messages between Romero and some visiting Americans. "Montoya stood embarrassed. He wanted me to say something." Jake offers up the desired response: "'Don't give Romero the message,' I said." Then, within the space of four pages, Jake consents to introduce Romero to Brett. At this point, Montoya comes into the room, starts to smile, sees what is happening, and does "not even nod." At the end, after Brett has gone off with Romero, "Montoya did not come near us." In seeing himself through Romero's eyes, Jake subjects himself to a severe and withering self-judgment.

Hemingway so often asks his characters to behave in awkward and embarrassing ways as to make it difficult to speak of their operating on behalf of any sort of "code." This cliché of criticism has nevertheless served to promote a potted reading of Hemingway's texts in which a character is understood in terms of living up to or down to some agreed-upon set of standards. But Hemingway makes it clear through the figure of Jake that the characters in his early work simply find themselves "in it" and operate with little sense of what it is "all about." However good or bad the behavior, it would be a mistake to conflate what his characters do with an unvarying coping style being promoted by their author. Nick's or Jake's or Frederic's behavior is not being recommended to us but is instead being held up for our empathetic scrutiny.

In the nature of his wound, Jake lives out an embarrassment that cannot even speak its name. The reticence of all involved converts Jake's predicament into an uncanny "something" generating a low-grade mystery. Critical commentary has attempted to solve the mystery by appealing to evidence extrinsic to the novel itself. Without such help, a reader is left to rely on words and phrases like "hurt in the war," "Che mala fortuna!," "impotent," "steer," and "joystick." In the case of Jake's wound, research into the writing process is, however, of no avail. Hemingway wrote most of the first draft of the novel in seven blue notebooks. As Frederic Svoboda notes, "by page 39" of the first notebook, "that masterful and much discussed narrative device, Jake's war wound, has already been introduced, although nowhere in the manuscripts is it any more clearly identified than in the published novel."

When Jake responds to Bill's use of the word "impotent" by saying, "I just had an accident," we can be reasonably sure he has suffered an injury of a sexual nature. But of what kind? A 1926 review in *Time* magazine called Jake a "eunuch" and described him as "unmanned," whereas a *New Yorker* piece in the same year found Jake to be "sexually incapacitated." Yet, in a letter to Fitzgerald written during the period of reworking the novel, Hemingway discoursed "on The Importance of Subject" and asserted that "a dull subject I should say would be impotence."

Our understanding of the nature of Jake's wound has been shaped in part by a rumor started by Hemingway himself. As Mark Spilka notes, "we have only Hemingway's word for the intended condition." In a 1951 letter to an editor at Rinehart, Hemingway explained his thinking during the period of writing *The Sun Also Rises*: "I wondered what a man's life would have been like . . . if his penis had been lost and his testicles and spermatic cord remained intact." He gave the rumor another spin in a 1958 *Paris Review* interview, where he maintained that Jake "had been wounded in quite a different way" from the way in which a steer is wounded and that "his testicles were intact and not damaged. Thus he was capable of all normal feelings as a *man* but incapable of consummating them." Jake has been deprived of the ability to perform sexually but not of his capacity to feel sexual desire. Hence, the painful scene in his room when he begins "thinking about Brett and my mind stopped jumping around and started to go in sort of smooth waves. Then all of a sudden I started to cry. Then after a while it was better and I lay in bed and listened to the heavy trams go by and way down the street, and then I went to sleep."

In his room, alone, Jake experiences a number of sensations and feelings, none of them clearly articulated. "The old grievance," as he calls it, has made his head start "to work." Far from depriving him of the capacity to feel, Jake's wound has left him more than capable of all the normal feelings. Hemingway understood that by allowing Jake's injury and feelings to surface only indirectly he had in fact written a book deeply evocative of the tears of things. In November 1926, Hemingway wrote to Max Perkins on this very point. "It's funny to write a book that seems as tragic as that and have them take it for a jazz superficial story. If you went any deeper inside they couldn't read it because they would be crying all the time."

Writing for Hemingway "*was the greatest pleasure*" because, in the years when he felt he had control over the writing process, it was an activity that never ended. Instead, he made sure to stop writing before he had used up the will to continue. "I had learned already never to empty the well of my writing," he wrote in *A Moveable Feast*, "but always to stop when there was still something there in the deep part of the well, and let it refill at night from the springs that fed it." On the other hand, "by then I knew that everything good and bad left an emptiness when it stopped." How, then, to survive the end of writing? "I learned," Hemingway tells us, "not to think about anything that I was writing from the time I stopped writing until I started again the next day. That way my subconscious would be working on it." It was also good to turn to other pleasures, "to get exercise" and "to make love." But the core strategy focused on the scene of writing itself. By learning when to stop, and by then allowing some part of the mind to keep working, Hemingway managed to devise a practice in which he was never not writing.

Hemingway may have taken the greatest pleasure in an ongoing writing project, but what happened after the subconscious had stopped "working on it" and he was faced with having to edit the thing done? Revision involved pleasures and challenges altogether different from those of the initial creative act. The workings of a second will required Hemingway to submit not only to self-criticism but to the advice of wives, editors, and friends. *The Sun Also Rises* was written quickly, in less than two months, and it was thereafter subjected by its author to a prolonged period of revision. Crucial to this process was Hemingway's new friend, F. Scott Fitzgerald.

On the second day of 2012, I walked over to the Department of Special Collections at the University of Virginia and checked out the "Ribbon typescript setting copy" of "the unpublished first two chapters" of *The Sun Also Rises*. I knew that Fitzgerald had responded sharply to the opening pages of the novel and that Hemingway had reluctantly followed his advice. But I was unprepared for the impact of the typed pages set before me on the long, smooth cherry table, pages that Hemingway did not type but which he had surely touched. "This is a novel about a lady," chapter one began. The chapter proceeded to offer a biography of Elizabeth Brett Murray, telling the story of husbands who found Brett "much too expensive," of her going off with Mike Campbell, of her "grand vitality" as a drinker, and of her never being "very good at being alone."

Chapter two of the typescript begins as follows: "I did not want to tell this story in the first person but I find that I must. I wanted to stay well outside of the story so that I would not be touched by it in any way and handle all the people in it with that irony and pity that are so essential to good writing." With a degree of self-consciousness ruthlessly cut from the published novel, Jake admits to "the unfortunate mistake, for a writer, of being Mr. Jake Barnes. So it is not going to be splendid and cool and detached after all." A newspaper man who has always wanted to write fiction, he now supposes that his "novel will have that awful taking the pen in hand quality that afflicts newspaper men when they start to write on their own hook."

It was this taking the pen in hand quality Fitzgerald objected to in his carefully detailed letter to Hemingway about the novel. There was "a feeling of condescending *casualness,*" Fitzgerald explained, in the narrative voice. Too much of the backstory provided was "of no importance." "You can't *play* with peoples [sic] attention," he added, with these "sententious preliminaries." Fitzgerald recommended the removal of entire scenes: "Ernest I can't tell you the sense of disappointment that beginning with its elephantine facetiousness gave me."

Fitzgerald's comments had largely to do with the beginning of the book. It may be hard to believe that *The Sun Also Rises* could have begun in any other way than with its famously "snooty" opening:

> Robert Cohn was once middleweight boxing champion of Princeton. Do not think that I am very much impressed by that as a boxing title, but it meant a lot to Cohn. He cared nothing for boxing, in fact he disliked it, but he learned it painfully and thoroughly to counteract the feeling of inferiority and shyness he had felt on being treated as a Jew at Princeton. There was a certain inner comfort in knowing he could knock down anybody who was snooty to him, although, being very shy and a thoroughly nice boy, he never fought except in the gym.

"He could knock down anybody who was snooty to him," Jake writes. By the logic of this claim, Jake is here inviting Robert to knock him down, since his narrative snootiness toward his character just misses being absurd. That Hemingway is in full control of Jake's tone and means to make him sound as he does is indicated by the fact that, in the course of reworking his novel, the word "snooty" came to replace "snotty," the adjective originally chosen, as Item 194 in the Kennedy Library's Ernest Hemingway Collection reveals. As the substitution of the one word for the other makes clear, the point was to keep the emphasis on Robert's *snoot* – on his nose.

Hemingway met Fitzgerald in the spring of 1925 and, in early June, wrote Perkins to say "I've read his Great Gatsby and think it is an absolutely first rate book." While Jake Barnes and Nick Carraway are both narrator figures who begin by talking about somebody else, Hemingway's opening expresses none of Carraway's powerfully conflicted affection for a man toward whom he also feels "an unaffected scorn." There is a feeling at the beginning of *The Great Gatsby*, and throughout, of unrequited love. Jake's responsiveness to Cohn is of quite another kind. His condescension toward Robert redounds furiously back upon Jake himself; the feelings being attributed are clearly feelings being projected.

Nothing is more embarrassing here than Jake's snooty attempts to explain how Cohn's nose became "permanently flattened." Perhaps it did not happen during a boxing match, Jake surmises, "maybe his mother had been frightened or seen something." A birth libel so gratuitous can only make the reader question the intentions of the narrator. "Why I felt that impulse to devil him I do not know," Jake will later admit. "Of course I do know," he continues. "I was blind, unforgivingly jealous of what had happened to him." Robert Cohn can have sex with Brett while Jake Barnes cannot, and, as a consequence, his jealousy of him takes the primitive form of flattening Robert's most salient body part. Given the ugliness of this beginning, Jake will have to make a considerable effort to regain the reader's trust. He does so in chapter X by openly sharing the feelings he so carefully displaces away from himself in the novel's opening paragraphs.

Grudgingly, inexorably, Hemingway worked his way round to taking Fitzgerald's advice about revising the opening of his novel. In the event, he would cut fifteen pages of the ribbon typescript setting copy in order to begin with the words that can be found on the top of page sixteen: "Robert Cohn was once middleweight boxing champion of Princeton." "I have commenced with Cohn," he wrote Max Perkins in August 1926, after receiving the proofs at Cap d'Antibes. "I believe the book loses by eliminating this first part but it would have been pointless to include it." Five days later, he wrote Perkins in a more resolved state of mind: "I believe that the book is really better starting as it does now directly with Cohn and omitting any preliminary warming up."

Hemingway was becoming accustomed to reworking his beginnings: the pages Fitzgerald had seen were a second try at a novel that in its earliest draft began with a scene at the Hotel Quintana, one in which two Americans have been invited by the proprietor of the hotel to meet a matador. The first-person narrator finds the matador to be "the best looking kid I have ever seen." Hemingway later recast the scene as a third-person account before abandoning it for the version of the beginning read by Fitzgerald.

Hemingway claims in *A Moveable Feast* that Fitzgerald did not see the novel "until after the completed rewritten and cut manuscript had been sent to Scribner's at the end of April." The ten-page handwritten letter sent by Fitzgerald to Hemingway in June 1926 proves otherwise. The letter makes clear reference to pages that had not yet been cut, and it ends with Fitzgerald writing, "Please do what you can about it in proof."

In the generosity of its concern and in the accuracy of its critique, Fitzgerald's letter to Hemingway has assumed an iconic status. Yet the letter itself almost missed seeing the light of day. It did not appear, for instance, in the 1963 *The Letters of F. Scott Fitzgerald*, edited by Andrew Turnbull. It turned out that Hemingway had folded the letter into one of the notebooks containing the first draft of *The Sun Also Rises*. The letter was discovered in the late 1960s by Philip Young and Charles Mann as they began an inventory of the Hemingway papers and is reprinted in full in Frederic Svoboda's *Hemingway and* The Sun Also Rises (1983).

In responding to a story so attentive to the making and losing of friends, it is a tribute to Fitzgerald's emotional courage that he would risk arousing Hemingway's sensitivity to criticism with the candor of his comments. Their exchanges about the novel may have marked the beginning of the end of one of Hemingway's most intimate and conflicted friendships. Years later, in a letter to Max Perkins, Fitzgerald wrote: "I'd like to see him too and I always think of my friendship with him as being one of the high spots of life. But I still believe that such things have a mortality, perhaps in reaction to their very excessive life, and that we will never again see very much of each other."

By the time Hemingway began remembering back to the days of awe, Fitzgerald had long since been operating out of the authority of failure and Hemingway out of the authority of success. Still, it somehow felt necessary to cut Fitzgerald down to size. The task is performed in *A Moveable Feast* with remarkable efficiency in a chapter called "A Matter of Measurements." Scott comes to Ernest with "something very important to ask me." They meet at Michaud's. Zelda has told Scott that "the way I was built I could never make any woman happy." Ernest responds, "Come out to the office." After they return from "*Le water*," he says to Scott, "You're perfectly fine."

As in *The Sun Also Rises*, the word "penis" is never used. But whereas Jake's predicament is gently and even jokingly indicated, there can be no ambiguity in *A Moveable Feast* about what is at stake for Fitzgerald. He is thereby subjected to an embarrassment more acute than anything experienced by Jake Barnes. It is one thing to have one's joystick shot off, but it is quite another to be accused of having a small one. It is not Zelda here who takes revenge on Fitzgerald, it is Hemingway, and in a chapter immediately following the one in which he has misrepresented both the timing and the extent of his friend's assistance with the revision of his first novel. Hemingway takes his revenge by indulging in one of Jake's forbidden pleasures, his "rotten habit of picturing the bedroom scenes of my friends."

From the start, *The Sun Also Rises* was read as a *roman a clef.* Hemingway had based his story on real people: Brett Ashley is Duff Twysden, Robert Cohn is Harold Loeb, Mike Campbell is Pat Guthrie. In a coda to the novel written in the year after its publication, Jake is drinking in the Dingo Bar when Mike and Brett walk in. They allude to being written up as characters in a novel. It is a "dreadful bore," Brett tells Jake, to be pointed out "as a character in a book." Robert E. Fleming reads this fragment "as an attempt to come to terms with what some have seen as an act of betrayal by which Hemingway settled the score with his former friends by libeling them." In a novel so concerned with how to do things well, the one "how to" it appears to have perfected was how "to get rid of friends."

The greatest pleasure registered in *A Moveable Feast* is felt when Hemingway is writing alone. In a chapter called "Birth of a New School," the activity is represented as self-generated and self-sufficient, an almost god-like act of building out. Then a voice pipes up:

> "Hi, Hem. What are you trying to do? Write in a café?"
>
> Your luck had run out and you shut the notebook. This was the worst thing that could happen.

Feeling that he has "to make a stand or move," Hemingway tries to continue writing while talking with the friend. The friend complains about being unable to write, and Hemingway finally tells him to "keep the hell away from this café." The next day, he decides not to take any chances and so stays home and works at the dining room table. "I worked better than I had ever done," Hemingway continues, and he does so by reclaiming control over when he will experience the end of pleasure.

In *A Moveable Feast*, friends either support or interfere with the writer's work. Support, however, comes to feel like interference, and so an early teacher, like Gertrude Stein, must be discarded. Despite its tender evocation of Hemingway's first marriage, the memoir, like Hemingway's first novel, often devolves into a settling of scores with former friends.

In the spring of 1926, Fitzgerald took the risk of interrupting Hemingway just at the point where he might have considered his novel to be finished. A friend in the life now became the conscience of the work. But Fitzgerald had made the mistake of involving himself in the one activity where Hemingway was at his best and also at his most vulnerable. Too many embarrassments were thereby revealed. The tenderness shown to Jake Barnes, a man beyond all concern for matters of measurements, could not be summoned when remembering the friend who had rescued Hemingway from a less than true beginning by having him cut fifteen pages expressive of an aspiring novelist's awkward attempt to distance himself from his friends.

CHAPTER 4

False Surmise

A Farewell to Arms

"Why does he have to lose everything?" my wife Ann said about Frederic Henry, after finishing *A Farewell to Arms*. She was re-reading it following our return from Friuli in the spring of 2012, a trip on which we had sought out some of the places Frederic lived in and retreated through: Udine, Codroipo, Gradisca d'Isonzo. Thinking I should try to answer her question, I said something like, "Because we all will." I said it because I believe that losing everything is the consequence of living in a world without heaven to follow, that Hemingway understood this, and that, like Elizabeth Bishop and Wallace Stevens and the other artists who share this view, he had so studied the art of losing as to come to believe that death is the mother of beauty. Or, in Hemingway's case, the mother of *pleasure*, an experience he renders with such force as to be able to interpose a little ease within the ever-present sense that everything will eventually be lost.

The pleasure, as we have seen, depends upon the loss: only the impermanent can have value. Hemingway's task is to get us to accept the passingness of a mortal existence and even to savor it. "Again" becomes for him the big word, and the hope that a pleasure can be experienced again continually vies with the knowledge that, for everything, there will be a last time.

"In *A Farewell to Arms*, the reader is never taken by surprise," Michael Reynolds writes, "for all the major pieces of action are economically foreshadowed." Reynolds sees Catherine's death-by-pregnancy as bodied forth in the scene in chapter XV when she visits Dr. Valentini. The doctor tells Frederic, "she will make you a fine boy." While the scene is telling, the foreshadowing of Catherine's doom begins long before it, in the novel's opening paragraph:

> In the late summer of that year we lived in a house in a village that looked across the river and the plain to the mountains. In the bed of the river there

> were pebbles and boulders, dry and white in the sun, and the water was clear and swiftly moving and blue in the channels. Troops went by the house and down the road and the dust they raised powdered the leaves of the trees. The trunks of the trees too were dusty and the leaves fell early that year and we saw the troops marching along the road and the dust rising and leaves, stirred by the breeze, falling and the soldiers marching and afterward the road bare and white except for the leaves.

At first, this voice appears simply to report what it sees. It sounds in touch with seasons and elements. We stand aside here and conserve ourselves as the water flows, the troops pass, the leaves fall. Everything else spends itself. Yet somehow high summer – a time of ripeness – becomes late fall. We are manipulated into the season of loss as parallel syntax presents an army of falling leaves. Men are "marching" and leaves are "falling," and, through this easy parataxis, they become all too easily confused. The men disappear; the leaves stay. What remains is the emptiness of landscape – a "road bare and white" – that the human presence interrupts but cannot master.

Even before he sets in motion the metaphor of men as falling leaves, Hemingway conveys a sense of the already over in the phrase "that year." In saying this, Frederic's voice begins by placing the time of the story altogether in the past. If Frederic "dictates *A Farewell to Arms*," as Rose Marie Burwell maintains, he does so from a perspective almost posthumous. "I could not tell it," he says a few pages further on; "I cannot tell it now." When is this "now"; at how many light years beyond the time of the story itself? Perhaps the most heart-breaking evidence of this sense of stunned retrospect comes in a sentence interrupting Frederic's reverie in chapter XXXIV about being able to feel alone with Catherine even when they are together: "It has only happened to me like that once." Like "that year," the phrase "has only happened" situates the experience being remembered at a considerable temporal remove, while the word "once" defines it as unique and seems to foreclose such a happening from ever occurring again.

The sentence "It has only happened to me like that once" originally appeared in the final paragraph of one of the variant endings Hemingway wrote for the novel. It appeared there as part of "The Fitzgerald Ending," as Bernard Oldsey calls it, an ending Hemingway tried out at the suggestion of his friend. "Why not end the book with that wonderful paragraph on P. 241," Fitzgerald had written, after reading the typescript of the novel. "It is the most eloquent in the book + could end it rather gently + well." In the passage Fitzgerald admired, Frederic broods on a world that "kills the very good and the very gentle and the very brave impartially." Urging

Hemingway to end his book with this "burst of eloquence," Fitzgerald described it as "one of the most beautiful pages in all English literature." In considering and then rejecting his friend's idea, Hemingway also preserved the force of "It has only happened to me like that once," allowing it to retain its status as a shocking flash forward into all the upcoming and unimpassioned years rather than using it as a solemn end note.

Imagery, syntax, and tone work together from the beginning of *A Farewell to Arms* to create the sense of an ending – and yet we read on. In this, Hemingway reveals to us, reading is like living: it is, ultimately, and to use a phrase from *Across the River and Into the Trees*, "a movement without hope." And yet, of course, we hope and care and invest in outcomes nevertheless; the novel could be said to measure our fierce will to cling to these motions of mind and heart in the face of all that is evidenced against them. Grace under pressure reveals itself as the courage to keep faring forward into a narrative in which "there is no end except death."

Frederic fends off hopelessness with surmise, a word I use in its Miltonic sense, one first established in "Lycidas." There, as the elegizing poet nears the end of his poem, he calls upon the vales and valleys to "hither cast" their "bells and flowerets of a thousand hues." He is staging a funeral in which the mourners are being invited to throw flowers as the procession passes. In the process, Milton names many of the beauties of an English spring. The surmise is maintained for some sixteen lines, until it runs up against its concluding line, the line in which we are reminded of what we have agreed, with the speaker, to do: "To strew the laureate hearse where Lycid lies." But the line is self-consuming, since Lycid lies not here – in front of us, in the hearse – but elsewhere. He has drowned in the Irish Sea, and his bones have found only a "watery bier." As the line is uttered, the entire scene collapses, but not before granting us the pleasure of gathering and strewing flowers on an empty hearse.

Milton proceeds to acknowledge his own practice:

> For so to interpose a little ease,
> Let our frail thoughts dally with false surmise.

In other words, in order to make the reader and myself feel better, I have just indulged in this (impossible) act of paying tribute. Milton both gives us the surmise, with all the ease it interposes, and then reminds us that it is only a surmise. Poetry cannot raise the dead, but it can, with its fictions, help us to live with the loss of them. "False," Milton writes, not as in "untrue," but as in "fictio," a fiction, something made, and also made up.

Life itself is a little interposed ease as we make our way toward death, and the false surmises of our fictions are offered to aid us in the living of it.

A surmise like Milton's is the opposite of a fantasy or an illusion since, having the nicer knowledge of belief, it knows itself to be untrue. In this double motion of mind – in the suspension of disbelief and in the acknowledgment of the suspension – it acquires the dignity of a fiction that can stand the test of experience rather than offering an illusory escape from it. Such fictions have to be true to what we want and to what we get.

One example from Hemingway's novel to show how surmise can work: after the deserting Frederic jumps on the train and lies beside the guns, he imagines himself "lying with Catherine on the floor of the car." He takes the "hard floor for a wife." Then he separates the tenor from the vehicle. No, he thinks, "you did not love the floor of a flat-car . . . you loved some one else whom now you knew was not even to be pretended there." In entertaining and then distancing himself from his surmise, Frederic anticipates his declaration of "a separate peace." As he says to himself on the train, "You were out of it now."

The most ambitious surmise interposed into the novel is the experience we call "love." Love creeps up on Frederic, catching him off guard, and it can be said to begin for him in the complex surmise dropped into the middle of chapter VII. On the previous afternoon, he has "lied" in telling Catherine he loves her; he is still perceiving it all as a "game." Now, back in his villa and thinking about writing a letter to the States, his mind begins to work and to wish. "I wished we had a Napoleon," he thinks. He tells himself he will not be killed and then wanders into thoughts of visiting the Black Forest and Spain after the war. Finally, he gets to Catherine: "I wish she were here now." As Frederic imagines arriving with Catherine at a hotel in Milan, the surmise takes flight in one of the longest and most beautiful sentences Hemingway ever wrote:

> Maybe she would pretend that I was her boy that was killed and we would go in the front door and the porter would take off his cap and I would stop at the concierge's desk and ask for the key and she would stand by the elevator and then we would get in the elevator and it would go up very slowly clicking at all the floors and then our floor and the boy would open the door and stand there and she would step out and I would step out and we would walk down the hall and I would put the key in the door and open it and go in and then take down the telephone and ask them to send a bottle of capri bianca in a silver bucket full of ice and you would hear the ice against the pail coming down the corridor and the boy would knock and I would say leave it outside the door please.

In an unpunctuated sentence unfolding through a cascade of twenty "and's," Frederic refuses the pause of even one comma for fear that the loss of momentum might derail the wish. Yet the sentence also very much takes its time in the careful notation of each step in the progress leading toward the arrival of the ice bucket. The goal is to maintain and lengthen the surmise – all this takes place under the cover of a *Maybe* – for as long as breath can manage it. Hemingway's power to move us, as Reynolds Price discerns, "is always built upon *breath*, long breath." "What the words are ostensibly saying," he explains, "is less true, less complete, than the slow arc of their total movement throughout their length." Here, the slowness of the arc makes a key point about the pleasure Frederic takes in his surmises. They are all about buying time, since it is "against time" and its inexorable march that Frederic makes his doom-burdened and yet hope-filled way.

Of course, Frederic and Catherine have so little time. But the point Hemingway is beginning to make about love is that its value cannot be measured solely in terms of its duration. Love is a pitching into life and against and in spite of the odds, odds thrown into relief by the intensities and extremities of the claims each character makes upon the other.

Our fore-understanding of love's doom is stimulated on the novel's second page in one of the most extraordinary similes – a rare trope in the early work – Hemingway ever wrote. Frederic prepares us for the simile with a little piece of irony when, in the novel's second paragraph, he says, "the nights were cool and there was not the feeling of a storm coming." Yes, the storm is denied – but why is it ever envisaged? To say that something may not happen is to raise the possibility that it might, and here, as so often in Hemingway, the reader is invited to feel more than she understands, to engage in a reading through the "not" that culminates in the following chapter, when the storm inevitably breaks. "It came very fast and . . . suddenly we were in it and it was snow." Implied futures arrive very fast, and they often come in the form of bad weather from the sky, like the rain in which the novel will end.

Frederic's simile further complicates our expectations. He is watching the troops march by his house when he notices something strange about them. "Their rifles were wet and under their capes the two leather cartridge-boxes on the front of the belts, gray leather boxes heavy with the packs of clips of thin, long 6.5 mm. cartridges, bulged forward under their capes so that the men, passing on the road, marched as though they were six months gone with child." Through abundant detail, Frederic attempts to establish the probability of what he sees, but the metaphoric leap from carefully measured cartridges to carefully measured pregnancy is so idiosyncratic as to reveal more about the mind of the beholder than what it beholds. Knowing what is coming and yet wanting to buy time for remembering the pleasure he took in loving Catherine, Frederic cannot prevent or perhaps even subtly intends this uncanny comparison. As swiftly as that, the engines of death are conflated with the opportunities of birth. So, at the end, Catherine will both give birth *and* die, thus fulfilling the terrible pun latent in Frederic's concluding phrase, "gone with child."

Frederic and Catherine live out a romance. The romance is as much a product of their inner fears and resistances to love as it is shaped by the existential and biological traps lying in wait for them. Catherine has already lost a boy in the war; Frederic "had not wanted to fall in love with her." Still, they both fall, and fall suddenly. The resulting story becomes an inquest into the uses and value of romantic love.

And it is deeply embarrassing, so much so, even to Hemingway, that he will cut away from every sex scene. Frederic uses the word "embarrassed" to describe his feelings about the big words "sacred, glorious, and sacrifice and the expression in vain," but he might better apply the word to the behavior of lovers indulging in fantasies that can easily be described as regressive. Frederic and Catherine court total oneness: "There isn't any me. I'm you. Don't make up a separate me." "We really are the same one." She promises compliance: "I'll say just what you wish and I'll do what you wish." She becomes his home, tenting him with her hair as Nick Adams is tented by his canvas, "and it would all come down and she would drop her head and we would both be inside of it, and it was the feeling of inside a tent or behind a falls." The two experience an instant intimacy when, in their first meeting, Catherine suddenly punctures Frederic's irony by asking, "*Do* we have to go on and talk this way?" The question is followed by an even more arresting one: "Have you ever loved anyone?" So we watch them falling in love, whether or not they know it to be happening.

Of the major literary modes, romance continues to solicit the most stubborn misunderstandings and casual dismissals. Romance is that mode in which a writer's imagination converts the world into an object of fulfilled desire, and to call these desires infantile or regressive is to miss the point, to refuse to entertain the offered fallacy. Romance expresses the longing for union and return and represents these longings as given to both genders. Romance offers, above all, to carry us away, and the resistance to being so caught up speaks through those readers who would reduce the love in *A Farewell to Arms* to mere neurosis. Mark Spilka proves eloquent on this point: "Catherine is believable, as well as the object of male fantasies, since she is also the subject of female fantasies that we know to be 'true,' that do exist, however embarrassing we may find her enactment of them." We know such fantasies (I prefer the less pejorative word "surmises") to be true – as in compelling and attractive – from our continual assent to them when reading romance, the literary mode most responsible for having created them.

If a surmise gains strength by the qualifications to which it is subjected, then the romance of Frederic and Catherine's love proves a strong surmise. Catherine dies, and Frederic loses everything. What makes this bearable and meaningful is the way in which Hemingway both prepares us for and protects us against his novel's promised end.

"The rains" arriving in the novel's third paragraph prepare us, for instance, for Catherine's later uncanny and predictive admission, "I'm afraid of the rain because sometimes I see me dead in it" and for Frederic's final walk home alone in the rain. Such a structure of imagery converts a *Farewell to Arms*, in Hemingway's phrase, into "a study in apprehension." We have already seen how Frederic in his role as narrator imposes upon the novel an excruciating sense of mournful retrospect. As a character in the story, however, he is asked, like everyone else, to summon the courage to move forward into existential time. "Well, we were in it. Every one was caught in it and the small rain would not quiet it." Sounding its sinister refrain throughout, the phrase *in it* figures time as an irresistible and hope-crushing force. Yet, even within Frederic's despairing expression of a sense of entrapment, Hemingway has already embedded the means by which he can temporarily escape from it into an interval of freeplay. Acting as a counterforce to Frederic's sense of foregone conclusion, such intervals plunge us back into the immediacy of the story and provide access to how Frederic thought and felt as he lived through it.

The phrase "small rain" itself acts as such a counterforce as Frederic's poetic allusion spirals into an extended reverie during the retreat from Caporetto. He and his men have picked up two girls along the way:

> A retreat was no place for two virgins. Real virgins. Probably very religious. If there were no war we would probably all be in bed. In bed I lay me down my head. Bed and board. Stiff as a board in bed. Catherine was in bed now between two sheets, over her and under her. Which side did she sleep on? Maybe she wasn't asleep. Maybe she was lying thinking about me. Blow, blow, ye western wind. Well, it blew and it wasn't the small rain but the big rain down that rained. It rained all night. You knew it rained down that rained. Look at it. Christ, that my love were in my arms and I in my bed again. That my love Catherine. That my sweet love Catherine down might

> rain. Blow her again to me. Well, we were in it. Everyone was caught in it and the small rain would not quiet it.

In this experiment with free association, Hemingway embarks on one of the projects he assigned himself during the 1930s, the expansion of the textual space devoted to exploring what he calls the "inner life."

Frederic here transports his thoughts into Catherine's bed. In doing so, he creates a "meantime" world in which the pressures of being "in it" fall away. In quoting and playing with "Western Wind," he also unearths a source for the rain imagery so pervasive in the novel. Telling the story of a man separated from and wishing to get back to the woman he loves, the poem – and it is surely the greatest very short poem in English – anticipates the plot of the novel Hemingway is writing. Hemingway quoted the following version of the poem in a letter written to Ernest Walsh in the winter of 1926:

> O western wind, when will thou blow
> That the small rain down can rain?
> Christ, that my love were in my arms
> And I in my bed again!

Unlike Frederic and Catherine, however, the poem's speaker wants the small rain down to rain, since it brings with it the wind blowing in the direction of home. The actual rain of a front moving in from the west also provokes, in the return it helps to accomplish, another, smaller kind of rain, the tears that will be shed by the beloved when she experiences the speaker's arrival.

The wind blows us back. As the novel unfolds, the words "back" and "ahead" acquire a powerfully ambivalent force, measuring as they do both the constraints on and the possibilities for mobility in space and time. The book opens with a series of returns. "When I came back," Frederic says, "when I got home." Being able to go or get back becomes one of Frederic's longed-for pleasures, with Catherine becoming the primary object of the wish. The wish expresses the conviction that good things are especially good if they can happen again. "We'll be back," Frederic tells the barman as he borrows his rowboat and heads up the lake, a promise and a wish he can scarcely believe to have much chance of coming true.

Frederic also begins as a man who thinks he can control or at least see what is ahead. He is noticeably alert in this way during the retreat from Caporetto, when knowing where he is heading becomes a matter of life and death. "Ahead the road turned off to the left . . . . We walked along together all going fast against time." "Ahead across the wet countryside," Hemingway writes, "Ahead across the plain was the hill of Udine." Much earlier, during the second meeting with Catherine, Frederic finds himself "angry and yet certain, seeing it all ahead like the moves in a chess game." Falling in love teaches him differently and allows him to surrender control. "God knows I had not wanted to fall in love with her," but, in spite of his foreseeings, "when I saw her I was in love with her." The question becomes: can he learn to learn anything from being self-surprised?

Chapter III ends with a counter-surmise, a passage in which Frederic admits to himself that "I had wanted to go to Abruzzi" but that he had somehow failed to do so. He proceeds to conjure the place, complete with a landscape "where the roads were frozen and hard as iron, where it was clear cold and dry and the snow was dry and powdery and hare-tracks in the snow and the peasants took off their hats and called you Lord and there was good hunting." In converting a missed opportunity into something almost had, Frederic also begins to acquire the instructive lessons of regret. Morality can perhaps become something more than a matter of things one feels badly about afterward; it can be a forward-looking and creative act. The priest from Abruzzi has been "suddenly hurt" that Frederic has not gone there as promised, and, in thinking about him, Frederic realizes "he had always known what I did not know and what, when I learned it, I was always able to forget. But I did not know that then, although I learned it later."

What Frederic learns goes unnamed here and is in any case secondary to when it is learned. Does learning always arrive as belated, "later" rather than sooner? At his most despairing, when Catherine lies dying, Frederic repudiates any hope of preparing for what is up ahead. "That was what you did. You died. You did not know what it was about. You never had time to learn. They threw you in and told you the rules and the first time they caught you off base they killed you."

Frederic's one memory of home appears to repudiate the possibilities inherent in moving either back or ahead. It occurs during the retreat after Aymo is shot and Frederic has taken cover in a barn:

> The hay smelled good and lying in a barn in the hay took away all the years in between. We had lain in hay and talked and shot sparrows with an air-rifle when they perched in the triangle cut high up in the wall of the barn. The barn was gone now and one year they had cut the hemlock woods and there were only stumps, dried tree-tops, branches and fireweed where the woods had been. You could not go back. If you did not go forward what happened? You never got back to Milan. And if you got back to Milan what happened?

The passage echoes the scene in *The Sun Also Rises* when Jake Barnes crosses the town square and remembers coming home from an out-of-town football game to find it "all strange."

The two memories have much in common. First, we are invited to consider them as representative because they are so singular: at no other time in either novel does the protagonist remember his past. Second, the two memories share a quality of déjà vu: "I felt as I felt once," Jake tells us, while Frederic lies in hay the way he had "lain in hay." Each man experiences his home-memory as a repetition, as something that recurs. And what recurs is a feeling of strangeness within a homelikeness. Jake returns only to find it "all different," whereas Frederic's recall of warmth in a barn is superseded by it being "all gone," with the woods cut down.

Remembered only as an uncanny place, home becomes for each character the not-had-thing. Frederic continually attempts not to refind home but to experience it for the first time: "in a little time the room felt like our home"; "feeling that we had come home"; the hotel in Lausanne is made to feel "like our home." After jumping into the Tagliamento, he even attempts to create an intimacy with the "heavy timber" he holds on to. When Frederic says, "I hoped we would move toward the shore," and repeats the pronoun "we" five more times, he asserts an uncanny familiarity with an inanimate object. In this desperate and touching surmise, he summons an instant community to replace the one he has lost during the retreat.

In repeating the pattern of Jake's memory of return, Frederic also refines it. Having arrived in "a good place," as he describes the barn, he now feels the fruitlessness of moving either "back" or "forward." Frederic remembers so little of his past because what is remembered paralyzes rather than empowers him, reminding him, as it does, of a sense of primal uncanniness too unsettling to wish to recall.

Frederic ends up loving Catherine as best he can and against his habitual ironic resistance, but the attachment can at best be a tenuous one, since he appears to have never had and then been required to surrender a love he will later search to refind. Manuscript evidence supports this speculation. In a long meditation on his love for things that are "*perishable*" and on his inability to believe in "*the kingdom of heaven*," a passage Hemingway eventually decided to cut, Frederic makes a striking omission from the list of the things he has loved: "*you were born loving nothing and the warm milk of your mother's breast was never heaven and the first thing you loved was the side of a hill and the last thing was a woman and they took her away.*" Catherine here is very clearly not imagined as a substitute for the had and lost "good place" of mother-love.

Frederic stands at the end rather than at the beginning. His narration's continual intimations and apprehensions of loss, along with its sense of being told from a position of great remove, combine to render his love for Catherine not as something refound but as something already over. Brave as he is in surmising against death and in risking romance, he remains, finally, an ironic figure. In *A Farewell to Arms*, romance pushes back against irony and is finally defeated by it. It would not always be this way. As he turned toward the nonfictional experiments of the 1930s, Hemingway began to allow himself the freedom "to stop a story anytime" and in ways not previously imagined possible and even to tell the story of a life, however "short," that could be called a "happy" one.

"Don't touch a thing," Owen Wister wrote, after reading the ending Hemingway had finally settled on for *A Farewell*. The date was June 23, 1929. Hemingway had completed a draft of the novel that January, one complete except for its final paragraphs. During the following six months, he would generate more than forty variant endings for the story, all of which are contained in the archives of Boston's Kennedy Library. It is difficult to conceive of the novel ending in any other words but these:

> But after I had got them out and shut the door and turned off the light it wasn't any good. It was like saying good-by to a statue. After a while I went out and left the hospital and walked back to the hotel in the rain.

Hemingway followed his usual practice in revising his beginning as well. Arguing that "Hemingway made an even more drastic adjustment in the opening of *A Farewell to Arms* than he did in *The Sun Also Rises*," Bernard Oldsey bases his claim on a careful scrutiny of Item 240 in the Ernest Hemingway Collection, a "two-chapter fragment" he takes to be "an early – perhaps the original – opening of the novel." In the first of these chapters, a wounded Emmett Hancock (he is not yet Frederic Henry) arrives in Milan; in the second, he wakes the next morning and is cared for by nurses. These events were eventually incorporated into chapters XIII and XIV of the published novel. In Oldsey's view, the opening that has come down to us was an "afterthought."

Once again, an original beginning had to be cut or repositioned. The opening finally chosen, with Frederic on the Isonzo rather than in Milan, was also to be carefully revised. In Item 64, which Oldsey reads as the first pencil draft of the final opening, there is no separation between chapter I and chapter II. While the novel's famous opening sentence appears to have been fully formed when it hit the page, the following sentence, about the appearance of the river, was to be heavily reworked, and the opening paragraph displays in manuscript at least seven deletions and insertions.

Even during the typescript phase, Hemingway was still making changes to his beginning. In the published novel, the sentence ending with the words "six months gone with child" concludes a paragraph. In the typescript, the sentence is run on with the following one. Hemingway then inserted a handwritten paragraph mark into the typescript to indicate a setting off of the crucial phrase. With this change, the opening chapter became one of five paragraphs, each of which ends in a downbeat: the fallen leaves, the "storm coming," "gone with child," the war "going very badly," and seven thousand men dying of cholera in the Italian army.

These hesitations at the beginning appear minor indeed, however, when compared with the trouble Hemingway took with his ending. How many versions of it did he attempt? In a book published in 1973, Sheldon Grebstein writes of "the original ending," one he deems to be "inferior" to the ending in the published novel. Two years later, in *Hemingway's First War*, Michael Reynolds upped the count of variant endings from one to thirty-five. In 1979, Oldsey brought the count to forty-one and grouped the variants into categories: "The *Nada* Ending," "The Live-Baby Ending," "The Morning-After Ending." In 2012, the website at the Kennedy Library numbered the novel's variant endings at forty-four.

On the day I visited the Hemingway Room for the first time, in July 2012, Seán Hemingway brought out the Hemingway Library Edition of *A Farewell to Arms*. The edition contains an Appendix attempting to bring before the public all the locatable variant endings, a number it fixes at forty-seven. Armed with this new figure, although not yet in possession of the new edition of the novel, I sat down at my desk overlooking the Boston harbor, opened Box 7, and removed Item 70. "A Farewell to Arms," the cover page read. "Drafts of Ending. Miscellaneous pencil and typed manuscripts. 38 pp."

The pages in the folder were photocopies of original manuscripts tucked safely away in the vault. They were numbered with pencil in the bottom right-hand corner in a librarian's hand. At first, I did not notice that the pages were out of order. After realizing this, I counted all the numbered pages and came up with thirty-five. I also discovered that nine pages in the folder were unnumbered. When I asked about this, I was told, "Oh, that's because they get a lot of use." The only thing I was now sure of was this: the folder contained forty-four pages, not, as indicated on the cover sheet, thirty-eight.

Out of Oldsey's forty-one variant endings, I was able to locate every one. Then I found eight endings unlisted by him. Some of these were mere fragments, like the words written on the back of another provisional ending: "Nothing was changed then ~~except that~~ as I woke completely I had an ~~strange physically~~ empty feeling." Did this count as an ending? Had Oldsey dismissed it, or overlooked it? I duly added it to my list. (It would later turn out that the Library Edition numbers this sentence as Alternative Ending 44.) When I had finished with the folder and had inspected the available typescripts and galleys, my total number of endings found was forty-nine. By the close of my first day working in the Hemingway Room, it had begun to appear to me that the search for these endings would never end.

A week after my first reading of Item 70, a librarian at the Hemingway Room handed me an advance copy of Seán Hemingway's Library Edition. "All of the alternative endings are published here for the first time," the Introduction claimed. I checked all endings found by me against those printed in Appendix II. The Appendix followed Oldsey closely, relying on his groupings, combining two of his endings into one (V-32 and V-33 had become No. 27), and adding seven endings not listed by Oldsey. The count of alternative endings now stood at forty-seven.

My count had been forty-nine. I was able to reconcile my count with Seán Hemingway's by accepting the emendation to Oldsey as well as the decision to treat two fragments counted as endings by me as subsets of other endings. While a crux had been temporarily resolved, I left the library believing that what counts as an "ending" to *A Farewell to Arms* will remain a matter of some debate.

But what of the ending Hemingway finally chose to publish? It can be said to begin a few paragraphs into chapter XLI, when, after Catherine has been given a room in the hospital, she says to Frederic, "Please go out and get something to eat." He demurs, but finally consents to go. This is how he will spend the time as the action gathers to a close: trying to get into a room and being asked to leave. Meanwhile, he eats.

On his first departure, Frederic walks to a café and has wine and brioche and coffee. When the second glass of wine is poured, he notices the barman overfilling it so that the wine runs down onto the zinc. Outside, he sees a dog nosing at a refuse can and looks to see if there is anything he can pull out for him. Then he returns to the hospital.

The eating and drinking scene will be repeated in greater detail a few pages later when Frederic goes out for lunch and orders choucroute and beer. "The waiter brought a dish of sauerkraut with a slice of ham over the top and a sausage buried in the hot wine-soaked cabbage." He eats and again returns to the hospital. Catherine's pain has intensified, and she asks desperately for more gas. "*Give it to me*," she says.

Frederic leaves the room and watches it grow dark outside. Then his mind starts to work: "This was the price you paid for sleeping together," he thinks. "This was the end of the trap. This is what people got for loving each other." People do not die in childbirth nowadays, he reminds himself, before falling into a question he will repeat nine times over: "But what if she should die?"

The doctor proposes a Caesarean. Frederic steps outside the operating room and sees that it has begun to rain. When the child is taken from Catherine's body, he sees it as "a freshly skinned rabbit." "I had no feeling for him," Frederic admits. "He did not seem to have anything to do with me. I felt no feeling of fatherhood."

In the recovery room, Catherine asks Frederic what the baby looks like and he replies: "He looks like a skinned rabbit with a puckered-up old-man's face." Catherine again tells Frederic to get something to eat. In the hall, the nurse informs him that the baby had never been alive. Frederic then engages in his final reverie, a deeply anguished counter-surmise: "Poor little kid. I wished the hell I'd been choked like that. No I didn't. Still there would not be all this dying to go through. Now Catherine would die. That was what you did. You died. You did not know what it was all about. You never had time to learn. They threw you in and told you the rules and the first time they caught you off base they killed you."

A nurse tells Frederic that Catherine is "all right" and to "go and have your supper." For the third time, he walks to the café, where he is offered ham and eggs. He orders a demi-blonde and the waiter says, "I remembered . . . .You took a demi-blonde this noon." When his supper arrives, Frederic describes it: "The ham and eggs were in a round dish – the ham underneath and the eggs on top."

Frederic drinks beer until there is "quite a pile of saucers" on his table. Then he suddenly knows it is time to get back. At the hospital, he is told that Catherine has had a hemorrhage. "Everything was gone inside me," he thinks, as he begins his desperate prayer: "Please, please, please, dear God, don't let her die," a prayer like the one made by the soldier in chapter VII of *In Our Time* as he lies under the bombardment at Fossalta.

Frederic goes in to see Catherine. "I'm going to die," she says. He takes her hand and she says, "Don't touch me." He lets go, she smiles and says, "You touch me all you want." Frederic promises he will not "do our things with another girl." Then the doctor orders him to leave the room. After waiting outside, Frederic re-enters the room and stays with Catherine until she dies.

The final chapter of the novel offers an experience of strange mixtures – of, above all, food and terror. The intervals spent walking to and dining in the café allow the terror to build. Frederic goes about the business of going out and coming back largely in response to Catherine's and the nurse's promptings. It is as if he is performing a prescribed chore: loving Catherine has now become indistinguishable from killing time. It is an ironic reprise of the assessment Frederic makes to himself after feeling obligation washed away in the river. "I was not made to think. I was made to eat. My God, yes. Eat and drink and sleep with Catherine."

The ending mixes two orders of noticings; things that cannot quite be seen or said and things that are articulated and repeated. "I do not think that I could have watched them cut," Frederic admits. The price a woman's body can pay for sleeping with a man is not one he feels able to take in. But he remains willing to voice to himself and to others his bitterness against the resulting child. As he says to himself before learning that the boy has been born dead, "I felt no feeling of fatherhood."

In having Frederic remain so stubbornly loyal to a woman rather than to her child, Hemingway offers his reader an honest depiction of one man's incapacity to share love. Frederic's dismissal of the child as a skinned rabbit is not simply competitive and resentful but is expressive of the fear of vulnerability any further human attachment might produce. It will be a long time before a Hemingway male feels anything as intense for a child as he feels for a woman. Reynolds Price locates that moment in the 1970 *Islands in the Stream*, a book beginning with a father dedicated to enjoying and instructing and protecting his young sons. Here, for the first time, Price writes, we see Hemingway engaging an emotion previously omitted, "parental devotion, filial return."

In a number of the discarded endings, Hemingway attempts a direct address to the reader, as in "You will die and I will die and that is all I can promise you." As another rejected ending admits, and in a sentence Hemingway eventually crossed out, "You can stop a story any time." And the way a story stops is not at all the way a life stops: "It all keeps on as long as your life keeps on and then it keeps on. It never stops. It only stops for you. ~~A lot~~ Some of it stops while you are still alive. ~~A lot~~ The rest goes on and you go on with it. ~~You can stop a story any time. Where you stop it is the end of that story~~. On the other hand you have to stop a story. You stop it at the end of whatever it was you were writing about." It should be pointed out that my version of this ending is based upon an inspection of the original manuscript – not a photocopy – and that it differs from the version of the ending printed in the Library Edition.

The language of this rejected ending steps out of the dramatic action to comment on the fact that we have now reached the end. Hemingway continues to ring the changes on the meanings of words like "stop" and "end" in a number of the alternative endings. The cumulative effect is of a prolonged and unfinished essay on the question of how stories should end.

On the other hand, many of the discarded endings also address Frederic's future. "It goes on," they maintain, about life. Frederic admits to the "going on with everything that had happened since." But to be reminded that life goes on is an awareness neither wanted nor needed at this particular end. Frederic's life is effectively over ("It has only happened to me like that once"), and a reader can have no earned investment in a sense of its continuance.

This is why the ending Michael Reynolds calls "false ending with child" may be the truest of the endings Hemingway was to write and set aside. Here is the ending as quoted in *Hemingway's First War*:

> There are a great many details starting with my first meeting with an undertaker and all the business of burial and continuing on with the rest of my life – which has gone on and will probably go on for a long time. I could tell about the boy. He did not seem of any importance then except as trouble and god knows I was bitter about him. Anyway he does not belong in this story. He starts a new one. It is not fair to start a new story at the end of an old one but that is the way it happens. There is no end except death and birth is the only beginning.

Of course, many kinds of fictions start a new story at the end of an old one, fictions we call comedy or romance. In *this story,* Hemingway is arguing – in *A Farewell to Arms* – a new start at the end would be unearned. There is too much bitterness to be overcome.

"He did not seem of any importance then except as trouble and god knows I was bitter about him," Frederic says about the boy. The bitterness is the result of the fact that the boy has "killed his mother." It is an explicable but not an attractive emotion. But it turns out that Hemingway may not have written "bitter" after all.

Reynolds's "false ending with child" is numbered as the seventh alternative ending in the Hemingway Library Edition and is called "The Live-Baby Ending." Seán Hemingway's transcription differs from Reynolds's on a few small points; one version capitalizes the word "God," one does not. There is, however, one vital difference between the two transcriptions, and it has to do not with God but with bitterness. In the Library Edition, the relevant sentence reads as follows: "He did not seem of any importance then except as trouble and God knows that I was better about him."

The substitution of "better" for "bitter" had gone unnoticed by me until I assigned an undergraduate class a paper on the alternative endings to *A Farewell to Arms*. Because my students were working with the Hemingway Library Edition of the novel, and because they had never seen Reynolds's "false ending with child," the students who chose to write about "The Live-Baby Ending" naturally referred to the word "better" when beginning to discuss the ending in class. I immediately corrected them – the word, of course, was "bitter." The momentum of the sentence, I told them, calls for a word like "bitter"; it is as if Frederic is admitting to one more failure of feeling.

I had been committed to this reading ever since coming across it in Reynolds's wonderful book. But Reynolds and I appear to have got it wrong, a possibility brought home to me when my students referred me to Figure 6 in the Hemingway Library Edition, a photograph of the handwritten ending in question. And there, on the unassailable page, was a word that could well be read as "better." It made no sense, but there it was.

In my second summer of working with the Hemingway Collection, I went straight to the folder containing the variant endings of *A Farewell to Arms*. I showed a librarian the photograph of the "Live-Baby Ending" in the Library Edition – the "better" ending – and then asked her to take a look at the photocopy of that ending available in the files. She agreed that the copy had so distorted the letters of the word in question that it was necessary for us to consult the original manuscript.

Once the manuscript was retrieved from the vault, we were joined by the head librarian. After scrutinizing the original page, the three of us agreed that the word as written could be "better"; the loop in the "e" seemed a little more open than in the photocopy, and we could find no dot over an "i." Hemingway, however, tends to dot his "i's" with a high dot, so it could have been effaced by the generous stroke with which he had crossed the two "t's." On page 40 in the same folder we also found the phrase "see if that makes it any better," and there the loop in the "e" was unquestionable, open and wide.

I had discovered a real crux, one not likely to be resolved. And the more I thought about the crux, the less I wanted it to be resolved. A tight loop in an "e" or a missing dot over an "i" had generated an uncertainty in Hemingway's text that shaded nicely into a complementarity. Michael

Reynolds reads the "false ending with child" in one way, and Seán Hemingway reads "The Live-Baby Ending" in another, and those of us who come after are left not to split the difference but to contend with the offered surmise.

Of course, there is a world of difference between "bitter" and "better" – we might call it the Hemingway difference. For Frederic to feel bitter about the child is to be confirmed in his preemptive irony. But for Frederic to move from experiencing the boy as trouble to feeling better about him in the space of seven words is to signal a radically new capacity for sudden changes of heart. In this reading, and in one sentence, Frederic is allowed to own up to bitterness and to forgive himself for it.

Of course, all this happens in an ending Hemingway finally put aside. The baby was not to be allowed to live. But the possibility of feeling better rather than bitter about how lives end, and about the price women and men are sometimes called upon to pay for loving each other, had nevertheless been broached, and the endings to come could be, therefore, altogether different.

CHAPTER 5

Making a Wound

A Farewell to Arms and "Now I Lay Me"

In his 1966 *Ernest Hemingway: A Reconsideration*, Philip Young wrote, "It is still too early to know which of all the worlds our writers offer will be the ones we shall have turned out to have lived in." Looking back from the early twenty-first century, Hemingway appears to have foreseen more clearly than most that the looming story of the twentieth century was to be the extension of American power out into the world. His novels and stories had long figured forth a prediction made in 1943 in a letter to Archibald MacLeish: "Actually I think we will be at war for the rest of our lives." The prediction about the growth of the American Imperium was to come true in a shockingly literal way as the United States elected to engage in "small war on the heels of small war," in Robert Lowell's words, a perpetual series of wars fought on behalf of a perpetually elusive peace. "I don't see any end until we destroy them, there and here and everywhere," says a character in "The Strange Country," a story Hemingway began in 1946. "I don't see any end to it ever, he thought."

Hemingway imagined the price of the adventure as one registered upon the male body, in wounds: a hit in the spine, a gone penis, a knee no longer there, a crushed leg, a riven hand. The gains made by the nation by way of its foreign wars were to be measured against these vivid and painful physical losses.

A price initially paid by the body had to be lived out by the spirit. Ground had been gained, power displayed, and money made, but the winners looked to take away nothing but guilt, depression, lovelessness, nightmares, and loss of faith. Winning, it turned out, proved difficult to distinguish from losing. "Ever since I had been a boy," Hemingway wrote in 1946, "I had been in retreats, holding attacks, retreats, victories with no reserves to follow them up, etc., and I had never known how winning can make you feel." He had come to prefer situations in which the options were life and death rather than victory and defeat. The Second World War had promised to deliver up the first set of options but ended up delivering the second. Victory had somehow turned the whole thing into a game. "We, in games," he wrote in *Death in the Afternoon*, "are not fascinated by death, its nearness and its avoidance. We are fascinated by victory and we replace the avoidance of death by the avoidance of defeat. It is a very nice symbolism but it takes more cojones to be a sportsman when death is a closer party to the game."

For a writer, the consequence of perpetual war is "a depreciation of all our terms." Henry James spoke the following words in a newspaper interview with the *New York Times* in 1915:

> One finds it in the midst of all this as hard to apply one's words as to endure one's thoughts. The war has used up words; they have weakened, they have deteriorated like motor car tires; . . . and we are now confronted with a depreciation of all our terms.

Hemingway read the James interview and typed the passage quoted above onto an unnumbered page of the manuscript of *A Farewell to Arms*. After making this discovery, Michael Reynolds wrote: "Hemingway's novel is an answer to James's question of what language will remain."

It is James, then, who stands behind Frederic's famous renunciation of rhetoric in chapter XXVII:

> There were many words that you could not stand to hear and finally only the names of places had dignity. Certain numbers were the same way and certain dates and these with the names of the places were all you could say and have them mean anything. Abstract words such as glory, honor, courage, or hallow were obscene beside the concrete names of villages, the numbers of roads, the names of rivers, the numbers of regiments and the dates.

Against the depreciation of words, one fought back with style. A writer's choice of tone and image and sentence sound and story structure became a kind of war against war, a struggle to rescue its particularities from words seeking to rationalize its purposes or to anaesthetize its pain.

Hemingway also understood that it was not necessary to go to war in order to be able to write well about it. Michael Reynolds's *Hemingway's First War* has definitively established *A Farewell to Arms* as a work of the imagination, not a documentary record of some actual lived experience. Reynolds demonstrates that a landscape so concrete that it must have been seen and a retreat so accurate to the facts that it must have been experienced were neither seen nor experienced by Hemingway. The house in the village that looked across the river and the plain toward the mountains was in a town and on a river Hemingway had never visited. The retreat from

Caporetto so carefully reconstructed in Book Three occurred months before Hemingway arrived in Italy. Hemingway had "not experienced the military engagements in which Frederic Henry takes part," Reynolds writes. Hemingway's brief war was fought on the Veneto plain, above Venice, while Frederic's took place along the Isonzo River, in the vicinity of what was to become, by the end of the century, the border with Slovenia. "Yet," as Reynolds writes, Hemingway's "geography is perfectly accurate."

It is accurate because the novelist carefully researched the informing context of his wartime experiences. Like Krebs in "Soldier's Home," he began reading about his war after returning from it. He immersed himself in books like *The Story of the Red Cross in Italy* (1920), *With British Guns in Italy* (1919), and *Battlefields of the World War* (1921). He also "located accurate topographic maps of northern Italy" so as to be able to reproduce Frederic's retreat as a "seemingly firsthand experience." While the art of the novel only makes it *seem* as if its author must have experienced Caporetto firsthand, surely with the central trauma in the story it is different, since as everyone knows, Ernest Hemingway, like Frederic Henry, was wounded in the war.

On the evening of July 8, 1918, an eighteen-year-old Red Cross ambulance driver serving with the Italian Army along the Piave River found himself at a forward listening post. He had been in Europe a little over a month, docking at Bordeaux, making his way to Milan by train, and finally barracked on the plains above Venice, near a town called Fossalta. On an overnight visit with other American drivers staying in a neighboring village, he lay on the floor in a room like the one in which Nick Adams would one day listen "to the silk-worms eating." He befriended a priest from Florence; he watched the shelling in the mountains. It was a kind of trench warfare, and it was either deadly or dull. Nothing much happened until the night of July 8, when, near midnight and as the Austrian bombardment intensified, the young man headed toward the front lines with some cigarettes, chocolate, and postcards.

He was joking with the Italian soldiers when he heard an incoming shell from the Austrian batteries across the river. It exploded with the force of a hurricane. He tried to move but he could not. An injured soldier was crying nearby, and the young man managed to pick him up in a fireman's carry and turn back toward the command post. After moving about fifty yards, he was hit by machine gun fire in his right knee. Later, he could not remember how he covered the final one hundred yards, but he did so, delivered his man, and then passed out.

Two stretcher bearers carried him to a roofless shed. There he recited to himself the child's prayer, "Now I Lay Me." Twenty-eight shell fragments were removed from his legs and feet after an ambulance conveyed him to a makeshift medical station. During his long convalescence in Milan, doctors would remove two machine gun bullets and hundreds of shell fragments from his lower legs. The convalescent even worked out some of the smaller fragments with the point of a pen knife.

Carlos Baker tells this story in his 1969 biography, *Ernest Hemingway: A Life Story*. It is a good story, full of fine behavior, even heroism. Being wounded is one thing, but acting to save another injured man is altogether more impressive. The striking display of strength within vulnerability could be taken to define what a man might mean by grace under pressure.

But the story is unverifiable, perhaps even untrue. On his return to the United States in January 1919, Hemingway told a reporter from the New York *Sun* a quite different story. After being hit by mortar fire, he had been picked up by two Italian stretcher bearers. His bearers were then hit by Austrian machine gun bullets, "one of which got Hemingway in the shoulder and another in the right leg." While he had been hit by machine gun fire, it was while lying down. There had been no picking up of anyone in a fireman's carry. "The surgical chart of his battered person shows 227 marks," the reporter noted.

A third version of the wounding came ten years later, in *A Farewell to Arms*:

> I ate the end of my piece of cheese and took a swallow of wine. Through the other noise I heard a cough, then came the chuh-chuh-chuh-chuh – then there was a flash, as when a blast-furnace door is swung open, and a roar that started white and went red and on and on in a rushing wind. I tried to breathe but my breath would not come and I felt myself rush bodily out of myself and out and out and out and all the time bodily in the wind. I went out swiftly, all of myself, and I knew I was dead and that it had all been a mistake to think you just died. Then I floated, and instead of going on I felt myself slide back. I breathed and I was back. The ground was torn up and in front of my head there was a splintered beam of wood. In the jolt of my head I heard somebody crying. I thought somebody was screaming.

Frederic Henry hears his fellow drivers screaming, but he cannot move. He feels much the way Hemingway had himself felt: "My legs felt warm and wet and my shoes were wet and warm inside." He reaches for his knee but his kneecap is not there. Two stretcher bearers pick him up and begin carrying him toward the listening post. They drop him twice. On the operating table, he is told that his blood coagulates beautifully. Then the pain sets in and "all that was happening was without interest or relation."

All this happens to Frederic Henry in the ninth chapter of *A Farewell to Arms*. In chapter X, he recounts the incident to his friend Rinaldi. "Did you do any heroic act?" Rinaldi asks.

> "No," I said. "I was blown up while we were eating cheese."
> "Be serious. You must have done something heroic either before or after. Remember carefully."
> "I did not."
> "Didn't you carry anybody on your back? Gordini says you carried several people on your back but the medical major at the first post declares it is impossible. He had to sign the proposition for the citation."
> "I didn't carry anybody. I couldn't move."

So which is the true war story? The answer given may depend upon the kind of war story one has come to prefer. If you like heroism, take the first story. If you like heroism corrected by ironic afterthought, you may prefer the second. And, if you like a surprising mixture of suffering endured, tenderness offered, and skepticism as an ever-available default position, you will probably like the third.

The emergence of the more accurate version of what happened on a July night in 1918 is a good story in itself. In 1976, when he published *Hemingway's First War*, Michael Reynolds was still relying on Baker's version of the wounding. "Suffering severe shrapnel wounds in his right leg," Reynolds writes, Hemingway "managed to carry a wounded Italian soldier back to the dressing station." Bernard Oldsey repeated the claim three years later: "carrying another wounded man, Hemingway made his way toward the rear."

A 1982 article by Robert W. Lewis, "Hemingway in Italy: Making It Up," was the first to question Hemingway's "alleged heroism" in carrying a wounded soldier to safety. In an American Red Cross report located by Lewis, Hemingway is described as "wounded by the explosion of a shell which landed about three feet from him, killing a soldier who stood between him and the point of explosion." Describing as "bogus" the story of Hemingway's carrying another man, Lewis also points out Baker's reliance in his account of the wounding on two letters written by Hemingway himself, one sent to his parents on August 18, 1918, and the other composed thirty years later and sent to Malcolm Cowley. "The two sources are, in part, contradictory," Lewis concludes, "and notably so on the point of Hemingway's alleged carrying of the wounded Italian."

Much of the power and beauty of Carlos Baker's biography derives from his relying throughout on a skillful paraphrase of Hemingway's letters. If you were to check any colorful paragraph in *Hemingway: A Life Story* against a letter by Hemingway describing the same experience, you would be impressed by Baker's ability to ventriloquize his subject. In his end "Notes," Baker is candid about his method of composition: "EH's wounding: the most trustworthy account is EH's own, contained in a letter to his parents, Aug. 18, 1918. The substance of that letter is followed here. EH describes the Austrian trench mortar in a letter to Cowley, Sept. 5, 1948. In this same letter, he vouches for the autobiographical accuracy of the passage on the wounding of Frederic Henry in *A Farewell to Arms.*"

In relying as it does on a letter *and* a novel by Hemingway, Baker's footnote would have it both ways. In the letter written to his parents, a convalescing Hemingway promoted the myth of carrying his wounded to the rear: "The machine gun bullet just felt like a sharp smack on my leg with an icy snow ball. However it spilled me. But I got up again and got my wounded into the dug out." The letter cannot therefore be deemed trustworthy, as Baker claims, or, at the least, it cannot be squared with "the autobiographical accuracy of the passage on the wounding" as provided in the novel. In *A Farewell to Arms*, as Frederic says to Rinaldi, "I didn't carry anybody."

A decade after publishing *Hemingway's First War*, Michael Reynolds chose to begin his five-volume biography with the date on which nineteen-year-old Ernest Hemingway landed in New York on his return from Europe. Chapter One of *The Young Hemingway* is titled "The End of Something: January 21, 1919." By 1986, Reynolds had located the New York *Sun* article and had in consequence decided to open his narrative with extensive quotation of it. In commencing with the moment of homecoming and with Hemingway's interview with the reporter from the *Sun*, Reynolds signals his intention to attend both to the facts of the life and to the construction of the Hemingway legend.

Reynolds is generous about the many embellishments generated by Hemingway or others about his war experience. "Not a lie exactly," Reynolds concludes, about Hemingway's allowing people to believe that he had actually served with the Italian army. Back home in Illinois, Hemingway even promoted himself to First Lieutenant when responding to a questionnaire sent out by the Memorial Committee of Oak Park and River Forest. In March of 1919, he told an assembly of students at his former high school, "I picked up the wounded man and started back toward the trenches." Over the years, the story of the wound would be amplified or diminished by Hemingway depending on the mood of the moment. "In the *Sun* interview," the account in which Hemingway admitted to having been picked up by two Italian stretcher bearers, Reynolds concludes, "he came closest to the truth."

"His lies were quite unimportant lies and consisted in attributing to himself things other men had seen, done or heard of, and stating as facts certain apocryphal incidents familiar to all soldiers." Hemingway writes these words about Krebs in "Soldier's Home." Back home in Oklahoma, Krebs, a veteran of trench warfare on the Western Front, feels an acute pressure to exaggerate his wartime experience so as to feed the popular appetite for "atrocity stories." "Krebs found that to be listened to at all he had to lie." In this way, "he lost everything," Hemingway writes, although Krebs will recover from his self-induced nausea, as his author himself was to do, by beginning to read about and to study the war.

The embellishments Hemingway lavished upon his rite of pain pale in comparison to those visited upon it by his critics. What they managed to construct was "not a lie exactly," as Reynolds might say, but a severely inhibiting myth. The Wound of War hypothesis dominated Hemingway criticism for most of the twentieth century and still constitutes, for many readers, the salient biographical fact. How this story earned such pride of place is itself a kind of romance, although one less revealing about Hemingway than about an interpretative community's need to fend off the profound uncanniness of an author's work by reducing it to the response to a single traumatic event.

In my battered teaching copy of *In Our Time*, I find these words written in pencil on the inside cover: "personal trauma on which all traumas are based – shrapnel wound near Fossalta, July 8, 1918." In writing this in my mid-twenties, I was simply chiming in with a chorus of voices dedicated to "making a wound." The phrase "making a wound" can be found in the description of Pedro Romero's first *quite* in chapter XVIII of *The Sun Also Rises*, although it did not appear in the initial draft of the scene. As Frederic Svoboda has shown, that draft contains a long sentence in which Jake describes a picador driving into the bull with his hickory shaft, his horse pulling "sideways as he pivoted on the pic, enforcing the iron into the bulls shoulder." Three additional words, here italicized, were later added to the sentence: "and pulled his horse sideways as he pivoted on the pic, *making a wound*, enforcing the iron into the bull's shoulder." On second thought, in revising the sentence, Hemingway found words descriptive of a profession dedicated to making a wound.

The Wound of War hypothesis was given its first big boost in Edmund Wilson's "Hemingway: Gauge of Morale," an essay published in 1939 and then reprinted in Wilson's 1941 book, *The Wound and the Bow*. Spinning a theory of artistic development out of the myth of Philoctetes, Wilson argues for a "conception of superior strength as inseparable from disability." In this openly compensatory model of how art gets made, "the hero with the incurable wound" becomes the prototype for the creative artist. It is the energy generated out of living with the wound that empowers the artist to draw his bow.

While Wilson made no direct reference to actual wounds suffered by a young American at Fossalta, his "trauma theory of literature," as Hemingway later described it, became a central feature of the Hemingway industry. Malcolm Cowley made specific reference to the wound of 1918 in the Introduction to his 1944 *The Portable Hemingway*. He amplified his position in a 1984 article, "Hemingway's Wound – And Its Consequences for American Literature." In trying to account for a "haunted" quality in Hemingway's prose, "the first clue I found," he wrote, "was clearer than others: it was the wound he had suffered in Italy." In *The Twenties* (1955), Frederick J. Hoffman also chimed in: "The experience of the wound and the circumstances in which it had happened," Hoffman wrote, "radically altered Hemingway's entire view of the world he re-entered." When reprinted, Hoffman's pages appeared under the title, "The Secret Wound."

Philip Young's *Ernest Hemingway*, published in 1952, elaborated the Wound of War hypothesis across the length of an entire book. Citing the wound inflicted on Nick Adams in chapter VI of *In Our Time*, Young is led to conclude, "From here on the Hemingway hero is to be a wounded man." Fourteen years later, in *Ernest Hemingway: A Reconsideration*, Young described the "two arguments" of his first book in more explicit terms. "First, the notion that the so-called 'Hemingway hero' as I have defined him was pretty close to being Hemingway himself." "Second, the one fact . . . necessary to any real understanding of either figure . . . is the fact of the 'wound,' a severe injury suffered in World War I."

No genetic theory of the growth of a writer's mind can hold forever, and, in due course, the Wound of War hypothesis would give way to other explanatory schemes. What "if the 'wound' is androgyny and not, as Philip Young so early established, the actual physical wounds that Hemingway himself sustained at Fossalta?" Mark Spilka centers *Hemingway's Quarrel with Androgyny* (1990) on this question and makes considerable headway in trying to answer it. Kenneth Lynn had preceded him in his 1987 biography, where much is made of the fact that, during his early years, Hemingway's mother enjoyed attiring him in dresses. Extending this tradition, Debra Moddelmog reads "masculinity itself" as "a wound," one magnifying "the very anxiety it is meant to protect."

Why not, then, speak of Hemingway's wound as an aliveness to the pathos of gender? That we have bodies and come out of bodies is scandal enough, one to which Nick is made privy in "Indian Camp." But that we can only be engendered because sexual difference exists and that much of human happiness depends upon the acceptance and exploitation and even prizing of these differences was a predicament deeply arresting to Hemingway's imagination. As he grew older, he was to strive mightily against the tacit assumption that being born "male" required one to be only a "man." For a writer so driven by the demand to survive the end of pleasure, gender must have recommended itself to him as a powerful threat to the demand, since to be born as one sex and not the other was to be denied from the beginning access to an entire range of pleasurable experiences. When Frederic and Catherine talk about there being "no me" or lay claim to being "one," they are attempting to push back against the complex of feelings arising out of their awareness of this division of divisions.

The complex of feelings described by Freud as "uncanny" or by Hemingway as "mysterious and homelike" is an expression of the wound of *having* a beginning. The wounds of war suffered by his adult characters are no doubt traumatic, but they are exceptional rather than foundational, a unique "password," as Hemingway was to describe them, not a universal bequest. The dynamics of memory as they play themselves out over a career's worth of work reveal being wounded as an experience leading unendingly back. While Jake Barnes and Frederic Henry experience no primal scene at an Indian Camp, they are each granted a single memory of home pointing back to an uncanniness at the source. Adult life is thereafter punctuated for each man with a sense of "something repeated." There is a "feeling of going through something that has all happened before." When the wound of war comes, it arrives, then, not as an originating trauma but as a repetition, one more invitation to remember back.

Hemingway's fascination with the process of "remembering back" is most in evidence in "Now I Lay Me," a story published two years before *A Farewell to Arms*. It is a Nick Adams story. Unable to sleep after having "been blown up at night," Nick occupies himself by thinking of trout streams once fished. "Sometimes I would fish four or five different streams in the night." Much attention is given to the kind of bait being used; the act of return resembles the situation in "Big Two-Hearted River."

"But some nights I could not fish," Nick admits. Without the comforting displacements provided by memories of fishing, the mind is drawn "to the earliest thing you remember." In Nick's case, this is the attic of the home where he was born. The attic contains the mother and father's wedding cake in a tin box and jars of snakes and other specimens the father has collected. Nick prays for the people he remembers, the dark lightens, and he finds himself in a place where he can sleep.

In imposing this sleep-inducing work of memory upon himself, Nick discovers a limit to the process:

> On those nights I tried to remember everything that had ever happened to me, starting with just before I went to the war and remembering back from one thing to another. I found I could only remember back to that attic in my grandfather's house. Then I would start there and remember this way again, until I reached the war.

Here, the process sounds complete: Nick remembers back to his earliest memory of early childhood, and then he remembers forward until arriving at the present.

Any illusion of closure is immediately undone, however, by the following sentence. "I remember, after my grandfather died we moved away from that house and to a new house designed and built by my mother." In the ensuing paragraph, it is as if Nick's mind, sensing it has not gone deep enough, involuntarily recommences its work. Nick then remembers the burning scene.

The destruction of a man's "things" by a wife was to become, after Hadley's inadvertent loss of her husband's manuscripts in 1922, an injury refigured in the prose and one that became central to the making of *The Garden of Eden*. Here, in Hemingway's first iteration of the trauma, Nick will "remember those jars from the attic being thrown in the fire, and how they popped in the heat and the fire flamed up from the alcohol. I remember the snakes burning in the fire in the back-yard. But there were no people in that, only things."

On Nick's first try at delving deeper, he is unable to imagine any agents for the action at hand. "I could not remember who burned the things," he admits. In this version of the past, a man's carefully assembled specimens are unaccountably destroyed.

Then comes the second try. "About the new house I remember how my mother was always cleaning things out and making a good clearance. One time when my father was away on a hunting trip she made a good thorough cleaning out in the basement and burned everything that should not have been there." Nick remembers his father coming home and seeing the fire still burning. "What's this?" he asks, as he dismounts from his buggy.

"I've been cleaning out the basement, dear," Nick's mother replies. She is standing there smiling. The father kicks at the fire, leans over, picks something out of the ashes. "Get a rake, Nick," he says. Then the father carefully rakes through the ashes, pulling out stone axes and skinning knives and tools for making arrow-heads. "Take the gun and the bags in the house, Nick, and bring me a paper," the father says. "I took the shot-gun," Nick remembers, "which was heavy to carry and banged against my legs."

Nick finally supplies the agents of this primal scene. They have been implicit from the beginning of his attempt at remembering back, the mother present in the image of the wedding cake, the father in the jars and the other specimens. What a man makes or collects is subject to a woman's furious lust for housekeeping, a process she presides over with a smile.

But there is a third agent here – Nick himself. His second try at remembering back is actually his third one; the fully recalled burning scene is a revision of one Hemingway composed and discarded. The manuscript version of the story shows Nick acting not as his father's sidekick but as his mother's accomplice. "'I've been cleaning out the basement dear,' my mother called from the porch," JFK Item 618 reads, "and ~~Ernie's~~ Nicky's helped me burn the things." As Paul Smith writes, "I can recall no other Hemingway manuscript in which he inadvertently has Nick's mother call him Ernie."

The history of the composition of "Now I Lay Me" reveals a story struggling not to know what it knows, since Nick's work of courageous uncovering also functions as an act of concealment. Imagining Nick as assisting the mother in the act of clearance is troubling enough, since it positions the Hemingway protagonist on the side of a figure and a force with which he is never elsewhere identified. But the slip of the pencil is more troubling still. For Hemingway to insert his first name into "Now I Lay Me" is to reveal a younger Ernest as somehow complicit in an act of destroying a man's "things," an act anticipating the burning of David Bourne's writings in *The Garden of Eden*.

Most telling here, as so often in Hemingway, is a character's motion of mind. The content of Nick's complex act of remembering back matters a great deal, of course, although having it center on the triangle of mother, father, and child is hardly a surprise. Hemingway's achievement in "Now I Lay Me" has rather to do with his uncovering of how a mind works and with the ways in which it hides from and finally cannot defend itself against all it knows. Screen memories play their important part, and many minds will remain content to allow the work of remembering to carry them only so far back. Hemingway chooses instead to expose his character and his reader to the discovery that beyond every seeming limit on the process of remembering back a prior memory can loom up, as the mind moves ever closer to things it has chosen to forget.

The various wound hypotheses, including my own, are not so much inaccurate as they are reductive of a situation in which the writer's behavior as a writer is overdetermined. What caused Hemingway's unique take on human experience will never be known. The very nature of the question assumes that life causes art when Hemingway, along with Henry James, believed that "it is art that *makes* life." What happens in a life is, in any case, unverifiable, subject as we all are to the mind's continuous intermingling of fact and fantasy, whereas how we take things counts for as much as what is done to us. Hemingway entertains this view when he has Pilar say to Maria, a saying she then repeats to Robert Jordan, "nothing is done to oneself that one does not accept and that if I loved some one it would take it all away." In this deeply romantic formulation, the human imagination is seen as having the power to make experience mean what it will and to "not accept" as determining the traumas that come its way.

Still, Hemingway did experience something he called "the big wound," and he can, at times, appear to endorse the Wound of War hypothesis. While remaining contemptuous of "Bunny Wilson writing about some mysterious thing that changed or formed my life," in looking back on his "first war" in a letter written in 1948, he could say, "I now see, I was hurt very badly; in the body, mind and spirit and also morally.... Big-Two Hearted River is a story about a man who is home from the war. But the war is not mentioned."

Then there was the 1926 letter to Maxwell Perkins about the manuscript of *The Sun Also Rises*. Perkins had queried Hemingway about the wording of a passage dealing with an injury suffered by Henry James. James comes up in chapter XII during a conversation between Jake Barnes and Bill Gorton. Jokingly, Bill refers to rumors that Jake is impotent.

> "No," I said. "I just had an accident."
>
> "Never mention that," Bill said. "That's the sort of thing that can't be spoken of. That's what you ought to work up into a mystery. Like Henry's bicycle."

As they continue talking, Jake and Bill speculate on what "Henry" was riding when he had his accident – maybe it was a tricycle. "Well," Jake replies, "A plane is sort of like a tricycle. The joystick works the same way." By way of this series of substitutions, Jake and Bill come as close as the novel ever will allow to indicating that his joystick is what Jake has lost.

Perkins had objected to the use of James's surname in the manuscript version of the exchange, and Hemingway was eventually to cut the word "James" as well as a fair amount of detail about the event James himself once called his "obscure hurt." Hemingway's response to Perkins's concerns about the passage as originally written is telling:

> As for the Henry James thing – I haven't the second part of the Ms. here – it is over at Scott's – so I can't recall the wording. But I believe that it is a reference to some accident that is generally known to have happened to Henry James in his youth . . . . If Henry James never had an accident of that sort I should think it would be libelous to say he had no matter how long he were dead. But if he did I do not see how it can affect him – now he is dead. As I recall Gorton and Barnes are talking humorously around the subject of Barnes' mutilation and to them Henry James is not a man to be insulted or protected from insult but simply an historical example.

But if he did, Hemingway writes, as if the point at issue were a mere matter of fact. Perkins was concerned rather with a question of decorum and with whether or not to use a writer's life as a means of explaining his work.

On this point, Hemingway was to remain fairly consistent, at least in reference to himself. What was being depreciated by those who refused to "lay off the Biography" were his powers of imagination. As he had written as early as 1924, "*the only writing that was any good was what you made up, what you imagined . . . . That was what the family couldn't understand. They thought it all was experience.*"

Hemingway was especially impatient of those who confused him with his characters. "If I write about *anybody*," he complained to Perkins in 1933, "automatically they label that character as me." After Philip Young began his researches in the late 1940s, Hemingway wrote an editor at Rinehart about his misgivings. "When I hear from Malcolm Cowley that Mr. Young is writing a book which proves that I am all my heroes it occurs to me that it would be as well to dissuade him as early as possible so that he would not have lost his time and his work." Earlier in the same letter, he had made the more general point: "there has been too damned much written about my personal life and I am sick of it." And yet he went on to admit, "Every writer is in much of his work."

The force of this last claim turns upon the meaning of the word "in." One way a writer can be said to be in his work is as a researcher. Take "the whole genesis of The Sun Also Rises," Hemingway continues. "It came from a personal experience in that when I had been wounded at one time there had been an infection from pieces of wool cloth being driven into the scrotum. Because of this I got to know other kids who had genito urinary wounds and I wondered what a man's life would have been like after that if his penis had been lost and his testicles and spermatic cord remained intact." A private infection may provoke a concern, but only getting to know and to study the experience of "other kids" leads to the "inventing," as Hemingway calls it, of a "foreign correspondent in Paris" and "his problems."

In this account of the creative process, being wounded does not direct the imagination into inward terrain. Instead, the wound provokes curiosity, a movement away from the self and toward the "other." What to call such a wound? Chary of the word "trauma" and the biographical reductions it could encourage, Hemingway came to settle on a surprisingly modest term: password. The following sentences can be found in "The Restored Edition" of *A Moveable Feast* (2009), in a sketch called "On Writing in the First Person":

> In Italy when I was at the war there, for one thing that I had seen or that had happened to me, I knew many hundreds of things that had happened to other people who had been in the war in all of its phases. My own small experiences gave me a touchstone by which I could tell whether stories were true or false and being wounded was a password.

Again, the emphasis moves away from the self and its small experiences and toward "the experiences and knowledge of my friends and all the people I had known." The wound-as-password brings the writer a measure of credibility with these friends and people and assists him in determining the truth or falseness of their stories.

Hemingway expended considerable energy descrying the notion that in order to imagine something one had to have experienced it. Having to make his defense of the imagination was the ironic payoff of the power of his style to create an effect of verisimilitude. Again, from "On Writing in the First Person": "If the stories are made so real that people believe them, the people reading them nearly always think the stories really happened to you. That is natural because while you were making them up you had to make them happen to the person who was telling them. If you do this successfully enough, you make the person who is reading them believe that the things happened to him too." "Happen to," Hemingway writes, in a phrase that resonates with the word "in." A writer is "in" his work to the extent that, in creating it, he has the almost physical sensation of entering into his imagined world. "Some days it went so well that you could make the country so that you could walk into it," Hemingway writes in "Birth of a New School." Landscape often serves as the occasion for such claims because writing creates an experience felt to be dimensional. "Country" refers to a realm only reachable when the external is fully internalized in an act of the mind and that happening in the mind of a writer produces a second happening in the mind of a reader.

The made thing has a life as consequential as life itself since both writer and reader can live *in* it. "If you make it up instead of describe it you can make it round and whole and solid and give it life. You create it, for good or bad. It is made; not described." It is an illusion to believe that a writer's books are receptacles for actual happenings; they are instead experiences that happen to us. Hemingway could well have said what Alan Bennett says in *The Uncommon Reader* (2004): "You don't put your life into your books. You find it there."

PART II

Embarrassment

CHAPTER 6

Awkwardness and Appreciation
Death in the Afternoon

Death in the Afternoon offers itself as a book about learning how to see. To read it is to replace "the eye of a person unfamiliar" with that of an aficionado. While Hemingway admits, some sixty pages into the book, that "at this point it is necessary that you see a bullfight," his project rests on the assumption that we have not seen a bullfight, will probably never see one, and may even abhor the very idea of seeing one. He therefore begins by recalling his own resistance: "At the first bullfight I ever went to I expected to be horrified and perhaps sickened by what I had been told would happen to the horses." Admitting that some will turn away in sheer "disgust," he maintains that a balanced judgment of bullfighting can only be made once readers have "seen the things that are spoken of" and know "truly what their reactions to them would be."

By admitting that he, too, expected to be horrified and even sickened by "the killing of the horses," and by implying that his responses to the bullfight have evolved through and beyond such responses, Hemingway initiates one of the central arguments of his book: our encounters with works of art involve feelings, and, as we re-encounter these works of art, our feelings are subject to change. Hemingway's early letters about bullfighting, when compared with the voice he adopts in *Death in the Afternoon*, vividly make this point.

In a long letter dated March 8, 1925, Hemingway begins by informing Bill Smith, "I'm at work on a book on de bull ring" and asks him to "preserve the enditers screeds on bull battles." He ends the letter by reaffirming his ambition: "I'm going to write the whole thing from the start – Origins – the different parts – all the dope." The heart of the letter deals, however, with the response of his friend Chink Dorman-Smith to seeing his first bullfight, in Pamplona. A career soldier in His Majesty's Fifth Fusiliers, Dorman-Smith had commanded troops on the Asiago Plateau, had been wounded three times, and held the Military Cross for extraordinary heroism:

> In the afternoon fight the picador work was vile and there were a lot of horses killed.
>
> It nearly killed Chink. He was white as a sheet in rage and horror that people would do such things. Made me miserable, the horses didn't bother me but the sight of Chink did. I expected he just might leave the feria. He was hit hard. We had to just keep off the subject. He talked sarcastic and like hell about it. I told him he'd better just stay away from the corridas. No, he said he was going just to study these people. He said it made him understand the inquisition and the Auto da Fé. I wished to hell he hadn't come down he was taking it hard and a moral atmosphere was being injected.

This dismissive casualness comes to a head in a letter addressed to Ezra Pound in the summer of 1925:

> Bulls kill for fun and are killed the same way etc. To me bulls aint exotic. They are normal. And such a goddam relief from all this horseshit about Art etc. Bulls know how to knock the horseshit out of a horse. They know how to open a horse up and see what makes him go. They are not sorry for the horse after they have killed him. They nose and poke to make sure he is dead. Bulls are not sentimental.

By the time he came to write his "good book," Hemingway had learned enough about both bullfighting and writing to take a more considered tone.

As the years pass away and as the practice of bullfighting passes away as well, it becomes increasingly likely that any appreciation of bullfighting will depend upon the experience of seeing afforded by Hemingway's book, and this despite its author's admission that bullfighting is a "thing which it is impossible to make come true on paper." The word "impossible" haunts Hemingway's task, as when he writes: "It is impossible to believe the emotional and spiritual intensity and pure, classic beauty that can be produced by a man, an animal and a piece of scarlet serge draped over a stick." Here, a sentence beginning with an absolute claim and building in its rhythm toward an eloquent climax deflates in the bathetic surprise of a harsh and inelegant monosyllable. It is an awkward ending. Throughout *Death in the Afternoon*, the admission of awkwardness as an essential element of both what is being described and what is being said works to draw in resisting readers, who come to acknowledge their own awkward attempts at learning to appreciate art.

Hemingway's project takes its inspiration from Oscar Wilde's counter-intuitive claim, "it is much more difficult to talk about a thing than to do it." In choosing to write about the performance of something he cannot do himself – "I was too old, too heavy and too awkward," he tells the Old Lady, when she notes that he writes about bullfights and "yet are not a bullfighter yourself" – Hemingway becomes The Critic as Artist. While he makes repeated appeals to the primacy of actual experience – one must *see* a bullfight – his actual practice argues instead for the efficacy and the necessity of another kind of seeing, the kind afforded by the after-experience of art we call "criticism."

Only by way of criticism, Hemingway demonstrates, can any member of an audience develop taste. The initial encounter with the work of art is too overwhelming to allow for a complete and sufficient response. Criticism – any kind of thoughtful reflection on and analysis of the thing just done – stands in relation to the experience of the work of art as revision does to the writing of a book. It, too, is a kind of second will: the spontaneous overflow can only acquire its full force and meaning during the recollection in tranquility.

Taste emerges as a crucial subject early in chapter one, when Hemingway segues from a taste for bullfighting to a taste for wine. "Wine," he writes, "offers a greater range for enjoyment and appreciation than, possibly, any other purely sensory thing which may be purchased." This enjoyment depends upon "the education of one's palate." The palate is like the eye, "capable of transmitting constantly greater enjoyment to the brain because of the knowledge or ability to see that it has acquired." The pursuit of the education *becomes* the enjoyment; as the palate becomes more educated, it becomes more "capable of appreciation."

Hence the importance to Hemingway's project of the word "study." The study of an art form or of a sensory thing allows us to rid ourselves of the "preconceived opinions" forming the primary barrier to an act of true appreciation. When he began to write, Hemingway tells us in the opening paragraphs of his book, he found "the greatest difficulty, aside from knowing truly what you really felt, rather than what you were supposed to feel, and had been taught to feel, was to put down what really happened in action." The challenge became to produce "the emotion that you experienced." As a newspaper man, Hemingway had learned various tricks but he had never been able to capture "the sequence of motion and fact which made the emotion." Taking the true subject of his time to be "violent death," believing that once the wars were over the bullring was the only place where you "could see life and death," and seeking an education in emotion, Hemingway therefore decided "to go to Spain where I could study it."

In studying the bullfight, Hemingway learns a number of things: the difference between obligatory and uncensored feeling, a preference for empathy over identification, the necessity of intuiting the whole of an experience even while taking in the constituent parts, the power of a choreographed activity to have its "effect" long before one may have developed a taste for it, the value of surrendering to "awkward sights." Having learned about these things, a spectator will have acquired taste and will no longer want any "sweetening" in the wine.

By the end of chapter one, Hemingway has compared watching bullfighting to looking at paintings, drinking wine, watching movies, and listening to music. The practices allowing for the appreciation of any one of these art forms, he implies, allow appreciation of any of the others. And yet Hemingway must finally admit that bullfighting is "kept from being one of the major arts," remaining a minor art not because it is cruel but because "it is impermanent." After it is over, a bullfight "exists only in the memory of those who have seen it." "Suppose a painter's canvases disappeared with him and a writer's books were automatically destroyed at his death and only existed in the memory of those that had read them. That is what happens in bullfighting." In saying this, Hemingway reminds us of another impermanent experience that continues to exist only in memory. In its impermanence, the art of bullfighting comes closer than any of the major art forms to approximating the art of living. A life, like a bullfight, ends with a death, and individuals then exist only in the memory of those who loved them.

It took some time for Hemingway to make the connection between the end of a bullfight and the end of a life. When he first started writing, he "was working very hard to try to get" the sequence of motion and fact that made the emotion and trying to learn to do this by watching bullfights was no easy thing. "I believe I saw more than fifty bulls killed with various degrees of facility before I consciously saw one killed well." "I could see the bull had to be killed to make the bullfight" and yet "the sword business" that was supposed to be the climax of the fight "looked like a trick and gave me no emotion at all."

Hemingway saw his first bull fight in Madrid in the late spring of 1923 at 4:30 in the afternoon and wrote up the experience in the *Toronto Star*. Robert McAlmon and Bill Bird were with him; they had barrera seats. Villalta had been gored at Malaga in the previous week, but in Madrid he stood straight as a lance and walked like a young wolf. When the bull came out of its dark pen, he charged, "and as he charged, I suddenly saw what bullfighting is all about." It was the first bullfight Hemingway had ever seen, "but it was not the best." The young journalist then proceeds to discourse on how to approach the bull, about "all sorts of complicated passes that must be done with the cape," about "the three absolute acts of the tragedy." The reader is even informed about which usages are "obsolete" and that gypsies are "the greatest killers." The writer is clearly a man who knows what bullfighting is "all about."

The account of his inaugural act of seeing in *Death in the Afternoon* is quite different:

> at the first bullfight I ever saw, before I could see it clearly, before I could even see what happened, in the new, crowded, confused, white-jacketed beer vender passing in front of you, two steel cables between your eyes and the ring below, the bull's shoulders smooth with blood, the banderillas clattering as he moved and a streak of dust down the middle of his back, his horns solid-looking like wood on top, thicker than your arm where they curved; I remembered in the midst of this confused excitement having a great moment of emotion when the man went in with the sword. But I could not see in my mind exactly what happened and when, on the next bull, I watched closely the emotion was gone and I saw it was a trick. I saw fifty bulls killed after that before I had the emotion again. But by then I could see how it was done and I knew I had seen it done properly that first time.

The key words in this recollection of Hemingway's first bullfight are the words "consciously" and "mind." As with so many initial encounters with an unfamiliar mode of art, the onlooker has an emotion without being able to account for how it is being produced. And this is the value and purpose of criticism, or the corrective self-criticism Hemingway administers here as, through writing, he recovers an experience that would otherwise have remained lost to him. Criticism allows him "consciously" to "see in my mind" what has already been seen with the eyes but remains unnoticed until it is acknowledged through an act of second will and valued fully for the first time.

While learning how to see it done properly is the heart of the matter, not every member of an audience will prove competent to do so. The complex process we call "identification" stands in the way of such learning. Having "taken many people" to bullfights, Hemingway has come to notice a difference between "those that were affected and those that were not affected" by the treatment of the horses.

"People may possibly be divided into two general groups," he then proceeds to argue, "those who, to use one of the terms of the jargon of psychology, identify themselves with, that is, place themselves in the position of, animals, and those who identify themselves with human beings." In nodding toward the jargon of psychology, Hemingway reminds his reader that Freud brought the term "identification" into common usage in order to describe a dynamic largely unconscious in nature. In "Mourning and Melancholia," Freud defines identification as "a preliminary stage of object-choice." The "ego picks out an object ... wants to incorporate this object into itself" and "wants to do so by devouring it."

"I just devoured that book," we sometimes say. It sounds like a pleasurable thing, the appeasing of a hunger. Or, alternatively, we say, "I really identified with that character." Many readers claim this feeling as one of the more sought-after pleasures of reading.

However, Hemingway means to show that identification between a reader and a figure in a text is often, as Freud would have it, a "preliminary" affair. To identify with "The Poor Horses" – Hemingway's original title for chapter one – is to indulge in the preconceived. It is to respond not to the bullfight but to a something felt before the onlooker has crossed the threshold (*pre-liminary*, L. "before the threshold") of the ring. While such identification may be comforting and self-validating, it prevents us from opening ourselves to new experiences and thus from learning and changing. At their best, Hemingway's fictions work to discourage the easy "feeling like" of identification and to encourage instead a more strenuous and self-aware experience, the "feeling with" of empathy. As we develop this capacity, we learn to care about "objects" unlike ourselves.

The entire point of bullfighting as Hemingway understands it is to reveal the difference between animals and human beings and to remind the human onlooker that he is the only animal who lives with the knowledge that life ends with a death. The meaning of the bullfight resides less in the death of the bull than in the administering of that death by a man. The sword thrust "furnishes" a pleasurable and a prideful "emotion ... the feeling of rebellion against death which comes from its administering. Once you accept the rule of death thou shalt not kill is an easily and a naturally obeyed commandment. But when a man is still in rebellion against death he has pleasure in taking to himself one of the Godlike attributes; that of giving it."

In its promise to end with a death, bullfighting would seem to enact a continual embracing of the reality principle. "We owe God a death," Robert Wilson says, at the beginning of "The Short Happy Life of Francis Macomber." Yet Hemingway understands bullfighting as engendering something like the opposite of Wilson's recognition. In a sentence eventually cut from *Death in the Afternoon*, Hemingway had written: "Men search consciously or unconsciously for some sort of immortality." He may have deleted the sentence, but he retained its key word. A great matador "is performing a work of art and he is playing with death, bringing it closer, closer, closer, to himself, a death that you know is in the horns because you have the canvas-covered bodies of the horses on the sand to prove it. He gives the feeling of his immortality, and, as you watch it, it becomes yours. Then when it belongs to both of you, he proves it with the sword."

The manner in which death is administered in the bullring creates a complex interplay between empathy and identification. To side with the bull is certainly possible. As Hemingway acknowledges early on, many people identify themselves with animals. But to do so without qualification is to deprive oneself of one of the most pleasurable surmises afforded by the watching of a bullfight. We may feel like the bull, Hemingway allows, while also feeling with the matador. Bullfighting inevitably results in a "tragedy" for the bull; he is given the "gift" of death. But a spectator comes to a far different end, gaining a feeling of immortality as he participates through the matador in the administration of that death. In this sense, the bullfight is a romance, as nothing could be more romantic than to be indulged in the enduring human wish that one might live forever.

Hemingway's repeated use of the words "feeling" and "emotion" in *Death in the Afternoon* places considerable emphasis on the audience's receptivity: a matador "feels" a feeling during a bullfight, "gives the feeling of his immortality, and, as you watch it, it becomes yours." Whether or not we seek the peculiar and extreme feeling afforded by bullfighting, the dynamic played out between matador and spectator enacts Hemingway's most complex argument for the affective power of his own art. *Death in the Afternoon* both makes a case for the strategies and effects of Hemingway's early style and, in the last chapter of the book, also reveals his art to be in transition away from those strategies and those effects.

Hemingway's work of the 1920s invited readers to "feel something more" and did so through the art of leaving things out. "Krebs looked at the bacon fat hardening on his plate," Hemingway writes in "Soldier's Home." He does not write, "Krebs felt depressed." Relying on his own version of Eliot's "objective correlative," in such a moment Hemingway invites his reader to acknowledge a feeling by way of his own power to infer it. The result is not numbness – what Krebs may be striving for – but its opposite, the full influx of an awareness arising out of our ability to process the sequence of motion and fact which made the emotion.

As Robert Paul Lamb reminds us, "subjective feelings were the real omitted element of his fictions, present in their absence, evoked by carefully selected details, and filled in by readers who . . . recall similar such experiences from their pasts." Lamb's summary is persuasive until its last phrase, where he makes the error of assuming that a reader needs to have experienced a thing – like a bullfight – in order to supply the omitted feeling. But Hemingway's entire project is to offer not the memory of an actual experience, but the immediacy of the experience of reading: "I am trying, always, to convey to the reader a full and complete feeling of the thing I am dealing with; to make the person reading feel it has happened to them." The sentence appears in a letter to a librarian who had questioned Hemingway about the use of "certain plain words" in *Death in the Afternoon.*

While Hemingway practiced the art of omission most scrupulously in his early career, he gave his theory its most succinct explanation in *A Moveable Feast*:

> This was omitted on my new theory that you could omit anything if you knew that you omitted and the omitted part would strengthen the story and make people feel something more than they understood.

Words gain the power to do "something more" when they transport people into the gap between feeling and understanding. In this passage, Hemingway's use of the second person "you" has the effect of including the reader as if he or she had initiated the strategy being described. The work of art, he claims, possesses a deeply affective dimension and involves readers in an act of co-creation in which they infer fullness out of an apparent absence. Hemingway's sentence does not merely talk about his original theory of writing and reading here. As if to enact its central claim, the passage becomes the cry of its occasion when it gently includes the "you" in the Hemingway Sublime, an interactive encounter in which readers can come to feel they have created what they have merely heard.

These are claims made by a writer at the end of his career looking back at its beginning. The original articulation of Hemingway's "new theory" was made thirty years earlier, in *Death in the Afternoon*, and occurs in the chapter on the picadors. The passage does not rely on the generalized and inclusive "you" but instead articulates the transaction as one taking place between a "writer" and a "reader":

> If a writer of prose knows enough about what he is writing about he may omit things that he knows and the reader, if the writer is writing truly enough, will have a feeling of those things as strongly as though the writer

> had stated them. The dignity of movement of an ice-berg is due to only one-eighth of it being above water. A writer who omits things because he does not know them only makes hollow places in his writing.

Here, the repetition of the word "things" asks readers to enact the invoked experience, requiring us to hold in suspense the question of any concrete referent as we take in the point being made. What "things" might mean, that is, has been omitted. As in *A Moveable Feast*, the passage from *Death in the Afternoon* makes a claim about the importance of a reader having a feeling and promotes the experience by leaving something out. But the possible fusion or confusion of the two partners in the transaction is also spelled out – articulated in the two role-words reader and writer – in such a way as to create a more distinct division of labor. The intimacy of function indicated by Hemingway's "you" is here rendered more as the performing and the receiving of a service.

Long after he had ceased to adhere to any art of omission, Hemingway continued to appeal to the metaphor he had first deployed in *Death in the Afternoon*. In 1958, in the *Paris Review* interview, he told George Plimpton, "I always try to write on the principle of the iceberg." Given the central role the iceberg principle has played in Hemingway studies, readers may be surprised to discover its origin in a letter written to him by Hadley Richardson in the month before they were married. In the letter, she praises his ability to "find the scheme behind any subject tackled. I found something like that in music a little once, but you've got a magnificent grip on it – a magnificent grip on the form back of the material no matter how strange it is, like icebergs."

The two passages about Hemingway's art of omission differ on the question of how fully to include the reader into the writer's act of making. In *Death in the Afternoon*, the seven repetitions of the word "writer" and "writing," along with the three repetitions of the word "knows" or "know," indicate a prizing of know-how, a pride in artistry, before which the reader, as the audience at a bullfight, can at best play the role of passionate spectator. Given his shifting imaginative aims over a career of forty years, Hemingway was not able to achieve a stable balance between the writer and the reader who together complete the Hemingway text. Knowledgability was at times the enemy of feeling, and it is not difficult to single out those performances where Hemingway seems to put too much in and reduce his reader to the role of eager student or admiring auditor, as when we are asked to bear with Colonel Cantwell's reminiscences in *Across the River and into the Trees*.

At his best, Hemingway believed that "erudition shouldn't show.... Ideally a man should know everything, but when he writes make something so that it will really happen to the reader; be *made* (not described); so that afterwards the reader will have had the experience." A writer departs from knowledge, he does not end there: "You make something through your invention that is not a representation but a whole new thing truer than anything true and alive." Here, in this extraordinary utterance, Hemingway acknowledges the deepest thing he knows: that the stories and novels he makes are living sites of enactment rather than representations abstracted from something more true and alive. Writing became for him not a substitute for experience but rather the act of affirming his love of being in the world.

Does *Death in the Afternoon* afford its reader a chance to enact the experience of feeling more? Given its position as a transitional work between the imperatives of the early and the mid-career, the answer can only be "Yes" and "No." In the passages where Hemingway describes actual bullfights, he gradually naturalizes us into both an unfamiliar vocabulary and terrain. We learn, thereby, "the profundity of unseen detail"; that is, we learn to see what previously would have remained invisible to us, given our lack of an adequate schema. In so doing, in learning to follow "it easily in all its details," we have the by now familiar experience of coming to feel something more than we might otherwise have understood.

On the other hand, *Death in the Afternoon* contains so great a quantity of exposition and outright theorizing as to deny to its reader many of the customary pleasures of the Hemingway text. As a talky, digressive, and topic-ridden book, it has none of the feeling of sly inexorability that propels a reader of the early novels toward the promised end. Instead, we are treated to chapters on the raising of bulls, "horn knowledge," cape work, the placing of the banderillas, the use of the muleta, and, finally, how to kill cleanly. At one point, an entire short story is interposed into the text. At the end, Hemingway appends sixty-four pages of photographs, an Explanatory Glossary, and seven pages of "Some Reactions of a Few Individuals to the Integral Spanish Bullfight."

The form of *Death in the Afternoon* is, at best, awkward. "It is useless," Edward F. Stanton argues, "to expect here an orderly progression of well-organized chapters." Yet Stanton also discerns a vestigial narrative impulse, at least at the beginning of the book. He reads the opening two chapters, with their stories of gorings, slain horses, and gypsies roasting and eating a bull's testicles, as "tests of the reader's fortitude." This introductory ordeal then gives way to a discussion of technique revolving around a "secret structure of primordial symbols – blood, wine, sun, cojones." So far, so good. But Hemingway then makes the mistake of falling for the bullfighter rather than the bull and digresses into an "overemphasis on the personalities of toreros."

Stanton makes an impressive effort to resolve the relationship between the overall experience of the book and the diverse contents of its twenty chapters. In attempting to discern an unfolding pattern, he may perhaps be responding to the discussion of parts and wholes initiated in chapter one and continued throughout.

At the end of his book, Hemingway actually inverts his normal practice of concluding with an expectation fulfilled and comes to prefer an unlooked-for surprise. "Let it all change," Hemingway writes, as he closes in on his ending:

> We'll all be gone before it's changed too much and if no deluge comes when we are gone it still will rain in summer in the north and hawks will still nest in the Cathedral at Santiago and in La Granja, where we practiced with the cape on the long gravelled paths between the shadows, it makes no difference if the fountains play or not. We never will ride back from Toledo in the dark, washing the dust out with Fundador, nor will there be that week of what happened in the night in that July in Madrid. We've seen it all go and we'll watch it go again.

For a writer so concerned to ensure the repeatability of experience, this ending takes a remarkable turn. The many things he has loved to do in Spain, Hemingway admits, may well never happen again. In acknowledging the approaching imminence of his own death – "when we are gone" – and the acquisition of an ever-lengthening past, Hemingway turns to memory rather than to repeatable experience as the vehicle of return. Memory, especially as it is captured in writing, has the capacity to save the world from change. "Let those who want to save the world if you can get to see it clear and as a whole. Then any part you make will represent the whole if it's made truly." He writes four more sentences, and then his book ends.

Hemingway chooses to end by invoking the interdependency of parts and wholes. In doing so, he also circles back to a claim made near his beginning:

> I believe that the tragedy of the bullfight is so well ordered and so strongly disciplined by ritual that a person feeling the whole tragedy cannot separate

> the minor comic-tragedy of the horse so as to feel it emotionally. If they sense the meaning and end of the whole thing even when they know nothing about it; feel that this thing they do not understand is going on, the business of the horses is nothing more than an incident.

In responding to a "well ordered" work of art, Hemingway maintains, a spectator should not separate a disturbing "incident" from the "feeling of the whole." There is a patience involved, a willingness to remain in bafflement or in suspense. An audience may "feel that this thing they do not understand is going on," but this feeling is an inescapable and educative aspect of reading and living. The felt "not-understanding" is, in any case, manageable if readers allow themselves to trust an emerging sense of "the meaning and end of the whole thing."

Hemingway begins *Death in the Afternoon* by addressing the fundamental circularity of interpretation. In taking on the crux at the heart of the hermeneutic circle – the part can only be understood by inferring the shape of the artistic whole and the whole only by experiencing its various parts – he reminds us of his acute sensitivity to the moment when a reader enters a text.

We know that Hemingway was afflicted by the anxiety of setting out: the opening of "Indian Camp" establishes as much. "Where are we going, Dad?" is a question anyone beginning to read *Death in the Afternoon* might ask as well. Hemingway opens his book by directly addressing the anxiety of setting out. He begins, as we have seen, with the problem of the horses. In the opening paragraph the reader must make his way through words such as "horrified," "sickened," and "indefensible." In one more brilliant example of Hemingway's sense of the awkwardness of beginnings, he offers an invitation along with the expectation that it may well be declined.

Hemingway contributes to our understanding of the experience of reading by converting it into a test of courage. The difficulties in moving ahead after a beginning are not simply interpretative – they are existential. In creating openings uncanny ("Indian Camp"), unfriendly (*The Sun Also Rises*), or doom-laden (*A Farewell to Arms*), he places maximum pressure on the reader's will and capacity to move forward. And, by drawing attention to his crafting of each part – to each sentence as a "true" one – he challenges the reader to notice "the details" without allowing any one moment of appreciation or confusion to derail an ever-increasing sense of "the effect of the whole."

Often, Hemingway's endings invoke his beginnings, underscoring the tendency of interpretation to redound upon itself. In *In Our Time*, the closing story, "Big Two-Hearted River," returns us to the landscape of the opening story, "Indian Camp." In the 1930 edition, "L'Envoi," the closing vignette, evokes the Greco-Turkish War of the newly inserted opening story, "On the Quai at Smyrna." In its second paragraph, *A Farewell to Arms* invokes through negation a storm that is "not coming" but that will arrive as rain in the novel's last sentence. And the final sentence of *For Whom the Bell Tolls*, surely the most circular of Hemingway's major fictions, repeats its first sentence almost word for word.

Within these encircling structures lies the uncertain middle. The work produced before *Death in the Afternoon* had been uneasy with middles and preoccupied itself with rehearsing for the promised end or reacting against an uncanny beginning. But the bullfight book, in the openness and awkwardness of its form and in its foregoing of sleek momentums, allows its reader to take pleasure in the windfalls of the drive. "It is not enough of a book," Hemingway confesses at the end, "but still there were a few things to be said." Listening to the things said comes to feel like attending a series of impassioned lectures opening onto new prospects, as the pedagogical impulse seeks to prepare an audience to appreciate the work that lies ahead.

That work attempts a more open embrace of awkward behaviors and embarrassing feelings. If Hemingway engages in what Stanton deems to be an overemphasis on the personalities of the toreros, perhaps he cites so many instances of awkwardly managed bullfights because of his deepening appreciation of the difficulty of standing still in the face of oncoming death.

In *Idearium Espanol* (1905), Angel Ganivet counsels the Spaniard to "remain firm and erect, and then the least we can say of you is that you are a man." Remaining firm and erect would seem to be the cultural work expressly assigned to the matador. His job is to display "grace under pressure," the famous phrase Hemingway coined in a 1926 letter to Fitzgerald about bullfighting. Given Hemingway's power to represent such grace under pressure, it is remarkable how few of the matadors in *Death in the Afternoon* maintain their composure. "I had compromised myself through awkwardness," Hemingway tells the Old Lady, in recalling his attempts to enter the ring. It is strange and revealing that the same could be said for most of the matadors depicted in his book.

Hemingway had originally captured the matador's work of remaining firm and erect in three memorable sentences from chapter XII of *In Our Time*:

> *Villalta became one with the bull and then it was over. Villalta standing straight and the red hilt of the sword sticking out dully between the bull's shoulders. Villalta, his hand up at the crowd and the bull roaring blood, looking straight at Villalta and his legs caving.*

Each of these sentences is headed by a proper noun; "*Villalta*" keeps his place. He is the unmoved mover. As the sentences unfold, the auxiliary verbs drop away; not "*Villalta* was *standing*" but "*Villalta standing*." By the final sentence, the participles have all shifted to the terrain of the bull: he is roaring, looking, caving. And that sentence is over before you know it, as the matador's expertise (and the writer's) cuts the process short.

The first matador encountered in *Death in the Afternoon*, on the other hand, is at once given "to fits of cowardice" but also has the capacity to stand "absolutely straight with his feet still, planted as though he were a tree." The next matador cited, Hernandorena, cannot "control the nervousness of his feet." Although he wishes to stand still, "his feet jumped away in short, nervous jerks." So he falls to his knees, and is gored – gored not because he assumes a pose in order to protect himself from ridicule but because in doing so he makes the mistake of not keeping the muleta between himself and the bull until the charge. "At the moment of jurisdiction," he makes "a simple technical error."

Gitanillo, Villalta, El Gallo – each matador either admits "fear" or betrays "awkwardness." When Villalta "does a great faena it is all valor; valor and that magic wrist and it makes you put up with the greatest awkwardness you could see on all bulls which will not allow him to get his feet together." The very structure of this sentence argues for awkwardness as inseparable from and even perhaps essential to the achievement of any artfulness.

"Technique . . . is always most visible in its imperfection," Hemingway maintains, and because *Death in the Afternoon* is a book about learning to appreciate technique, he is careful to rely for his examples on performances that are less than perfect. "What they call your style," he was to write in one of the endings projected for *A Moveable Feast*, "is only the awkwardness of how to make it new and truly." He can therefore admit a feeling as awkward as finding certain "disembowellings" to be "very funny." "This is the sort of thing you should not admit, but it is because such things have not been admitted that the bullfight has never been explained." For Hemingway, the admission of the previously inadmissible becomes an important part of the work of the 1930s.

Henry James once described Flaubert as committed to "extraordinary attempts at bravery of form." Hemingway's bravery consists in overcoming his fear of admitting awkwardness. The bravery involved in his achievement of form has little to do with the upholding of a code. Bullfighting certainly has its "rules" and its predetermined maneuvers called "suertes" and its centuries of tradition governing "the conduct of a matador." But the great bullfighter is one who imagines beyond the rules and who, in doing so, "uses everything that has been discovered or known about his art up to that point ... and then ... goes beyond what has been done or known and makes something of his own." As Eliot argues in "Tradition and the Individual Talent," when the new – "the really new" – work of art arrives, "the *whole* existing order must be, if ever so slightly, altered."

The figure of Maera provides Hemingway with his central example of an artist who alters tradition as he enters it. Serving as a banderillero for Belmonte, Maera one day asked for an increase in wages and was refused. "'All right, I'll be a matador and I'll show you up,' Maera said. 'You'll be ridiculous,' Belmonte told him. 'No,' said Maera, 'you'll be ridiculous when I'm through.'"

At first, Maera "had many of the faults and manners of a peon to overcome." But his knowledge of bulls was so complete and his valor so absolute that within two years he has corrected his faults to become "one of the best and most satisfying matadors I have ever watched." With Maera in the ring, bullfighting is restored to an art with "dignity and passion." His story, it would seem, is of awkwardness overcome.

The real story awaits, however. Maera "had trouble with his wrists." Killing one time, Maera drives in with the sword and strikes one of the vertebrae, causing the sword to buckle back and dislocate his right wrist. Now the awkwardness begins. Maera takes a second sword, profiles, and holding the sword and the muleta in his left hand, drives in. "Again he hit bone, insisted, and the sword buckled." He picks up the sword in his right hand and tries again. He tries two more times, always hitting bone, before, "on the sixth time," the sword goes in. As he walks over to the barrera someone asks about his wrist. He holds it up and sneers at it. "He was made out of cement," he says. "F- -king bull made out of cement."

Maera redeems the awkwardness of the performance with the gallantry of his disdain. The hitting of the bone makes for the story, but the matador's persistence in the face of embarrassment and pain is what makes for the bravery of form. Hemingway pays Maera the supreme compliment: "He gave emotion always and, finally, as he steadily improved his style, he was an artist."

This continual improvement and breaking of style is an awkward business. But it is the only way any art form can be rescued from the threat of "decadence" that haunts Hemingway throughout. A truly individual talent allows and requires a writer, like a matador, to be willing, as Donald Bouchard puts it, "to stumble and recover." It is the price that must be paid, this making of mistakes. But it is also an experience of gain-through-loss. If we shift our gaze a little, and begin to look for courage rather than composure, we may, as Bouchard argues, begin to see the 1930s as "Hemingway's most distinctive and lively period" rather than one heralded by a wrong turning into "inferior" experiments in nonfictional prose.

The most dramatic breaking of style occurs in chapter twenty. In it, Hemingway decided, against the theory that had governed his early practice, not to omit but to put everything *in*. As Susan Beegel has shown, Hemingway worked hard to achieve this unlooked-for end, eventually cutting the "nine paragraphs that originally opened the final chapter." So, an act of inclusion was preceded, as so often in Hemingway's writing, by an act of exclusion. The result, according to Michael Reynolds, was "an ending richer than anything he has ever written."

"If I could have made this enough of a book it would have had everything in it." Opening the final chapter in an apologetic tone, Hemingway appears to be regretting a failure: if I could have, I would have. But then, in a cascade of semi-colons, he proceeds to do just what he says he regrets not having done:

> The Prado, looking like some big American college building, with sprinklers watering the grass early in the bright Madrid summer morning; the bare white mud hills looking across toward Carabanchel; days on the train in August with the blinds pulled down on the side against the sun and the wind blowing them; chaff blown against the car in the wind from the hard earthen threshing floors; the odor of grain and the stone windmills.

Hemingway begins by regretting that he has not put "everything" in and then proceeds to do just that. To say you are not going to mention a thing while also mentioning it is to adopt the rhetorical trope called *praeteritio*. Beegel was the first to identify the presence here of this "ironic device," one that "appears in many works by Hemingway," especially works from the later career.

As the chapter unfolds, as the lists accumulate, and as the tenses shift from the conditional to the indicative, Hemingway deploys the trope to maximum advantage, offering us, in spite of all the "not's" and "nothing's," as condensed and full a portrait of how it feels to love a country as he would ever write. *Praeteritio* allows a speaker to have it both ways: while claiming to omit, he actually gets to express. The trope is appropriate to a book so committed to admitting what has "not been admitted" before, and it allows Hemingway to register a somewhat conflicted response to his decision to say at last what has gone without saying.

"It is nice, every once in a while, to say a few of the things that go without saying." These words are from a letter Hemingway sent to Horace Liveright in 1925, at the height of his period of not saying. By the time Hemingway came to write *Death in the Afternoon*, he had clearly begun to question the cost to his imagination of remaining committed to the art of omission. Like *praeteritio*, "the omitted" in Hemingway's fiction performs a double function, at once not saying a thing and also working to "make people feel something more than they understood." But *praeteritio* is a much more openly manipulative strategy, one not reliant upon a reader to supply the unsaid. In adopting its more open ironies, Hemingway was also beginning to distance himself from the most striking feature of his early style.

The problem with the art of omission was twofold: it asked a reader to perform a work of which he might prove incapable, and it protected a writer from the awkwardness of saying precisely what was on his mind. The less said, the more felt: this was the central assumption behind the strategy. But what if the thing left out was, simply, left out: what if it bespoke a failure of feeling rather than a powerfully indirect expression of it?

By the time Hemingway finished the closing chapter of *Death in the Afternoon*, he had become aware that his art of omission was in danger of hardening into a kind of artistic ideology. When Roland Barthes defines ideology as that which "*goes without saying*," he offers up Hemingway's early art as the art of ideology itself. In allowing characters to hide from their own feelings, even while encouraging a reader to fill them in, Hemingway had risked allowing his audience to remain in a kind of bad faith. "Appreciation" of the work too often took the form of denying its uncanny power. Rather than being allowed to feel something more than they understood, readers of the early work were encouraged instead by a generation of critics to accept a character's lack of expressed emotion as a kind of higher stoicism. As a result of such readings, Hemingway was represented as recommending a set of behaviors he is actually inviting us to scrutinize.

It was time to come out from under the cover of "You'll lose it if you talk about it"; it was time to take the risk of saying a few of the things that had gone without saying. "Am glad you liked the last chapter," Hemingway wrote about *Death in the Afternoon* to the editor of *Esquire*. "It is what the book is all about but nobody seems to notice that. They think it is just a catalogue of things that were omitted. How would they like them to be put in?" The question forecasts a looming future. In the work to come, the said will seek its place alongside the unsaid. Hemingway signals the turn in his closing sentences: "No. It is not enough of a book, but still there were a few things to be said. There were a few practical things to be said."

CHAPTER 7

Hunting Shame

Green Hills of Africa

The manuscript of *Green Hills of Africa* I first encountered in the winter of 2012 remains for me a haunting terrain. Its 492 pages are handwritten on a brown unlined paper that tears easily, so the archivists in the Special Collections at the University of Virginia asked me to wear white cotton gloves and to sit at a table where my movements could easily be observed. In moving through the pages, it felt as if, after hearing a rumor about a landscape, I had driven around a bend in a road and suddenly found myself at "the edge of the salt-lick," there with Kandisky and his noisy truck; there when P. O. M. (Poor Old Mama, the narrator's wife) misses her lion and her husband has to finish it with his Springfield; there in the long, digressive middle of the story, "Pursuit Remembered," as Hemingway and Karl chase "the best buff, the best rhino"; and there at the end, when "Pursuit and Failure" becomes difficult to distinguish from "Pursuit as Happiness," titles Hemingway gave to the last two parts of his book.

The manuscript itself lacks chapter divisions. Hemingway did not divide it into its four named parts until July 1935, after receiving galleys from Scribner's. He had begun working on *Green Hills* in May 1934 and completed a draft of the book by mid-November, during what he called "a belle epoque of working." On the page, the big, looping hand moves confidently forward; when insertions and deletions occur, they have less to do with the pursuit of animals than with the pleasures inherent in the writing and especially in the reading life.

For a reader picking up *Green Hills of Africa* without benefit of such background knowledge, a simple question is likely to arise: what is *Green Hills of Africa* really about? Hunting? Moving through landscape? Eating, drinking, sweating – the narrator is often soaked through – talking? Hemingway's love of Africa? As South African novelist Nadine Gordimer maintains, in his African books and stories Hemingway "constructed for himself according to his own needs and desires something that had little relation to the reality of the object." Despite the many attempts to show Hemingway as responsive or unresponsive to the historical Africa, Hemingway's first big book about experiencing the continent aims at something other than its named subject.

Hemingway had far less interest in what we call "subject matter" than in the treatment of it. His art was engaged first and last in constructing, as Gordimer puts it, something according to his own needs and desires. Those needs and desires had to do with sustaining the work of the imagination for as long as he lived:

> The way to hunt is for as long as you live against as long as there is such and such an animal; just as the way to paint is as long as there is you and colors and canvas, and to write as long as you can live and there is pencil and paper or ink or any machine to do it with, or anything you care to write about, and you feel a fool, and you are a fool, to do it any other way. But here we were, now, caught by time . . . .

By the year in which he began *Green Hills*, Hemingway was feeling caught by time. It was time to shed the skin of his familiar style, time to experiment and to risk failure.

In the phrase "anything you care to write about," Hemingway brackets out the question of subject matter. It is "the way" one chooses to hunt or paint or write that engages him. *Green Hills* is a deeply competitive book, and the competition would seem to be between Hemingway and Karl: who will kill the biggest animals? Yet the obvious self-mockery brought to bear on this *mano a mano* lays something of a smoke screen. While a reader is, of course, free to invest in the shooting contest, in the Foreword to his book Hemingway directs attention toward a competition being staged between a past and an emergent writing self:

> Unlike many novels, none of the characters or incidents in this book is imaginary. Any one not finding sufficient love interest is at liberty, while reading it, to insert whatever love interest he or she may have at the time. The writer has attempted to write an absolutely true book to see whether the shape of a country and the pattern of a month's action can, if truly presented, compete with a work of the imagination.

The repetition of "true" and "truly" may distract attention from the much more telling word, "attempted." The early 1930s were for Hemingway an essaying time rather than a period of complete victories. "It is not enough of a book," he wrote at the end of *Death in the Afternoon*, and the same could well have been said of *Green Hills of Africa*. But each was nevertheless a courageous attempt at the breaking of style. The willingness to chance failure – one sentence in *Green Hills* uses the verb "failed" three times – cleared the ground for the sure successes to come.

Green Hills begins with a character named "Hemingway" and a character named "Kandisky" stopping to talk. "The literary discussion, though it contains some precious plums, is mostly bad," Bernard DeVoto wrote in his 1935 review. Once Kandisky realizes that Hemingway is the poet he has read in the *Querschnitt*, he asks about the concrete things that harm a writer. Hemingway answers: "'Politics, women, drink, money, ambition. And the lack of politics, women, drink, money and ambition,' I said profoundly." Since the book opens with this sort of badinage, it tends to stick in the reader's mind and can overshadow the good work up ahead.

"The most literary hunting trip on record," the *New York Times* wrote of *Green Hills*. Again, the objection is to Hemingway's self-described "verbal dysentery" at the start. Never mind that the most infamous claim – "All modern American literature comes from one book by Mark Twain called *Huckleberry Finn*" – has been quoted by generations of English teachers as usefully provocative, if not truly profound.

As Hemingway issues his pronouncements, he lards them with put-downs. Words like "profoundly" are offered up as a preemptive strike against a reader's anticipated disapproval. But of what, exactly, do we disapprove? Not, surely, of the Hemingway in the book, but rather of his performance as the author of it.

Green Hills of Africa begins as a bad book, and it is bad because the writing is coy, knowing, and self-conscious. In addition, the author of "Pursuit as Conversation" does not seem to understand that he has created a character for whom self-deprecation operates as a form of self-regard. It is as if the author cannot hear the self-consuming ironies built in to the ways in which he has chosen to have his character speak. None of the shame "Hemingway" will later feel or the awkwardness he will later display inflects this opening performance. Instead, he comes off as self-satisfied. By electing to begin in this way, Hemingway makes the tactical error of reducing one of the book's profound concerns – the place of reading and writing in our lives – to mere competitive chitchat. *Green Hills* may begin as a bad book, but it does not remain one. The Scenes of Reading that occur in chapters four and five will, in the possibilities for enactment they provide, more than make up for Hemingway's false start.

There is an established tradition of attempting to dignify the action of *Green Hills* by reading it as an allegory about the making of art. Here is Michael Reynolds: "Hemingway is writing a book about writing a book." And here is Donald Bouchard: "*Green Hills of Africa* is a book that examines the nature of the modern writer's career as an ongoing struggle to produce his text." To read the Africa book as *just* about writing would be to reduce it, however, to a somewhat sterile and postmodern exercise. It is important not to lose sight of the apparent vehicle as we go in search of its hidden tenor; it is important, as always in reading Hemingway, not to divert attention away from the fascinating surface in search of mere depth.

Hunting matters here. In drawing a parallel between hunting, painting, and writing, as Hemingway does in the sentence about an artist and his way, the pattern of a month's action of hunting is put forward as competitive with "anything" else a writer may "care to write about." As the experience on offer, hunting will prove a powerfully revealing one. And if it stands in for anything – besides the parallel so explicitly drawn with creative work – it stands in for experiencing itself. *Green Hills of Africa* can fairly be said to be about its narrator-hero's capacity for and repeated failure to live up to his best sense of the proper response to experience. In taking this as his subject, one that cannot be separated out from its subtext, Hemingway also constructs a book about the self's capacity to tolerate shame.

As for improper response and self-indictment: Hemingway jumps the gun, shoots too soon; he flies into unearned rages; he forms irrational dislikes; he makes *pronuciamientos*; he mistakes his targets; he is "poisoned with envy"; he omits "the steps in how it is done"; there is a slipping into bitterness; he behaves like "a smugly righteous bastard." Each of these admissions is shared candidly with the reader. And the bad behavior is not simply noted, but judged: as Hemingway says more than once, "I was ashamed."

The entire sentence reads as follows: "I had gotten excited and shot at the whole animal instead of the right place and I was ashamed." We are asked once more to entertain hunting as an activity capable of producing shame. It happens on his last day of hunting, as Hemingway attempts to bag a sable bull. The story unfolds through the confusions of chapter thirteen, the book's remarkably inconclusive final chapter.

Near the end of chapter twelve, as he eats a piece of roasted kudu liver, Hemingway indulges in a case of "the evening braggies." He spreads out six cartridges and then names the animals killed: "Lion, lion, rhino, buffalo, kudu, kudu." The point being made is that each has been killed with a single shot. "Tomorrow, sable," he and his companions agree.

But tomorrow is also the last day of the safari. Caught by time, and by his ambition to complete his list, Hemingway must now summon the grace with which to operate under the self-imposed pressure. But there is a problem, and it is one of vision. "I had never seen a sable," Hemingway admits, and this in the same book in which he hoards the handkerchiefs necessary for the continual cleaning of his glasses. Chapter thirteen turns out to be one in which it is "hard to see well."

Throughout his African book, Hemingway engages in an impressive and detailed remembering of landscapes being hunted through. "Terrain is what remains in the dreaming part of your mind," he writes in *Across the River and into the Trees*, and the hills and plains of Africa clearly did stay with him. In the fifty pages of the closing chapter, his preternatural ability to recall each step of a hunt operates to guarantee, however, that the reader will lose his way. The confusions of the hunt are virtually impossible to follow. And this is Hemingway's parting gift to his reader, one meant to instruct him once again in one of the ever-present subjects of Hemingway's art: the fate of reading.

"Where's the bull?" Hemingway asks, and then, five pages later, he sees "the biggest" one. The herd is spooked by the theatrical gun bearer, and he has "no choice" but to shoot. "I knew it was bad," he immediately adds. He shoots again, "and I knew I had him." Then he detects "something wrong"; as the herd trails up through the timber, "they all looked like the one I had shot . . . . They all looked about the same and they were crowding running and then came the bull." Hemingway shoots, hits the bull, sees him go down, and watches him head up the valley into the tall grass. He now realizes that the first sable he had shot was a cow, and it is this "excited shooting" that makes him feel ashamed.

Having wounded two animals, Hemingway sets out after the "big bull." He sees another cow and almost shoots it for a bull. Then he almost immediately shoots "another sable," but it, too, "was no bull." These confusions echo those of the buffalo hunt in chapter five, when Hemingway first mistakes a bull for a cow and is made to confess, "They all look like bulls to me."

Hemingway and M'Cola follow the bull's blood spoor but eventually lose the trail. The day heats up, and the other trackers lose enthusiasm for the hunt. "For a minute I began to doubt whether there ever was a bull." Then Hemingway sees him "again" in his mind's eye and confirms his belief in the shot. The sun is becoming "something serious by now"; they continue tracking, but "we had lost him."

The "old man" accompanying them sees the bull, and they are off again. The sun fills Hemingway's head with a "pounding ache." As he watches his primary guide shaving the sweat off his forehead with a grass stem, he knows him to be "immeasurably the better man and the better tracker."

They stop to rest in the shade of a tree. There, Hemingway faults himself for hitting the bull but not having "killed it cleanly." The "fault" lies in "the over-confidence in being able to do a thing and then omitting one of the steps in how it is done." "We were beaten," Hemingway concludes, as he decides to return to camp. On the way back, another herd of sable is sighted, but, by now, the hunter has learned enough to see that they are "all cows."

After quickly breaking camp, Hemingway and his party ride out of the country, and, while drinking German beer, he reviews the day. "That damned sable bull," he thinks. "I should have killed him." Then he says to himself, "Every damned thing is your own fault if you're any good." And then he imagines something extraordinary. In anticipation of the Robert Jordan who can say, "I do not like to kill animals," Hemingway imagines coming back to Africa and *not shooting*. "I'd see the buffalo feeding where they lived, and when the elephants came through the hills we would see them and watch them breaking branches and not have to shoot, and I would lie in the fallen leaves and watch the kudu feed out and never fire a shot." As for sable, "instead of trailing that sable bull, gut-shot to hell, all day, I'd lie behind a rock and watch them on the hillside and see them long enough so they belonged to me forever."

In this fantasy of return, the taking of literal trophies gives way to the pleasures of visionary possession. Hemingway has already begun to experience such a substitution in the moment when he visualizes the shooting of the bull in his mind's eye and so allows "the truth of Imagination," as Keats calls it, to trump the certainties of the doubt-ridden world of fact:

> For a minute I began to doubt whether there ever was a bull. Then I saw again his heavy, high-withered blackness and the high rise of his horns before they swept back, him running with the bunch, shoulder higher than them and black as hell and as I saw it, M'Cola saw it again too through the rising mist of the savage's unbelief in what he can no longer see.

The two hunters here see "again" through and in spite of the barriers of doubt and unbelief. They enact a reader's prerogative, the willing suspension of disbelief essential to being able to go "where you can never go except in books."

Where you can never go except in books: These words from the manuscript of *Green Hills of Africa* appear in a sentence eventually cut from the published book. Had the sentence remained in the text, it would have appeared on page 109 in the extended passage in chapter five where Hemingway describes himself "reading." Here is the manuscript sentence in full: "For we have been where you can never go except in books, it is a good way to go, better perhaps, and we will give you the books, as we have taken them from others." In this lovely fantasy of transmission – Hemingway is reading Tolstoi's "The Cossacks" – a writer imagines the life of literature as a give-and-take ending in writing and beginning in reading.

As Hemingway rides away from the last camp on the final night of the safari, he thinks about his desire to come back to Africa. "Here I could shoot and fish. That, and writing, and reading, and seeing pictures was all I cared about doing." Shooting, fishing, writing, reading, seeing pictures: it is not a long list. In its original form in the handwritten manuscript, the list had been even shorter. "Here I could shoot and fish. That and writing was all I cared about doing." Liking reading and seeing pictures was added as an afterthought.

The entire Scene of Reading beginning with Tolstoi in chapter five is itself an insert. As often happens in the book, Hemingway has gone out in search of one kind of animal, a rhino, only to chance upon another, a buffalo. When the buffalo takes cover in the thick jungle, the party decides to stop and read in the cool of the "large trees." Hemingway opens his book to "The Cossacks" and finds himself "living in that Russia again."

A long inserted paragraph follows the word "again." It begins with the words "I was thinking" and ends with the words "in the different seasons." The sentence is compelling for its content and for its motion of mind. "I was thinking how real that Russia of the time of our Civil War was," it begins. As reading quickly gives way to thinking, Hemingway presents himself not as processing the words on the page but rather as engaged in a reverie about how reading fits into a human life. Reading creates a Russia "as real as any other place," he thinks to himself, so real that "I knew that I had lived there, as I had been in the family Buddenbrooks, and had climbed in and out of her window in *Le Rouge et le Noir*." And so he is off, paying tribute to Turgenieff, Mann, and Stendhal. "I saw all that," he maintains, "and it was me they did not break on the rack that time because I had been polite to the executioner the time they killed Coconas and me." While Hemingway may seem to be making a point about a reader's identification with a character in a novel – "it was me" – the stronger claim circles around the word "real." The experience of reading is as real as any other kind of experience. It has nothing to do with the desire to escape. And its reality is testified to in the very structure of the ongoing sentence, one in which a memory of reading merges with a memory of "Italy, better than any book," a memory not of reading but of actually lying in chestnut woods and walking to the Ospedale Maggiore in hobnail boots and of walking to it again in "the dark from Sermione."

"For we have been where you can never go except in books," the next sentence might have begun but for the fact that Hemingway cut it and supplied the following sentence instead: "For we have been there in the books and out of the books – and where we go, if we are any good, there you can go as we have been." The sentence cut makes the more radical claim. Books create places where we "can never go" *except* in books; it is a "good way to go," Hemingway had originally written, "better perhaps" than the actual going. The word "better" in the sentence eventually cut is meant to echo and to qualify the claim made at the bottom of page 108 about experience and the remembering of it as "better than any book." In deciding against including the second "better," Hemingway diminished somewhat the assertion being made about the place of reading in a human life.

Hemingway sits down to read *Sevastopol* near the beginning of chapter four. In this first Scene of Reading, he engages in the motion of mind he will experience again under the shade of the large trees in chapter five. As he begins to read, he begins to think. Reading merges with memory: "Then Sevastopol made me think of the Boulevard Sevastopol in Paris," and so the digression begins, unfolding across a sentence over a page in length, one including the feeling of cobblestones in the rain and "*the sudden whine of the saw*" in the apartment over the sawmill and the embarrassment of "*all of the stories back in the mail that came in through a slit in the saw-mill door.*"

The two Scenes of Reading in *Green Hills of Africa* afford Hemingway an opportunity to engage in a freedom of association largely absent from his previous work. What has been an alien country for most of his fictional characters – the past – is now becoming available to a mind in new and startling ways. Instead of choking off the associations that lead back, as Nick Adams does with the coffee according to Hopkins, we see a man willingly thinking. Hemingway chooses to go with memory, and he does so as a result of the intensities and immediacies made available to him by reading.

"Hemingway attempts as unremittingly as anyone to control his reader," Reynolds Price maintains, "to station him precisely in relation to the visible and invisible actions of the story and to the author himself, and finally to trigger in him the desired response." Or, as Hemingway himself wrote to his father in 1925: "I'm trying in all my stories to get the feeling of the actual life across – not to just depict life – or criticize it – but to actually make it alive. So that when you have read something by me you actually experience the thing." In this endeavor, Hemingway chooses to compose in *Green Hills* the longest sentence he ever wrote, the almost two-page invocation, in chapter eight, to the Gulf Stream. As Susan Beegel notes, it is a sentence that "sees everything, throws nothing away."

In the sentence, one acknowledging the stream's unending capacity to flow despite having to accommodate an entire island's garbage, including "the empty condoms of our great loves," Hemingway prepares the way for Pilar's exuberant offer, in chapter nineteen of *For Whom the Bell Tolls*, of the "sack" containing "the essence of it all," the aromas of the slop jars and the "odor of love's labor lost" and the remains of a dead flower bed that together comprise "the smell that is both the death and birth of man." In asking his reader to negotiate sentences of such length and complexity, as well as chapters of such interrupted and digressive action, Hemingway converts the experience of reading *Green Hills of Africa* into one of *following*.

Reading-as-hunting: the implied analogy between the two activities permits the finding of similitude in dissimilitude. Reading and hunting involve sticking with a task; to kill the prey, to finish the book. Yet the inconclusiveness of the final hunt also invites a reader to locate the pleasure of the text elsewhere than in any simple sense of an ending. Reading-as-hunting invites a reader to invest in outcomes – to have expectations – but also to allow them to go unfulfilled. In learning to wait for the promised end and to enjoy the digressions offered along the way, the middle of things reveals itself as having a value equal to or greater than the act of having consumed it. Hunting, like reading, encourages an openness to the field and a capacity to "learn," as Hemingway puts it in his conversation with Kandisky, "as I go along." As the process becomes its own self-gratifying product, readers are offered an experience of thereness – "we have been there in the books" – as compelling as the portable meanings or bagged trophies that might be carried away.

Above all, Hemingway means to reveal, reading-as-hunting can operate as both the cause and the cure of shame. In not being able to follow or to figure out – "to get" – a difficult or an experimental book, readers can feel a frustration and bafflement that can shade into chagrin. In the title given to Part III of *Green Hills*, Hemingway calls this experience "Pursuit and Failure." Every reader of wide experience has felt such a failure of recognition. One can then turn away from one's shame and dismiss the book as flawed or unimportant. Or, one can acknowledge the failure to engage or to be engaged and then convert that feeling into an awareness of the shortcomings – the limitations of "taste" – comprising in each of us what we call "character."

In recalling "the man who lived" in Hemingway's stories, Tobias Wolff describes him as "in most respects an unremarkable, even banal man who got things wrong and suffered from nervousness and fear, fear even of the workings of his own mind, and who sometimes didn't know how to behave." For Hemingway to share these awkwardnesses with us is perhaps gift enough. But Wolff proceeds to make a more delicate and important point. In the next step in his argument, he cites Hemingway's *awareness* of the impression being made: "I judged him," he continues, "but I also understood that he'd allowed me to, and this was chastening. Knowing that readers like me would see him in Nick, he had given us a vision of spiritual muddle and exhaustion almost embarrassing in its intimacy." Most of the misreadings of Hemingway's work occur when a reader refuses to take that next step and therefore fails to appreciate that Hemingway has "allowed" him to take it.

In the first installment of *Green Hills* serialized in *Scribner's Magazine*, Hemingway provided a list of "The People in the Book." Among them is "Mr. Hemingway – A braggart." "Quite deliberately," as Michael Reynolds submits, "Hemingway was creating an exaggerated man with all faults exposed." It is in many ways a shameful performance. But it is one Hemingway also invites us to judge.

In *Death in the Afternoon*, Hemingway had begun to admit things that "have not been admitted." In *Green Hills of Africa*, he continues this work. The narration of his behavior on safari does make a case for the importance of admission and acknowledgment, especially of awkward behaviors and ugly feelings. "This ability to . . . distance himself from his own views with mockery is one of Hemingway's strong qualities as a writer," Nancy Comley and Robert Scholes write, "and one for which he is rarely given sufficient credit."

In *Green Hills of Africa*, Hemingway confesses to feeling "ashamed" on three occasions. In chapter five, he breaks into a "highly-righteous" diatribe about his wife's too-tight boots, which have caused her to limp. In the very act of behaving badly he also admits to doing so, "me ashamed at having been a four-letter man about boots." The couple quickly makes up, largely on the husband's initiative, "stopping to whisper about it, both of us grinning at what was whispered." Hemingway's liability to repeat such behavior is admitted some twenty-five pages later, however, when he becomes "irritable, righteous, pompous" about P. O. M.'s difficulties with a camera shutter. He must again devise an apology: "I took a drink of water and told P. O. M. I was sorry I was such a bastard about the camera."

Hemingway knows himself to be skilled at projecting shame as blame and shows himself twice turning such behavior against his wife. In doing so, he displays a "new openness to the sufferings of women at the hands of men like himself." He knows himself to have fallen short, as he has earlier confessed to the reader, of his wife's "ideal of how a man should be."

Two other shaming occasions have to do with shooting badly. They have to do, we might say, with work rather than with love. Hemingway is "ashamed" of his excited shooting at the sable just as earlier he was "ashamed" of gut-shooting the buffalo. "I'm afraid I gut-shot him," he says to Pop after the wounded buffalo disappears down the stream. The concern here cuts two ways: toward the shooter, who has aimed badly, and toward the animal in pain.

Rather than brazening out moments causing unnecessary pain, Hemingway chooses to own them: "Every damned thing is your own fault if you're any good." He also never claims to be cured of his "primitive emotions" and so confesses at the very end, as if he has learned nothing, to being "poisoned with envy" at Karl's having shot the "most unbelievable pair of kudu horns in the world." At the same time, one of Hemingway's more endearing traits as a character appearing in his own work is his capacity to move through his feelings: "But I was bitter and I was bitter all night long. In the morning, though, it was gone. It was all gone and I have never had it again."

In *Death in the Afternoon* and in *Green Hills of Africa*, Hemingway begins to open himself to the work he will take up in earnest in the postwar years, "the recognition of the determined shape of the life he has created for himself, with an implicit comparison with the uncreated potential life he has forsaken." This is one of Northrop Frye's more compelling definitions of "the discovery or *anagnorisis* which comes at the end of the tragic plot." During the postwar years, Hemingway may well have begun to look back on his life and his work as assuming the shape of a tragedy. But in the middle 1930s, he still found himself poised between the might have been and the what will be: there was the second chance of "The Short Happy Life of Francis Macomber" and the fatality of "The Snows of Kilimanjaro."

Frye again:

> Tragedy seems to move up to an *Augenblick* or crucial moment from which point the road to what might have been and the road to what will be can be simultaneously seen. Seen by the audience, that is: it cannot be seen by the

> hero if he is in a state of hybris, for in that case the crucial moment is for him a moment of dizziness, when the wheel of fortune begins its inevitable cyclical movement downward.

Hemingway invokes "the wheel of fortune" in chapter eighteen of *For Whom the Bell Tolls*, when Robert Jordan reflects back on Pablo and his many changes. Riding it is "making me dizzy," he concludes, and he decides it is time to be "off that wheel." While seeming to be caught in a tragic situation, Robert has far too much hope to feel caught between the two roads invoked by Frye. Remaining the self-aware critic of his tight situation, he also continually steps aside into romance and so remains alive and in the world until the end.

As we attempt to follow the twists and turns in *Green Hills*, on the other hand, dizziness rather than insight becomes our portion. The *Augenblick* of which Frye speaks can only be "seen by the audience" when that audience is asked to hold in mind the radically opposing senses of an ending to be found in the two great African stories to come. Francis Macomber represents the new-found might have been, in all its stupid hope, and Harry Walden the familiar what will be, in all its dead-end dignity. In the light of these later imaginings, Hemingway's self-chastenings in *Green Hills of Africa* can assume the appearance of a pose.

Is not Hemingway willfully hunting shame? He certainly repeatedly seeks out the opportunity to feel it. The moments of aiming badly or mistaking a cow for a bull may reflect some incipient ambivalence about how shameful it would one day seem to set out to kill animals for the purpose of being able to say that one had done so. To view Hemingway's performance in *Green Hills* in this way is to uncover a uniquely American shame, since he would then have converted the experience of killing in Africa into an allegory about the consumption ethic at the heart of the pursuit of happiness. As Joan Didion writes in her mordant essay about the empty mansions crowding the seacoast at Newport, Rhode Island, "'Happiness' is, after all, a consumption ethic." In promising pursuit, not arrival, our founding document imagines American life as an unending process of creative destruction, since the getting and the having of a thing – in this case a dead animal – produces only the desire for more getting and having.

Hemingway's Africa book then invites a reading in which it can be taken as a complex gloss on the meaning of one of his favorite adjectives, *happy*, as well as an investigation into how shaming our various pursuits of happiness can turn out to be. Hence, the fantasy of coming back to Africa and *not shooting*, a fantasy introduced at the end of the failed sable hunt in order to provide an alternative model for being in Africa and being in the world. "I'd lie behind a rock and watch them on the hillside and see them long enough so they belonged to me forever." Hemingway here imagines another way of having – of taking – experience. It need not necessarily involve the literal hunting down and killing – consuming – of something. This new kind of possession begins in an act of seeing and completes itself in a feeling of belonging. The fantasy is given only a brief life in Hemingway's text, however, since within a few pages he reverts to the imperatives of the hunt: "Here I could shoot and fish." Hemingway has nevertheless begun to articulate a crucial distinction between the pleasures yielded by literal and by symbolic action, one central to the stories and the novels to come.

That it might be too late for us – that we might have already used up all the good country – is a thought much on Hemingway's mind as he brings his book to a close. "A continent ages quickly once we come," he admits. Just where do Americans find themselves, as a people, in historical time? Are we closer to the end than to the beginning? In answering the question, Hemingway takes on the note of the autumnal artist: "Our people went to America because that was the place to go then. It had been a good country and we had made a bloody mess of it and I would go, now, somewhere else as we had always had the right to go somewhere else and as we had always gone. You could always come back. Let the others come to America who did not know that they had come too late." The rate at which Hemingway appears to be "using" up Africa converts the safari into an extension of this unfolding American tragedy.

A tragedy is a story in which the recognitions come too late. That a good timing of things was on Hemingway's mind in the mid-1930s and thereafter is indicated by the fact that *Green Hills of Africa* and the two big African stories each contain the word "late."

Hemingway opens up the question of the "too late" at the beginning of *Green Hills*, when the hunt is interrupted by Kandisky's noisy truck. The kudu bull scared off by "that exploding, clanking sound" might return "later, in the dark; but it would be too late." In "The Short Happy Life of Francis Macomber," after Francis has "gotten awfully brave, awfully suddenly," his wife asks him, "Isn't it sort of late?" And, in "The Snows of Kilimanjaro," after Harry Walden has his memory of Williamson, he thinks to himself, "everything you do, you do too long, and do too late."

As is typical of Hemingway's early books, *Green Hills* begins under the shadow of the already-over: "It is finished" is the first thing said. So speaks the theatrical tracker when he hears Kandisky's truck. With only two more days to hunt, the time has grown short, and Hemingway urges his men to "Wait a little." But the game has been scared away by the noise, and so, as it grows dark, Hemingway agrees to return to camp. Strangely, on the ride back he finds himself feeling "altogether happy."

He is happy because he knows what is coming: a flashback. "Pursuit Remembered" interposes a little ease between the reader and the imminent sense of an ending. The long middle of the book circles "back to the time" after Hemingway had come back from being ill in Nairobi and then moves forward through seven detailed chapters. While M'Cola's "estimations were only from day to day and required an unbroken series of events to have any meaning," narrative, as Hemingway is coming to understand it, depends for its force on digressions, interruptions, and deferrals. Through the simple narrative device of the flashback Hemingway shows how a work of the imagination has the power to buy more time. "Take your time," Pop will say, and, as readers enter the offered digression, they are allowed to avail themselves of his advice.

"That all seemed a year ago," Hemingway writes in the first sentence in chapter ten, as he returns us to what might be called the present time of the narrative. "Now" he continues, "I knew there were only two days more to hunt before we must leave." And so we are given Parts III and IV, "Pursuit and Failure" and "Pursuit as Happiness." Useful as they are, these divisions simply highlight the recursive structure Hemingway had already imposed on his narrative. The central digression was necessary not only to give the story a sort of second chance but to counteract another of the book's key formal features. Hemingway sailed for Africa in late November 1933, and he began his journey home from Mombasa in late February 1934. In writing about that time, he decided to condense it into "the pattern of a month's action." The sense of urgency and economy created by the condensation of time needed then to be counteracted by opening up the middle of the book to "Pursuit Remembered."

"Isn't it sort of late?" Margot Macomber asks. Belatedness can be said to be Hemingway's subject; it is there in the word "another" in the opening sentence of "Indian Camp," and it is there in Brett Ashley's, "Oh, Jake, we could have had such a damned good time together." Haunted from the beginning of his writing life by a sense of the already over, Hemingway found himself limited to the invention of characters all too skilled at seeing "ahead" to the inevitable and life-crushing promised end. They adapt to their predicament by learning to survive the end of pleasure and by digressing into false surmises, like love, that have the power to make "time stand still."

Hemingway comes up with the phrase "time stand still" in one of his typical already-over moments. It arises out of the first Scene of Reading in *Green Hills*, after he thinks of Joyce and of how "It was nice to see a great writer in our time." Then Hemingway falls into the habitual trap of feeling it is already too late for him. In Africa, and loving it, he finds himself already missing it, and so commits what he is coming to understand as the ultimate sin: the revenge against time.

This beautiful and heart-breaking passage deserves to be quoted in full:

> All I wanted to do now was get back to Africa. We had not left it, yet, but when I would wake in the night I would lie, listening, homesick for it already.
>
> Now, looking out the tunnel of trees over the ravine at the sky with white clouds moving across in the wind, I loved the country so that I was happy as you are after you have been with a woman that you really love, when, empty, you feel it welling up again and there it is and you can never have it all and yet what there is, now, you can have, and you want more and more, to have, and be, and live in, to possess now again for always, for that long, sudden-ended always; making time stand still, sometimes so very still that afterwards you wait to hear it move, and it is slow in starting. But you are not alone, because if you have ever really loved her happy and untragic, she loves you always; no matter whom she loves nor where she goes she loves you more. So if you have loved some woman and some country you are very fortunate and, if you die afterwards it makes no difference.

The passage begins by giving us a man habitually displaced in time. Still in Africa, all he wants to "do now was to get back to it." Experience is converted into nostalgia even as it is being had.

But Hemingway does not end there. Instead, manuscript evidence shows him striving to find words more accepting of the gift of the present moment. "I loved the damned place so I was as happy as after you have been with a woman that you really love," he had originally written. The manuscript passage continues: "when you feel that there is more of her and that you can never have all of her and feeling it again you want more and more and there it is and you can have it and can feel it." In the original passage, the emphasis falls upon wanting "more." In the passage as revised and published, the emphasis shifts from pursuit to immersion: "and you can never have it all and yet what there is, now, you can have, and you want more and more, to have, and be, and live in, to possess now again for always, the long, sudden-ended always." Only after consenting to live "in" the now, the final version suggests, can a man gain the experience of a love that will thereafter "always" exist.

Taken together, the two versions of this reverie create a palimpsest of Hemingway's writing future. He is Harry Walden, a man dying of his own nostalgia. He is Robert Jordan, who, in learning to "have it *now,*" creates a love that will go with him. And he is Francis Macomber, a man who can answer, when asked by his wife whether it is not in fact altogether too late: "Not for me."

CHAPTER 8

Empathy and Candor

"The Short Happy Life of Francis Macomber"

Francis Macomber and his wife are on safari in Africa. They are guided by professional "white hunter" Robert Wilson. On the night before his first lion hunt, Macomber hears the lion roar and is afraid. The next day, he wounds a lion and is required to track it into the high grass. He finds himself running after seeing the lion charge. At lunch that day, Margot Macomber looks "curiously at her husband" and that night she sleeps with Robert Wilson. Macomber feels "hate" for Wilson, a hate somehow trumping his fear. In a repetition of the lion hunt, Macomber wounds a buffalo that again takes cover. Instead of fear, he now feels "a wild unreasonable happiness that he had never known before." So, when the buffalo charges, he stands "solid" and shoots for the nose, while "Mrs. Macomber, in the car, had shot at the buffalo with the 6.5 Mannlicher as it seemed about to gore Macomber and had hit her husband about two inches up and a little to one side of the base of his skull."

"Every damned thing is your own fault if you're any good," Hemingway writes, near the end of *Green Hills of Africa*. He says as much to himself while mulling over the possible reasons for having gut-shot the sable bull. The claim made advances a stringent notion of responsibility. The fault that falls to us if we are "any good" stops only at "every damned thing," where the phrase appears to include all actions committed by a certain person, a "you." In such a view, intention does not play its mitigating part. A self can be held to be at fault for everything done by it, including things accidental or unintentional. If "we understand" and accept Hemingway's claim, we do so, as Bernard Williams writes, "because we know that in the story of one's life there is an authority exercised by what one has done, and not merely by what one has intentionally done."

Francis Macomber does not mean to run from the wounded lion. He hears a "swishing rush in the grass. The next thing he knew he was running; running wildly, in panic in the open, running toward the stream." He runs away as a man possessed; the phrase "the next thing he knew" invokes the doing of a thing of which he is unknowing. His unintended act is nevertheless one he will choose to see as part of his life: "It was there exactly as it happened with some parts of it indelibly emphasized and he was miserably ashamed at it." Macomber takes responsibility for his act and feels a consequent shame. "It is an agent's regret, and it is in the nature of action," Hemingway means to demonstrate, "that such regrets cannot be eliminated, that one's life could not be partitioned into some things that one does intentionally and other things that merely happen to one."

Bernard Williams advances these claims about an agent's regret in *Shame and Necessity* (1993). As a student of philosophy and of the ancient world, Williams takes as his project the stressing of "some unacknowledged similarities between Greek conceptions and our own." Basing his findings on the great poets – Homer, Aeschylus, Sophocles – rather than on Plato or on Aristotle, Williams maintains that "we are, in our ethical situation, more like human beings in antiquity than any Western people have been in the meantime." One thing we might understand ourselves sharing with the ancient Greeks is a sense of the regulating power of shame.

As Macomber and his wife and Robert Wilson enjoy their cool lime drinks on the afternoon after the lion hunt, they also avoid "one another's eyes." Their behavior at the lunch table conforms to Williams's concession that "the basic experience connected with shame is that of being seen, inappropriately, by the wrong people, in the wrong condition." In the case of Hemingway's story, the averted gazes are the result of a man having "just shown himself, very publicly, to be a coward."

While "The Short Happy Life of Francis Macomber" may indeed appear "founded on values that put a great weight on how you are seen," Hemingway, like Williams in describing the actions of Oedipus and Ajax, uncovers in the predicament of his characters a more complex set of concerns than "merely some exaggerated sense of looking ridiculous." Shame has to do with more than "the notion of losing or saving face." It has to do with the experience of living with and caring about an "internalized other" whose existence creates a necessity to act in certain ways. Williams again: "The source of the necessity is in the agent, an internalized other whose view the agent can respect. Indeed he can identify with this figure, and the respect is to that extent self-respect; but at the same time the figure remains a genuine other, the embodiment of a real social expectation. At the extreme, the sense of necessity lies in the thought that one could not live and look others in the eye if one did certain things."

Hemingway invokes the distinction between an outer-directed and an internalized sense of shame in the scene in which Macomber and Wilson hunt for impala on the afternoon following the bad morning. "It's not very pleasant to have your wife see you do something like that," Macomber says to Wilson. "I should think it would be even more unpleasant to do it," Wilson thinks to himself. Wilson's unspoken response affirms that one does what one does whether or not one is *seen* to be doing it. The unpleasantness invoked arises from the judgment of a fully internalized other whose view Macomber will learn to respect.

Hemingway arranges the elements of his story into a plot with a distinctly revealing shape. "It was now lunch time," the first sentence begins. Hemingway starts with the aftermath of an event and then produces its apparent cause: we first see Macomber's "red" face and are thereafter provided with the reason for the discoloration. Once again, we have arrived too late and must scramble to orient ourselves among all the portentous talking and looking that fill the opening pages of the story.

Using the same narrative structure deployed in *Green Hills of Africa*, Hemingway divides his story into three parts: the "now" of the lunch and the rest of the day after the lion hunt; the "before" of the hunt itself; the circling back to a moment in which the story appears to re-begin – "It was now about three o'clock in the morning" – and after which we are carried forward toward the final end.

Hemingway deploys what we might call the structure of the second chance: in re-beginning his story two-thirds of the way through it, he allows a character to revise his life. And by starting not with the lion hunt but its aftermath, he draws attention away from the shaming event itself and toward Macomber's response to it. Once again, he finds himself writing a story about *facing* shame.

"Now what in hell were you going to do about a man who talked like that, Wilson wondered." He thinks this to himself after Macomber says, "I bolted like a rabbit." Wilson seems to take the admission in the same way he has taken an earlier question: "I mean no one will hear about it, will they?" Feeling insulted by the question, Wilson explains that a professional hunter never talks about his clients. Macomber apologizes and adds, "There are lots of things I don't know." It is at this point that Wilson first thinks to himself, "So what could he do . . . He was all ready to break if off quickly and neatly and here the beggar was apologizing after he had just insulted him." Macomber then makes the comment about bolting like a rabbit.

By the time Wilson asks himself a second time what "to do" about a man who talks like this he is, however, undergoing a change of heart. It is a reversal. Macomber furthers this possibility by saying, "Maybe I can fix it up on buffalo." At this juncture, well after he has decided to break with Macomber, Wilson completes his change of heart: "Perhaps he had been wrong. This was certainly the way to take it . . . . He was all for Macomber again."

Wilson's turning back on his earlier resolution is the first of a number of reversals around which Hemingway organizes his story. Sometimes the reversals involve a shift in mood, as when Macomber passes from "fear" to "elation." These are reversals in thinking and feeling. On other occasions, there is a reversal of a pattern of action, as when Macomber stands solid instead of running. And sometimes the reversal involves a matter of appearance, as when Margot goes from having a "red" face to a "white" one.

I count eleven instances in the story of the adjective "red" or "redder" being applied to the color of a person's face. In a sinister shift near the end, Macomber also notes Wilson's "red neck" – Macomber himself will be shot from behind, while facing away from his wife. And, in a clear pun on what amounts to nothing less than the story's prevailing color scheme, Wilson converts a signifier of shame into a compliment when he describes Macomber, after discerning his willingness to go in after the wounded buffalo, as "a ruddy fire eater."

The color of a face comes up early on when Margot Macomber finds herself looking at her husband and then looking at the white hunter as though she had never seen Wilson before: "He was about middle height with sandy hair, a stubby mustache, a very red face and extremely cold blue eyes with faint white wrinkles at the corners that grooved merrily when he smiled." The paragraph given over to the survey of Wilson mentions twice more his red face.

Macomber also has a red face. He even makes a joke of it at lunch, after Margot suggests it might be time for Wilson to put on his hat:

> "You know you have a very red face, Mr. Wilson," she told him and smiled again.
>
> "Drink," said Wilson.
>
> "I don't think so," she said. "Francis drinks a great deal, but his face is never red."
>
> "It is today," Macomber tried a joke.
>
> "No," said Margaret. "It's mine that's red today."

Early on in the story, then, each of the three main characters has acquired a red face.

Surely our faces turn red in shame. This is the recognition behind Macomber's joke; he is acknowledging that he feels and ought to feel "miserably ashamed." Margot is in turn ashamed for her husband; hers is a vicarious emotion. Wilson's face is red from the sun, and perhaps, as he admits, from drink.

We see Wilson's face turning "redder" in embarrassment only once, after Margot kisses him in front of her husband. His normal color is heightened by way of a physical reflex that bespeaks a big emotion. For all his composure, Wilson will prove vulnerable to the experience of embarrassment, although these occasions are not ordinarily registered in the color of his face.

In two moments of candor Wilson foregoes his usual reserve and submits to feeling embarrassed. In the first, he tells Macomber that his men prefer being whipped to being fined. When Macomber finds this strange, Wilson answers: "Which would you rather do? Take a good birching or lose your pay?" It is after putting this question to his client that Wilson feels "embarrassed."

In the second incident, Wilson finds himself quoting Shakespeare on every man owing God a death. "Damned fine, eh?" he then says, as if to ease his way out of the moment. A brief paragraph follows:

> He was very embarrassed, having brought out this thing he had lived by, but he had seen men come of age before and it always moved him. It was not a matter of their twenty-first birthday.

Wilson habitually turns away from – finds it hard to face – moments of candid emotion. Lacking in the kind of courage that might prevent him from finding such moments embarrassing, he quickly navigates away from them. Macomber, on the other hand, appears driven to initiate and to prolong moments of excruciating candor. The emotional courage he displays in doing so is meant to contrast with the physical courage he initially lacks.

One of the many things Macomber does not appear to know is how to avoid exposing himself to embarrassment. "I'm just scared, you know," he admits after Wilson tells him he does not have to go in after the lion. Macomber has already shown a willingness to articulate awkward emotions a little earlier on, when he says flat out to the white hunter, "I don't want to go in there."

In Wilson's worldview, this is not "the way to take it." Even after he has his change of heart and is all for Macomber again, Wilson clings to a preference for wordlessness. Macomber becomes very talkative during the final hunt, providing Wilson and his wife with a blow-by-blow account of his surges of feeling. "You know I don't think I'd ever be afraid of anything again," he tells them, after the drunken elation of the buffalo chase. Wilson responds in kind: "Cleans out your liver," he agrees. Margot can only eye her husband "strangely."

In "The Short Happy Life of Francis Macomber," Hemingway imagines a facing forward with a lighter and less apprehensive heart. Yet, while Wilson admits to sharing Macomber's "feeling of happiness about action to come," he will not consent to going on about it. "Doesn't do to talk too much about all this. Talk the whole thing away," he says, adverting to the "You'll lose it if you talk about it" school of thought. Margot goes even further, saying, "you're both talking rot." Expressed emotion, even of an upbeat nature, is here seen as rotten, shameful. As both men agree to risk embarrassment in this scene, Margot is assigned the role of a censor speaking on behalf of the decorums observed by Hemingway's early style. But her husband has broken through to a messier and a fuller sense of life, one reliant upon the courage to put words onto feelings.

"What's in her heart God knows," Wilson thinks to himself about Margot, after he has resolved to stop sleeping with her. Candor is one way to discover what is in a person's heart. When candor is absent, the human imagination has available to it another way of knowing: empathy.

Empathy gives play to the fiction that we can gain access to how another person – or animal – might feel. It may be more of an aspirational ideal than an achievable state: to speak of it at all is to presume to a somewhat self-congratulatory capacity. As the characters in the story struggle to experience empathy or to fend it off, Hemingway finds it necessary to construct a narrative voice willing to go almost anywhere in pursuit of finding out how another might feel.

Early drafts of the "Macomber" manuscript have it being narrated in the first person. Item 689 in the Hemingway Room begins: "Of course by the third day the old man was gone about her." Paul Smith characterizes this ur-narrator as "an admiring assistant introducing the white hunter." In abandoning this first-person narrator, Hemingway opted instead for a third-person voice capable of astonishing shifts in focalization.

This voice proves willing to imagine how even a lion might feel. As Macomber steps out of the car and onto the ground,

> The lion still stood looking majestically and coolly toward this object that his eyes only showed in silhouette, bulking like some super-rhino. There was

> no man smell carried toward him and he watched the object, moving his great head a little from side to side. Then watching the object, not afraid, but hesitating before going down the bank to drink with such a thing opposite him, he saw a man figure detach itself from it and he turned his heavy head and swung away toward the cover of the trees as he heard a cracking crash and felt the slam of a .30-06 220-grain solid bullet that bit his flank and ripped in sudden hot scalding nausea through his stomach. He trotted, heavy, big-footed, swinging wounded full-bellied, through the trees toward the tall grass and cover, and the crash came again to go past him ripping the air apart. Then it crashed again and he felt the blow as it hit his lower ribs and ripped on through, blood sudden hot and frothy in his mouth, and he galloped toward the high grass where he could crouch and not be seen and make them bring the crashing thing close enough so he could make a rush and get the man that held it.

Macomber had not thought how the lion felt as he got out of the car. In this justly famous passage, Hemingway achieves an empathetic intimacy well beyond the capacity of any character in the story. The point is made explicit when he writes: "Macomber had not thought how the lion felt as he got out of the car."

In "The Art of the Short Story," Hemingway was later to claim, "I can think inside a lion, really." He had already displayed a capacity for getting inside of animals in "The Undefeated" (1925), where the point of view suddenly shifts from the matador to the bull. "The bull had light circles about his eyes. His eyes watched Manuel. He felt he was going to get this little one with the white face." In chapter eight of the Africa book, Hemingway remembers his pain from a broken arm and "thought suddenly how a bull elk must feel if you break a shoulder and he gets away."

Hemingway actually *becomes* an animal in an astonishing sentence that can be found in the handwritten draft of chapter four of *Green Hills of Africa*. "I knew that I could lead my own life to water and that I could make it drink." The conceit at the heart of the sentence – "You can lead a horse to water. . . ." – refigures a familiar cliché into something rich and strange. Perhaps it was the ingenuity of the comparison of his life to a thirsty animal that led Hemingway to omit the sentence from the published book.

The degree of empathy extended toward the lion is, however, something new. In flipping the normal subject-object dynamic – in rendering the man and the car as the "object" of the lion's gaze – Hemingway enters more fully than ever before into the feelings of the animals his characters set out to kill. He will do so again a few pages later, as he has his narrator imagine the wounded lion's eyes narrowing with "hate."

In the two passages that go "inside" the lion, the reader is made privy to a kind of awareness unavailable to any of the characters in the story. The characters' lack becomes the reader's gain, as he is allowed an experience of intersubjectivity with a being usually encountered as an opaque object.

This apotheosis of empathy sheds a somewhat bitter light back on the capacities of the main characters in the story. For all his candor, Macomber remains largely closed off to empathy. He does not think "how the lion felt." The phrase is twice repeated some pages later, when we are told that "Macomber did not know how Wilson felt" and "did not know how his wife felt."

How Margot feels remains a matter of controversy. Could we but penetrate her "female cruelty," as Wilson describes it, we might have some purchase on how to read the story's ambiguous ending. Does she or does she not mean to shoot her husband? While the either/or question remains a matter of critical debate, to frame the matter in this way misses Hemingway's more complex and unsettling point.

Just after categorizing American women as "the hardest in the world," Wilson makes an important concession. It happens after Margot returns to the lunch table: "When she left, Wilson was thinking, when she went off to cry, she seemed a hell of a fine woman. She seemed to understand, to realize, to be hurt for him and for herself and to know how things really stood." Here, we see a character, Wilson, empathetically extending to a second character, Margot, the capacity of feeling empathy for a third character, Macomber. It is a lovely fantasy, and then Margot returns to the table, makes a crack, and stands again, at least in Wilson's eyes, "enamelled in that American female cruelty."

These mood shifts regarding Margot are assigned to Wilson, not to the narrator. The white hunter has in any case little patience with kind thoughts about her; they last for twenty minutes. At only one other moment does another point-of-view on Margot attempt to feel with her. It occurs during the climactic exchange:

> "You've gotten awfully brave, awfully suddenly," his wife said contemptuously, but her contempt was not secure. She was very afraid of something.
>
> Macomber laughed, a very natural hearty laugh. "You know I *have*," he said. "I really have."
>
> "Isn't it sort of late?" Margot said bitterly. Because she had done the best she could for many years back and the way they were together now was no one person's fault.
>
> "Not for me," said Macomber.

I find myself resenting Margot's question and liking Macomber for his response. So I am brought up short by the interpolated sentence beginning with "Because." At a moment in which Margot solicits a minimum of readerly sympathy, the narrator extends to her a unique statement of empathetic understanding. And then I realize I have bought into Wilson's propaganda about her and that I have been reading a story in which, despite its brilliant manipulations of point-of-view, it still proves easier for Hemingway to think inside a lion than to think inside a woman.

Is Hemingway aware of this limitation, and, if so, is he then conducting in "The Short Happy Life of Francis Macomber" a sly self-critique? Any sort of answer to the question will probably depend upon how we consent to read the ending.

In the pause before Wilson and Macomber go after the wounded bull, Margot looks at the two men:

> There was no change in Wilson. She saw Wilson as she had seen him the day before when she had first realized what his great talent was. But she saw the change in Francis Macomber now.

Change, Hemingway twice writes. The word appears as well in the paragraph immediately preceding Margot's act of looking, one in which we are given access to Wilson's thoughts about Macomber. "More of a change than any loss of virginity," he thinks to himself.

Macomber certainly feels changed: "Something happened in me," he maintains, in recalling the chase. Then he repeats himself. "'You know something did happen to me,' he said, 'I feel absolutely different.'" Wilson picks up on the word "happened" at the beginning of his internal monologue: "It had taken a strange chance of hunting, a sudden precipitation into action without opportunity for worrying beforehand, to bring this about with Macomber, but regardless of how it had happened it had most certainly happened."

Throughout the interval of waiting before going after the wounded bull, Hemingway repeats three key words: "something," "happened," and "change." That change has happened is now obvious, and this is taken to be the case "regardless of how it had happened." Hemingway here falls back upon his familiar friends, "it" and "something." But to use these words in this context is not to evade or to omit but to admit. In deploying these abstract nouns, and in refraining from further analysis, Hemingway openly admits to not knowing how change occurs but to believing it can happen.

The change that happens to Macomber allows him to begin leading a happy life. The word "happy" appears only in the story's title, although another form of the word does appear when Macomber talks about a feeling of happiness about action to come. "Happy" derives from the Middle English word "hap," as in luck or happenstance. "Something happened" to and in Macomber, and he becomes happy.

"Isn't it sort of late?" Margot asks, and Macomber gives his marvelous answer. Given how little time is left in which to enjoy this happy life, the reader might well ask, "Isn't the time too short?" Of the twenty-seven titles Hemingway considered using for his story, including options like "The Coming Man," "Through Darkest Marriage," and "The Lion's Portion," it is striking that he eventually went with the one having to do with the shortness of the time.

In imagining Macomber, Hemingway comes to believe that it is never too late to change and that the value of the life lived cannot be measured in terms of its span of years. A happy life is of supreme value whenever you get it and for however long it lasts. For a writer so given to the sense of the already-over and so often unhappy about the prospect of action to come, embracing such a fiction is an act of considerable courage. It is as if Hemingway has finally discovered the future.

It is therefore with something of a heavy heart that I turn to the controversy over "the one issue that has so dominated critical commentaries on the story: whether Margot Macomber deliberately murdered her husband or shot him accidentally while aiming 'at the buffalo.'" Paul Smith traces the debate through more than thirty scholarly arguments. The question is indeed a serious one, although the focus on Margot's intention is, I believe, misplaced. To return to Bernard Williams: like her husband, Margot will learn through her act "that in the story of one's life there is an authority exercised by what one has done, and not merely by what one has intentionally done." Margot shoots and kills her husband. It will henceforth be a truth about her that she is a person who has done such a thing. Unlike her husband, Margot is not, however, afforded a second chance. After her act, the story quickly ends. It ends with her asking Wilson to "stop," a word repeated eight times. "Please stop it," she cries, as he taunts her with his reading of her act. Wilson knows no discretion in assigning intention to what she has done, and we may fault him for it. But his brutal reductions do have the benefit of reminding us that Hemingway has so structured his story's ending as to make it one about how we might read the ending of a story.

I find myself drawn, at the end, to Robert Paul Lamb's fine observation about Margot's repeated plea for Wilson to stop. "She is begging the author not to leave the ending open, with the reader questioning her motives."

While this gets the problem right, it seems to me to limit the locus of responsibility, since Margot's plea can also be taken as addressed to the reader. In creating a story operating as a projective test of the reader's will to be believe in change, Hemingway has done what he has done. If a reader chooses to read the ending as one soliciting the questioning of Margot's motives, he is free to do so as well, and he, too, will then have to live with being the person who has done such a thing.

As he lies in bed on the night after having run from the lion, Macomber thinks to himself: "It was neither all over nor was it beginning." Lost in a true middle, Macomber finds himself in a condition Hemingway's characters have sought to defend against. To live *in* time, and to have a feeling of happiness about action to come – this has been the difficulty and the challenge. In imagining a character who feels and thinks and acts otherwise, Hemingway is himself changing as well. As he sums up his findings about "the most arousing and the longest" controversy in the history of Hemingway criticism, Paul Smith finds himself asking the looming question: "whether we can or should consider the evidence of an authorial intention embedded in the general vision of experience we find in his other works, or deny that evidence to allow the possibility of other, perhaps momentary, glances at that experience that are as compelling and as demonstrative of his complex art." Readers of the present book who have not closed it by now will know that the question can have only one answer.

PART III

Forgiveness

CHAPTER 9

Taking Time

For Whom the Bell Tolls

In my summer of reading Hemingway, the one book I most looked forward to picking up again was *For Whom the Bell Tolls*. Ever since my first encounter with Hemingway's longest novel in 1975, I have loved the book with a kind of helpless love. I am grateful for its sweeping emotions. Robert Jordan is allowed to think and to feel in ways no other Hemingway character had ever before or would ever again be allowed to think and to feel, and what moves me in the performance, beyond the obvious appeal of its high romantic action, is the bravery required to imagine it.

Vulnerability on all sides – this is what the novel calls for, in the character, the author, and the reader. The novel continually exposes Robert and the reader to the awkwardness of wanting things and of hoping to have more than we can perhaps ever get. But, because it is Hemingway, there is also a sense of constraint. As lovers, Robert and Maria are not in and of themselves incapable of realizing their deepest fantasies and of converting them into a working love. It is simply that they are not given much time.

And yet even this constraint is made to yield to a sense of beneficence, since Robert will prove capable of accepting what he has been given as enough. How to live in time and, above all, how to accept that living in time must end are the novel's great subjects, a set of challenges made bearable and even pleasurable by way of Hemingway's decision to omit nothing from the account of Robert's last days on the earth.

In December 1939, in a letter acknowledging the break-up of his marriage to Pauline, Hemingway wrote his mother-in-law about his progress on his new novel: "Have had a very lonely time working on this book. Hope it will be very good. Anyway it is very long and so far it hasn't a bad word in it." Published in 1940, the 471 pages of *For Whom the Bell Tolls* cover only seventy hours of narrated time.

We learn early on that Robert Jordan has been tasked with blowing up a bridge. Hemingway is able to suffuse the whole with a sense of mounting urgency by having the action of the story turn upon the proper timing of an explosion. On the other hand, the sheer length of the book allows Hemingway to suspend the doom and to divert attention into a deep and satisfying experience of the meantime. The reader is given access to the moment-by-moment rituals of daily life, as well as to Robert's inner life, to his memories, his fears, his hopes, and even to his dreams.

The core story is simple enough: in the second year of the Spanish Civil War, an American college professor fighting on the side of the Republic arrives at Pablo and Pilar's camp in the Sierra de Guadarrama, a range of mountains north of Madrid. Robert Jordan quickly falls in love with Maria, disputes with Pablo about the efficacy of his mission, blows the bridge, is wounded in a fall from his horse, and must stay behind and man the machine gun while Maria rides away. It is enough action to fill a long short story.

For Whom the Bell Tolls also contains Pilar's narration of "the day of revolution in a small town," Maria's backstory, matador Finito and his fight against fear, El Sordo's stand on the hilltop, Golz's broodings, Andrés's mission through enemy lines, and, above all, Robert Jordan's thoughts and memories. None of these tellings and rememberings forwards the central narrative. Instead, they respond to Robert's expressed longing, one a reader comes to share with him as the novel unfolds: "I wish there was more time."

More time. The very element that has been our "misfortune," to use Faulkner's word, the element Frederic Henry makes his way "against," becomes in *For Whom the Bell Tolls* a kind of mercy. None of Hemingway's books spends so much time talking about "time," and none attempts as many experiments with how to fill rather than to kill it. Hemingway forsakes ellipsis in order to do something only a big novel can do, which is to bind together the times of a life.

The novel opens with a character being granted a long perspective:

> He lay flat on the brown, pine-needled floor of the forest, his chin on his folded arms, and high overhead the wind blew in the tops of the pine trees. The mountainside sloped gently where he lay; but below it was steep and he could see the dark of the oiled road winding through the pass. There was a stream alongside the road and far down the pass he saw a mill beside the stream and the falling water of the dam, white in the summer sunlight.
>
> "Is that the mill?" he asked.
>
> "Yes."
>
> "I do not remember it."
>
> "It was built since you were here. The old mill is farther down; much below the pass."

> He spread the photostated military map out on the forest floor and looked at it carefully. The old man looked over his shoulder.

Robert Jordan has been here before; the landscape is known, the mill is new. So, once again, we are treated to a mixture of the familiar and the strange. Yet, far from producing an uncanny effect, the scene unfolds as one more stage in its viewer's education as an old man gives information to a younger one. Nothing is melodramatically foreshadowed or withheld. In this scene of instruction, knowledge passes from one generation to another with no apparent loss of power.

One opens the first folder of Item 83 in the Hemingway Room only to discover the novel, as originally conceived, beginning somewhat differently:

> We lay there on the brown, pine-needled floor of the forest and the wind blew in the tops of the pine trees.

Handwritten revisions show Hemingway soon adopting a change of person: "He lay flat on the brown, pine-needled floor of the forest . . . ." It had quickly become apparent that a first-person narrative simply could not accommodate the flexibility Hemingway's long structure required: the freedom to range through many times and into many minds.

But writing in the third person was to prove by no means an easy thing. In the spring of 1940, as Hemingway approached the end of his labors, he wrote to his editor: "Christ I am tired though, Max. Me in the third person for a year and going on two months. Me that the third person can beat to death in a thousand words." Part of feeling exhausted may have been the result of operating within a narrative mode which, although offering the protections of distance, worked as well to compel Hemingway into his most intimate portrayal of how life goes, day by day.

Once everything goes quiet after the Loyalist cavalry completes its assault on El Sordo and Company, Maria brings a tin bucket of stewed hare and mushrooms up to where Robert Jordan and Primitivo are keeping lookout. They have heard the planes bombing the hill, and Primitivo has lost his appetite. He finally consents to fill his plate, and Maria and Robert, each knowing "how the other felt," shake their heads and say nothing. Then "Robert Jordan ate the stew, taking time to appreciate the mushrooms completely."

Even in this moment of unease, Hemingway shows a character taking time. It is in these small moments of pleasure-taking and reminiscence that the true achievement of the novel resides. Moreover, the having of good time does not feel stolen from an otherwise doom-filled continuum. While Robert's seventy hours could well have been assimilated into the "pattern of tragedy into which the whole operation had seemed grooved," Hemingway continually forgoes the opportunity to place the emphasis on misfortune and loss.

In Virginia Woolf's 1927 review of *Men Without Women*, she found Hemingway's treatment of character "faked" and wondered whether the work might eventually "broaden and fill out; it may take a little more time and going into things – human beings in particular – rather more deeply." Woolf's speculation anticipates the achievement in *For Whom the Bell Tolls* in a quite literal way, since, in writing it, and in order to broaden, fill out, and go into things more deeply, Hemingway found it necessary to "take a little more time."

He takes the time, for instance, to show his characters making love. The two instances of "*la gloria*" have provoked considerable resistance in some commentators and have proved for others to be a downright embarrassment. And these passages are embarrassing, if we set out to judge them by way of Hemingway's early style. Here, there is no cutting away from the act and what is felt while experiencing it. On the other hand, if certain kinds of embarrassment are precisely what Hemingway's characters are being invited to overcome, then both the style and the substance of these passages play their part in a reader's education.

The earth moves twice for Robert and Maria. It happens in chapter thirteen and again in chapter thirty-seven. I pick up the first passage some six lines in:

> and for her everything was red, orange, gold-red from the sun on the closed eyes, and it all was that color, all of it, the filling, the possessing, the having, all of that color, all in a blindness of that color. For him it was a dark passage which led to nowhere . . . .

Hemingway repeats the word "nowhere" ten more times before this last, long sentence completes itself with the words "they were both there, time having stopped and he felt the earth move out and away from under them."

From "nowhere" to "there": that does not sound so bad. And the attempt to represent the experience from Maria's as well as Robert's point of view is also commendable. Yet there is something awkward here, something perhaps built in to any attempt to represent in words the having of sex. I think here of what Billy Bathgate says to us in E. L. Doctorow's novel of that name. "You can't remember sex. You can remember the fact of it, and recall the setting, and even the details, but the sex of the sex cannot be remembered, the substantive truth of it, it is by nature self-erasing."

In attempting to remember sex, Hemingway falls back on colors, on strings of participles, and on the repetition of one word. The sex of the sex is beyond him, or perhaps beyond any words, but the fact of it, that it has happened and that it matters and will matter to Robert and Maria, this he can attempt to put across.

The second sex scene also rides on the repetition of a single word:

> This, that they were not to have, they were having . . . . Come now, now, for there is no now but now. Yes, now. Now, please now, only now, not anything else only this now, and where are you and where am I and where is the other one, and not why, not ever why, only this now; and on and always please then always now, always now.

Making love is no longer a "dark passage" to the unfamiliar. In the course of twenty-four chapters, Robert moves from nowhere to now. This can happen because, in the interval provided, a man has taken the time to get to know and to become present to the woman he loves.

"What amateurs call a style is usually only the unavoidable awkwardness in first trying to make something that has not heretofore been made," Hemingway told George Plimpton, in their 1958 interview. The taking on of awkward subjects in *For Whom the Bell Tolls*, subjects not before taken on, entailed as well an awkwardness of style. "The cultivation of deliberate awkwardness," a minor but salient feature in even the early works, as Richard Peterson argues, becomes in the big novel a carefully deployed strategy.

Hemingway had first written about the power of lovemaking to stop time and to transport us into a "sudden-ended always" in *Green Hills of Africa*. So that insight was not new. In *For Whom the Bell Tolls*, however, the attention paid to words like "nowhere" and "now" function as part of a larger study of the experience of human time. Hemingway in fact carefully revised the two love scenes in order to make this plain.

Thomas E. Gould describes both scenes as "not nearly as graphic or detailed in the first draft of the manuscript as in the final text." The first scene originally consisted of one sentence: "And there was the moment when they stood absolutely still in time and he could feel the earth move out and away from under them." The second scene was even more heavily revised, with the original lovemaking being described as follows: "Robert Jordan knew then that if there is any reward, that only those have it who merit it. That it is only to be given and only by giving can it be received. He felt proud and humble and altogether happy with an ecstasy of fulfillment. There are no words for such things." In neither first try does Hemingway attempt to deploy repetition and sentence rhythm in order to gesture toward the sex of the sex. His original language does not attempt to transport us into an experience but stands off and describes how someone might later think about it.

Writing *For Whom the Bells Tolls* involved the formal challenge of finding ways to "slow up the time." Hemingway met the challenge by dedicating himself to the art of digression, as in the four Andrés chapters interpolated near the end, chapters in which narrative time is doubled as the reader turns aside to follow the journey to Golz's headquarters. Much of the novel is spent digressing into thought and memory, as when Pilar recalls her days of eating and making love in Valencia, or when Robert drinks his absinthe and is carried, as if by tasting a *petite madeleine*, back to the chestnut trees and boulevards of Paris. On other occasions, the third-person narrator simply chooses to take us elsewhere, as in chapter thirty-two, when, "on that same night" that Robert and Maria talk over her past, we are suddenly transported to a scene taking place at Hotel Gaylord in Madrid. All of these digressions work to create "that reprieved feeling," a feeling Andrés remembers having on those mornings of the fiesta when it rained and he lay in bed knowing that he would not have to go out and bait the bulls. Hemingway offers so generous a supply of turnings aside that few readers will recall them as unique occasions except in one instance – the unforgettable chapter ten in which Pilar tells the story of the day of revolution in a small town.

That Hemingway thought of chapter ten as something of a set piece is indicated by a title he provided for it in Folder 7 of Item 83:

> "How We Killed the Fascists of the Village"
> Told by the Woman of Pablo
> From Chapter Eight of an asyet untitled
> novel by Ernest Hemingw

H. R. Stoneback describes the chapter as, "hands down, the most vivid, powerful, and memorable section of the entire novel." The chapter is, however, only capable of inspiring such responses because of its place and function in a larger whole, and the experience of that larger whole is one Hemingway is recommending to us as having a vividness and value beyond the power of any short story to create.

Courage is the ostensible subject of Pilar's story. After the taking of the town, Pablo executes four *guardias civiles*. "Show us how to die," he says, before telling them to kneel down and place their heads against the wall. One of the *civiles* says to another, "How does it seem to you?" He is asking whether or not it is seemly to kneel. The corporal responds: "'It is as well to kneel,' he answered. 'It is of no importance.'"

Knowing how to die matters a great deal in the novel, and Robert spends time thinking about how others, especially his father, have done so. Learning how to live proves, however, the much greater challenge. "I am an old man who will live until I die," Anselmo says near the beginning, and his putting the case in this way bespeaks a new patience, a willingness to wait for the end rather than to hasten or to anticipate it. In talking about Kaskin's death, Pablo has earlier said, "That is the way we will all finish." Anselmo had then responded, "That is the way all men end," and so reduces old shibboleth to self-evident cliché. Pablo's morbidity will repeatedly get the best of him, and his prevailing mood stems from his "true regret" over what he did on the day he took the town. "I would not have had it happen as it happened," he will later say. "I would restore them all to life."

There is a lot of dying well and badly in Pilar's story, especially as the various "fascists" are brought out of the city hall, made to walk between the lines of flails, and then thrown over the cliff into the river. "All of his style was gone now," Pilar will say, when she comes to Don Faustino, the "great annoyer of girls." We can concentrate on these various styles of dying and so can approach it all as a sort of competition. Or, with the *guardia civile*, we may see the style of dying as "of no importance." To focus on whether the enemy behaves well or badly is to divert attention away from the larger fact that Hemingway has so structured the interval as to cast a light back upon "What we did. Not what the others did to us." Pilar's story asks a reader to perform a double motion of mind: to empathize with the enemy and to be accurate about the behavior of those being sided with. In doing so, the story acts as an exemplum of the whole, a novel in which the experiences of empathy and self-judgment lead to the possibility of forgiveness.

"*Vaya*, a day that commences," Pablo says, as the sun comes up over the captured town. Hemingway's novel tells the story of a little less than three days. How to live out a day becomes a subject much more challenging to the imagination than killing or getting ready to die; Hemingway can do that, and we see him do it brilliantly in chapter ten. But, as El Sordo tells himself, "Dying was nothing and he had no picture of it nor fear of it in his mind. But living was a field of grain blowing in the wind on the side of a hill. Living was a hawk in the sky. Living was an earthen jar of water in the dust of the threshing with the grain flailed out and the chaff blowing. Living was a horse between your legs and a carbine under one leg and a hill and a valley and a stream with trees along it and the far side of the valley and the hills beyond."

If there is a unit of time Hemingway is learning to care for as he writes *For Whom the Bell Tolls*, it is the day. Robert talks a lot about "now." He even conjugates the word: "Now, *ahora, maintenant, huete. Now*, it has a funny sound to be a whole world and your life." And, of course, he moves from nowhere to now in his lovemaking with Maria. But this movement matters and has value because it arises out of and is folded back into a felt sense of dailiness. "The Last Good Country," a Nick Adams story from the 1950s, makes the point: "*He had already learned there was only one day at a time and that it was always the day you were in.*"

William Balassi maintains that "Hemingway tended to think of his writing in terms of one-day tasks, many of which formed units that he focused on as though they were short stories." Continuity in the writing practice was maintained by beginning each day with a reading of the work done on the previous one: "You read what you have written and, as you always stop when you know what is going to happen next, you go on from there." The continuity turns out, however, to have less to do with his mode of starting the day than with his way of ending it: "You write until you come to a place where you still have your juice and know what will happen next and you stop and try to live through until the next day when you hit it again." Hemingway only stops when he knows what will happen next but *before* he has written it. It is a deeply conservative and even an anxious practice, one governed by the writer's sense of how much more juice he has left to spend.

However much Hemingway was faithful to these self-strictures, they appear to have been modified in the writing of his Spanish novel. In the 1958 interview in which he talked about knowing what will happen next, he also described *For Whom the Bell Tolls* as "a problem which I carried on each day. I knew what was going to happen in principle. But I invented what happened each day as I wrote." Like Robert Jordan, Hemingway knew what was going to happen in principle – the writing of a novel, the blowing of a bridge. And, like Robert Jordan, Hemingway also learned to allow "each day" to bring whatever pleasures it could bring.

After the lovemaking scene in chapter thirteen, Robert begins to entertain "certain notions about the value of time." He thinks about having to "live a life in two days," about trading years for hours. "So if you love this girl as much as you say you do, you had better love her very hard and make up in intensity what the relation will lack in duration and in continuity." As Robert's thinking becomes abstract, we watch Hemingway developing something largely absent from his work up to this point – we watch him evolving an explicit theme.

In *For Whom the Bell Tolls*, Hemingway continues the experiment with radical shifts in point of view begun in "The Short Happy Life of Francis Macomber." In following these shifts, a reader's loyalties are questioned and tested; it is as if he is being asked *not* to take sides. The empathy extended to the enemy in Pilar's story makes the first contribution to this effect. But the most striking shifts in point of view are reserved for the writing about Lieutenant Paco Berrendo, the man who completes the assault on El Sordo and who will find himself three times under the sights of Robert Jordan's gun.

The first point-of-view shift to the other side occurs while Anselmo keeps watch over the mill in chapter fifteen. It is cold, he thinks about leaving his post, he stays put. And then, suddenly, we are seeing something Anselmo cannot see:

> Inside the sawmill one of the soldiers was sitting on his bunk and greasing his boots. Another lay in his bunk sleeping. The third was cooking and the corporal was reading a paper. Their helmets hung on nails driven into the wall and their rifles leaned against the plank wall.
>
> "What kind of country is this where it snows when it is almost June?" the soldier who was sitting on the bunk said.

After a page-and-a-half of conversation, the narrative switches back to the figure keeping watch: "This was how they were talking in the sawmill while Anselmo waited in the snow."

In itself, it is a passage of no great interest. Its function is to prepare us for Hemingway's much more ambitious attempt to think inside Lieutenant Paco Berrendo.

When the main body of Fascist cavalry appears, it is Berrendo who rides into view "over the blued steel barrel" of Robert Jordan's automatic rifle. He proceeds up the mountain and eventually assumes control of the assault on El Sordo. Second in command, Berrendo must wait and watch as the first officer is killed when he recklessly exposes himself to El Sordo's fire. We do not simply follow Berrendo's actions and conversation: we are transported into his mind. "I hate these pistol brandishers, Berrendo was thinking." After the planes have bombed the hilltop, Berrendo rides up, finds the wounded Joaquín, and shoots him in "the back of the head, as quickly and as gently, if such an abrupt movement can be gentle, as Sordo had shot the wounded horse."

Berrendo is then a man of gentleness and good sense. As he rides back down the mountain, he moves once more into "the sharp clarity" of Robert Jordan's vision. With him are the horses carrying a poncho bulging "as a pod bulges with peas." As before, we are transported into Berrendo's mind: "He was thinking: taking the heads is barbarous. But proof and identification is necessary."

Why this digression into the mind and heart of an enemy? In *Anatomy of Criticism*, in writing of our founding poem of war, Northrop Frye discovers the precedent for such a move:

> It is hardly possible to overestimate the importance for Western literature of the *Iliad's* demonstration that the fall of an enemy, no less than of a friend or leader, is tragic and not comic. With the *Iliad*, once for all, an objective and disinterested element enters into the poet's vision of human life. Without this element, poetry is merely instrumental to various social aims, to propaganda, to amusement, to devotion, to instruction.

For Whom the Bell Tolls will in fact end with the fall of an enemy, and it is Lieutenant Berrendo. "Lieutenant Berrendo," the final paragraph begins, "Lieutenant Berrendo, watching the trail, came riding up, his thin face serious and grave." There, to meet him, is Robert Jordan, lying "behind the tree." He is waiting until the officer reaches the sunlit place. Then he will fire.

Of course, we do not see Robert fire and kill Berrendo, nor do we see the cavalry kill Robert Jordan. Both characters are kept alive until the end. But we know what will happen. It is well and fitting that Berrendo is the man at whom Robert takes his final aim, since, given Hemingway's disinterested treatment of this enemy figure, there can be no joy and scarcely even any satisfaction at the thought that he will, surely, be killed. It is not an ending that takes revenge. Instead, it luxuriates in the fact that the hearts of two men on opposite sides of a war are still beating.

In his treatment of Paco Berrendo, Hemingway poses a series of looming questions. Can we effect a change of heart about a side against which our attitudes may have hardened? And, if so, how might we do so? Beyond this, can character change? And, if so, how does such change occur? Hemingway continues to explore these questions up to and including his novel's final scene.

Pablo is the most changeable character in *For Whom the Bell Tolls*. A moral chameleon, his ever-shifting behavior acts as a parody of the profound changes experienced by Robert and Maria. Hemingway is all for second chances, as the story of Francis Macomber reveals. It is possible to start again – as William James would put it, to be "twice-born." But a second chance is only a beginning, since how it is lived out determines its meaning and value. For Pablo, it turns out, it is already "too late."

Pablo twice abandons his mission and twice returns to it. The first abandonment comes early, when he tells Robert "Thou wilt blow no bridge," cedes control of the band to Pilar, leaves the cave, and then returns the next morning as if nothing has happened. In the interval, the gypsy has urged Robert to kill Pablo but Robert does not "approve of the moment," and the opportunity passes. Later, Pilar and Augustín discuss the necessity of working with Pablo, despite his having been "rendered useless by his fear and his disinclination to action." Pilar concludes, "forced to a change, he will be smart in the change." So Pablo is given another chance.

When Pablo leaves a second time and takes the detonators, he ensures an outcome in which Anselmo will be killed. Pablo will again return and again be reaccepted into the band. He brings with him more men, and Robert knows that they are needed. "I had a moment of weakness," Pablo admits. "I went away but I am come back." For Robert, Pablo's second return has "broken the pattern of tragedy into which the whole operation had seemed grooved."

Pablo's second departure and return actually marks his *third* chance. We have no discourse of the third chance; the chances that matter are second ones. For it to mean anything – for it to signify a true change of heart – after the second chance, there can be no other. We only get one shot at being twice-born; following that, the reversals become comic and even absurd. Real change is painful, public, and irreversible, and it cares about the eyes of others. "I was full of shame," Pilar says, after the day of the taking of the town. But Pablo has lost his capacity for shame; he is merely tired and unable to sleep with her. As a result, Pablo does not change, he simply vacillates: "He has shifted like the wind."

Robert Jordan is unique among Hemingway's characters in his avid seeking after education. "It will be quite an education when it's finished," he says to himself in chapter eleven. In *A Farewell to Arms*, Rinaldi denies the very possibility of being educated: "We are born with all we have and we never learn." As Catherine lies dying, Frederic echoes the belief: "You died. You did not know what it was about. You never had time to learn.

They threw you in and told you the rules and the first time they caught you off base they killed you." In disdaining Frederic's habitual invocation of an unnamed and all-controlling "they," *For Whom the Bell Tolls* reasserts the human capacity to teach, to learn, and to change.

One of the novel's central acceptances is that education results from embarrassment. There can be no coming to know for a character marooned in the familiar and somewhat world-weary Hemingway knowingness. The "instruction" Pilar provides for Maria provokes a lot of blushing, as is to be expected, but it also ensures that she is ready to meet the nights when they come. The value of education is to replace inhibiting fantasies with enabling fictions, as happens for Robert at Gaylord's, the hotel in Madrid where he meets so many "intelligent" men. "He liked to know how it really was; not how it was supposed to be."

Admitting that he has "only started his education," Robert remains open to unsettling and awkward awarenesses up to the very end. After the last love scene, he says to Maria, "You taught me a lot, *guapa*." He goes on to say to himself "I know a few things now" and to wonder whether "you only learn them now because you are oversensitized because of the shortness of the time?" Then he makes a typical self-correction: "There is no such thing as a shortness of time, though. You should have sense enough to know that too. I have been all my life in these hills since I have been here."

In giving *For Whom the Bell Tolls* such an extended ending, Hemingway defies, like Robert, the shortness of the time. A little before noon on Tuesday, Lieutenant Berrendo rides into view. The action of the last day begins at ten minutes to three in the morning, when Maria rolls up the sleeping robe and Robert picks up the packs and enters the cave. The ninety pages remaining cover only nine hours, hours filled with brilliantly described action and the deaths or woundings of Anselmo, Fernando, Eladio, all of the new men Pablo has brought with him on his return, and, finally, Robert Jordan himself. The most remarkable writing in these pages comes after Robert has said good-bye and is left alone to think in the time that remains.

Hemingway signals this shift to the interior with a rare use of formal ellipsis: "Robert Jordan waved and then Agustín, too, was out of sight . . . . Robert Jordan looked down the green slope of the hillside to the road and the bridge. It's as well this way as any, he thought." From here on, as indicated by the dissolve of the ellipsis, the story moves into Robert's mind.

The six pages remaining comprise an appreciation. As Robert prepares himself to meet the soldiers moving up from below, he casts his mind back over his "good life." He struggles against the growing pain in his leg by instructing himself to "Think about them being away." He thinks about Madrid, "just over the hills there, and down across the plain. Down out of the gray rocks and the pines, the heather and the gorse, across the yellow high plateau you see it rising white and beautiful. That part is just as true as Pilar's old women drinking the blood down at the slaughterhouse. There's no *one* thing that's true. It's all true." Knowingness is here abandoned in favor of a more inclusive imaginative scheme. The one truth that has dominated Hemingway's fiction – how all men end – is here absorbed into a multiplicity of truths.

While the Hemingway manuscripts often yield rich surprises, I find myself both gratified and taken aback by a note scribbled on the final, sure-handed pages of *For Whom the Bell Tolls*. The absence of excisions and insertions in these pages reveals a writer moving ahead in the full confidence of his chosen approach. And yet, despite all the ways in which Hemingway's closing scene speaks for itself, he appears to have felt it necessary to compose a note to himself on the last page in Folder 11 of Item 84. In it, he makes an explicit plea for his changing sense of an ending:

> People are not as they end up (finish) but as they are in the finest point they ever reach.
>
> It is an altimeter which registers the ultimate height that is reached.

In Robert Jordan's case, his finest point reached is coincident with the end of Hemingway's book.

As Hemingway completed the final chapter, he wrote to Max Perkins: "I hated to have that damned Jordan get what he got after living with the son of a bitch for 17 months. Felt worse than if it were me." But just what is it that Jordan gets? He will die; of this there can be no doubt. But, in one of the most affirmative plot decisions Hemingway ever made, he decided against having his hero die *in* his book.

Robert Jordan is alive until the end: "He could feel his heart beating against the pine needle floor of the forest." In writing these words, Hemingway returns to his beginning: "He lay flat on the brown, pine-needled floor of the forest, his chin on his folded arms, and overhead the wind blew in the tops of the pine trees." The last sentence in the book is a virtual copy of the first sentence in the book, except that in the interval Robert has earned the addition of the word "heart."

Given the beauty and power of Hemingway's refrain-ending, it is surprising to discover that he considered extending it with an epilogue. A summary written by Max Perkins for the Book of the Month Club provides a sense of what Hemingway had in mind:

> Two short chapters, amounting to 1, 500 words in all, will bring the book to a conclusion. In the first of these Karkov and Goltz meet after the failure of the attack, and in driving back from the front they talk together about it, and about Robert's message and his success in blowing up the bridge. In the second, Andrés and Gomez motorcycle back to the outpost and then Andrés makes his way over the ground he covered before, and eventually reaches the abandoned camp, sees the ruined bridge, and knows all that has happened there.
>
> These chapters are written, but not yet to the complete satisfaction of the author. He wished to wait until after reading the proof up to this point before perfecting the end.

In 2011, Perkins biographer A. Scott Berg traveled to Cuba. "There in an old file in the basement of the garage at the Finca Vigía remained a 12-page pencil draft of those very pages." Standing next to Berg at the time of his discovery was Jenny Phillips, the daughter of Peggy Perkins. It was Peggy Perkins who, after reading a copy of the epilogue, had convinced her father Max that Hemingway's novel ended perfectly without it.

Berg was fortunate to be allowed to examine this file, since not all of the holdings at the Finca are yet open to researchers. As of this writing, copies of the papers left behind in Cuba are, however, in the process of being shipped to the Kennedy Library and are being catalogued as Collection #357, Museo Ernest Hemingway, Finca Vigía, San Francisco De Paula, Cuba. A portion of the pencil draft read by Berg may have already made its way north: Box 1 of the accumulating collection contains a folder of eleven handwritten pages labeled "Manuscripts – For Whom the Bell Tolls." One page appears as follows:

> Epilogue.
>
> It was night ~~on the road~~ when Golz rode
> ~~back~~ in a staff car ~~down from the pass~~ on the road ~~to~~
> down from the pass to
> El Escorial.

At the bottom of this page, Mary Hemingway has written: "For Whom the Bell Tolls." This fragment appears to bear out Max Perkins's description of the proposed epilogue as beginning with Karkov and Golz driving back from the front after the failure of the attack.

After sending Perkins the completed manuscript, Hemingway had written his editor a somewhat anxious letter: "What do you think? Is it o.k. as it is? (I have fixed the emotion some and made it better.) . . . . Should I put on the epilogue? Is it needed? Or would it just be grand manner writing and take you away from the emotion that the book ends on." In replying to these questions, Perkins told Hemingway that his daughter had loved ending with Robert's beating heart. "She thought it was perfect."

Hemingway's letter to Perkins reads like one of Robert Jordan's internal monologues, with all the twists and turns of a mind thinking. In debating with himself about how and when his novel ought to end, Hemingway brooded on the contents of the epilogue and then concluded:

> But it really stops where Jordan is feeling his heart beating against the pine needle floor of the forest.
>
> You see every dammed word and action in this book depends on every other word and action. You see he's laying there on the pine needles at the start and that is where he is at the end.

Of course, between the first and the last sentence everything has changed, but Hemingway's closing words *say* the ending as if it had not. Formally, the novel does not end; it recommences. Without in any way depreciating all that Robert has felt, thought, and learned in the interval, the last words allow a return to a sense of beginning unshadowed by loss. In creating a fiction of return rather than of imminent departure, the ending allows the reader to stay with Robert, in the sunlit place, forever.

CHAPTER 10

Forgiveness

For Whom the Bell Tolls

As he moved deeper into the 1930s, Hemingway began to imagine characters no longer caught up in repetitive and inescapable patterns of behavior. The way out, he discovered, lay in a fuller understanding of the function and power of symbolic action. For Francis Macomber and for Robert Jordan, an act of the mind is allowed to respond to and to stand in for things done to and by the physical body. As these characters learn how not to repeat, the revisionary and forgiving activity of the imagination emerges as a force as great or greater than anything that has been or might be literally done.

It was William Faulkner who first paid tribute to this emerging understanding in Hemingway. He did so in his 1950 novel *Requiem for a Nun*. Temple Drake has come to plead for the life of the "ex-dope-fiend nigger whore" she invited into her house as a nurse only to have the woman kill her child. In pleading for "something even better, stronger, than tragedy to hold two people together: forgiveness," she seeks out an example of what she means by recalling a scene from *For Whom the Bell Tolls*:

> Because suddenly it could be as if it had never been, never happened. You know: somebody – Hemingway, wasn't it – wrote a book about how it had never actually happened to a gir – woman, if she just refused to accept it, no matter who remembered, bragged.

The event that "never actually happened" is Maria's rape by the fascists, an event recounted in considerable detail by Maria during the last night she spends with Robert Jordan. Herself a victim of a violent rape, Temple is drawn not to the story of the event itself but to the proposed response to it.

That response had earlier been articulated in the seventh chapter of Hemingway's novel. Robert and Maria have fallen into sudden love, and she comes to join him in his sleeping robe. They snuggle and talk, and, in the way of things, he asks her, "Hast thou loved others?" "Never," she answers. She then feels compelled to add, "But things were done to me."

Robert tenses when he hears this, and Maria knows it. He recovers quickly and says something fine to her: "No one has done anything to thee. Thee, they cannot touch." They continue to talk and to kiss. Eager to make love, Maria feels obliged to tell Robert that she is "not sick" and then returns to the question of the things that were done to her. At this point, she repeats to Robert what Pilar has told her, and it is these words that Temple will later remember: "She said that nothing is done to oneself that one does not accept and that if I loved some one it would take it all away."

Hemingway is here recommending a complex act of the mind making possible an unshaming of the self. In order for Maria to free her soul of the thing "done," she must acknowledge it and share the fact of it with someone she loves. Then the shame can be lifted. In the logic of the novel of which this scene forms a part, shame only accrues from "what we did," as Robert will later think to himself, "Not from what others did to us."

When Temple Drake invokes forgiveness as something better than tragedy to hold two people together, she is invoking a process like the one Maria and Robert enact in chapter seven. It is not that Maria is being asked or expected to forgive the men who have raped her: this is not of concern here. Instead, Maria is being invited to engage in an act of self-forgiveness in which she refuses to grant anyone the power to touch and define her from without.

It comes down to the meaning of one carefully chosen word, "accept." Acceptance, as Hemingway here understands it, is a matter of mind and heart, an internal activity of adjustment in which a self shoulders only those responsibilities that are truly its own.

For Hemingway, the movement toward such understandings had begun in "The Short Happy Life of Francis Macomber." Courage is surely the deep subject of that story, but it is not simply the courage to face a wounded animal. The kind of courage Macomber learns to display has to do with another kind of facing, that of his own shame. The character is not, however, offered a method of facing shame that would disavow the required act of violence: Macomber must face *and* kill. Hemingway is not yet quite ready to say that the thing done can be undone by a refusal to accept it. He is not quite ready, that is, to imagine atonement through a symbolic rather than a literal act. But he does imagine a response involving the possibility of a second chance in which the self is allowed to repeat, and in repeating to revise, and in revising to break through to a life free of shame.

What allows Robert Jordan to move through shame to forgiveness is his reliance upon the activity we call *thinking*. In early Hemingway, thinking had typically been an ordeal to which the self felt doomed or from which it had attempted to escape. By the late 1930s, however, Hemingway found himself required to imagine characters more at home in their own minds. Only there, and in a calm and deliberate fashion, could the conflicts and dilemmas central to each project be confronted and worked through.

Maria gives a full description of the day of her rape in chapter thirty-one of *For Whom the Bell Tolls*. The entire chapter is about thinking, and Maria's story lies at the heart of it: Robert Jordan is asked to think hard about something he would rather not think about at all. While the object of thought certainly matters here – a man is asked to confront and accept his belatedness with respect to a woman's sexual history – the order of thought proves equally compelling. Thinking, as Hemingway understands it, has less to do with having big ideas or unlooked-for insights than it does with surrendering to a certain motion of mind. Thinking *leads to* something. As readers follow these often wavering lines of thought, they not only get to know Hemingway's characters in a more intimate way but find themselves instructed in how a mind, through courageous thinking, might come to know itself.

Beginning with Wyndham Lewis and his "Dumb Ox" theory, the critical tradition has characterized Hemingway's characters as thoughtless. In his Epilogue to *The Inward Terrain*, Richard Hovey maintains that Hemingway "dodged the *Thinking*" part of Emerson's description of the American Scholar. Hemingway "dreaded that *Thinking* might unman him." In an essay called "Hemingway and the Pale Cast of Thought," Robert Evans goes even further: "Nowhere in Hemingway's work does there glimmer even the faintest suggestion that one's life can be ordered by thought." Such claims persist despite the obvious fact that "Hemingway creates Men of Thought," as Mark Cirino points out. His gallery of male characters includes writers, teachers, painters, journalists, and students of architecture.

"He felt he had left everything behind, the need for thinking, the need to write, other needs." Claims about Hemingway being uninterested in thought usually rest on taking such sentences at face value. But even a cursory reading of "Big Two-Hearted River" reveals it as a story in which an aversion to deliberate thought requires Nick Adams to engage in thinking of *another kind*. Nick mostly thinks through noticing: the entire landscape through which he moves is more projected than seen, an index of his haunted mind. His behavior is so shadowed by the effort not to think that Nick can scarcely be described as unconscious. Instead, he is half-conscious, suspended in an anxious state between awareness and unbound movement. There is a holding off from steady attention: "If he looked too steadily they were gone. But if he only half-looked they were there, the far-off hills of the height of land."

What Nick is not allowed to do is to engage in "mental conversation," as his author was to describe it, and when Hemingway strayed into the direct notation of this kind of thinking, as in the passage Philip Young entitles "On Writing," he then "cut it all out." But that Nick is thinking in his own characteristic and displaced fashion is made clear in a note Hemingway scribbled to himself on a page labeled

Black River
Manuscript.

Filed as Item 281 in the Kennedy Library collections, the note reads as follows:

Big two hearted –
He thinks, gets uncomfortable,
restless, tries to stop
thinking, more uncomfortable
and restless, the thinking
goes on, speeds up, can't
shake it – comes home to
camp – hot before storm –
storm – in morning creek
flooded, hikes to the railroad.

In trying so hard not to think, as the note reveals, and as any careful reading of the story will discover, Nick is also always thinking.

It may have taken another writer as adept at encoding thought to recognize the subtlety of what Hemingway was up to. In *Shadow and Act* (1964), Ralph Ellison acknowledges Hemingway as the "true father-as-artist of so many of us." Hemingway "knew the difference between politics and art and something of their true relationship for the writer." Ellison also honors him for writing "with such precision about the processes and techniques of daily living that I could keep myself and my brother alive during the 1937 Recession by following his descriptions of wing-shooting." In a 1957 interview with Robert Penn Warren, Ellison expanded his sense of Hemingway's craft to include his theory of mind: "there seems to be in the early Hemingway the conscious effort *not* to have a very high center of consciousness within the form of the novel."

Ellison's carefully chosen words reinforce a prevailing assumption about thinking in Hemingway even as they allow for a qualification of it. He makes the standard claim about the absence in the early work of a willing lingering in the mind. The claim is accurate enough, since Nick, Jake, and Frederic typically work hard to avoid many kinds of thinking. On the other hand, in representing this resistance to mindfulness as a "conscious effort," Hemingway also indicates the continual presence of a mind at work. While a high center of consciousness may be absent early on, what is present is Hemingway's great and original contribution to our understanding of how many kinds of ways there are to think, some accomplished paradoxically or by indirection, even while trying not to think at all.

These kinds of thinking include the unwilled free association that overtakes Nick at the end of "Big Two-Hearted River: Part I." Having just indulged in a long paragraph of unbidden memory of "coffee according to Hopkins," Nick sees that "his mind was starting to work. He knew he could choke it because he was tired enough." The choking off of thought only becomes necessary because Nick has been thinking, and in an unsettling way. The paragraph of remembering bespeaks a history of losses Nick proves spectacularly unable to forget.

Jake Barnes's nocturnal meditations are also unwelcome, and yet, as a narrator, he is precise in noting how they come upon him. Alone in his apartment, Jake finds himself remembering the scene where the liaison colonel visited him in the hospital and said, "You . . . have given more than your life." As Jake's sense of the "old grievance" returns upon him, he fails to take some self-administered advice:

> Not to think about it. Oh, it was swell advice. Try and take it sometime. Try and take it.
>
> I lay awake thinking and my mind jumping around. Then I couldn't keep away from it, and I started to think about Brett and all the rest of it went away. I was thinking about Brett and my mind stopped jumping around and started to go in sort of smooth waves. Then all of a sudden I started to cry. Then after a while it was better and I lay in bed and listened to the heavy trams go by and way down the street, and then I went to sleep.

The attempt to avoid thinking here performs a kind of mercy: deprived of the capacity to enact the physical motions of love, Jake sublimates them into a sequence of thoughts that mimics a pattern of arousal, climax, and release.

Frederic Henry's thinking about his "head" after he climbs onto the floor of the flatcar provides a final example of the role of thinking in early Hemingway. "The head was mine, but not to use, not to think with, only to remember and not too much remember." He then proceeds to "think about" Catherine, while telling himself to think "only about her a little."

Of two minds, he imagines the "hard floor for a wife" and also repudiates the surmise. "You loved some one else whom now you knew was not even to be pretended there." Seeing "clearly and emptily" – Frederic is capable of characterizing the nature of his thought – he makes a decision: "You were out of it now." And so Hemingway attends to a process of head-work by way of which Frederic begins to make his separate peace. While Frederic ends the chapter by saying, "I was not made to think," he does so only after having engaged in a complex act of the mind.

Despite once having made the decision to cut out the direct treatment of Nick's thinking at the end of "Big Two-Hearted River," Hemingway did thereafter choose to represent welcome and self-aware thought as taking the form of mental conversation. Robert Jordan is especially skilled at this. He thinks by talking to himself, and he often does so by splitting his thinking self into an "I" who addresses a "you." Sometimes he even adds in a third person, a "he." "*Who are you talking to?*" Robert can ask himself, once he has begun to think in this way. "Listen, he told himself. You better cut this out. This is very bad for you and for your work. Then himself said back to him, You listen, see? Because you are doing something very serious and I have to see you understand it all the time. I have to keep you straight in your head."

When carried to an extreme, these mental conversations begin to feel schizophrenic. Here is Robert recalling his failure of nerve after Pablo has disappeared with the detonators:

> But you were pretty bad back there. I was ashamed enough of you, there for a while. Only I was you. There wasn't any me to judge you. We were all in bad shape. You and me and both of us. Come on now. Quit thinking like a schizophrenic. One at a time, now.

These nine sentences comprise an insertion into the manuscript made by Hemingway during the process of revision (see JK/EH 83, chapter 38, page 8). They intrude into a passage in which Robert has been thinking about "the greatest gift that he had, the talent that fitted him for war; that ability not to ignore but to despise whatever bad ending there could be." So he is in something of a self-congratulatory mood. "Instead of the surety of failure," he now feels "confidence rising in him." The interpolated passage intrudes to cut across this mood and reminds Robert that his moods do not always believe in each other.

A self-amendment made by the author here makes possible self-amendment in a character. We see Robert as able to think while standing aloof from his own thought. Yet, in the added sentences, the motion of mind threatens to move past critical self-awareness into obsessive brooding. At such moments, a character is therefore justified in telling himself, as Robert does a few sentences further on, "So do not think." These frequent instructions made to the mind and scattered throughout Hemingway's work are, however, more honored in the breach than in the observance.

As the two or even three sides of Robert's mind muse, question, remember, and argue, he is able to arrive at resolutions and acceptances previously unavailable to characters unable or unwilling to bring to light the processes of their own thought. In doing so, Robert completes his education, a growing into selfhood that earns for him the ultimate tribute, one Hemingway renders on the novel's closing page: "He was completely integrated now."

The full sentence reads, "He was completely integrated now and he took a good long look at everything." It may be surprising to discover that a word given so much prominence in the narrative – the word *now* – did not originally appear in this sentence. In the manuscript, the sentence begins, "He was completely integrated again." In changing the word "again" to the word "now" during the typescript phase, Hemingway chose to represent Robert as just now coming into a felt sense of integration. The experience is not a repetition but a unique and climactic one.

An actual interpersonal exchange supplants Robert's habitual mental conversation in chapter thirty-one. Robert and Maria talk. The chapter's complex mix of talking, listening, and internal musing marks Hemingway's most ambitious attempt to represent the centrality of thinking in a fully integrated life.

The chapter is a joint creation made to meet a mutual need. It takes place on the last night Robert and Maria share together and begins with her apologizing for having too much "soreness" to be able to make love. "I am ashamed," Maria says, and then wonders whether her soreness comes "from when the things were done to me." Robert prefers not to "talk of that," thinks to himself that her condition is not good luck for a last night, and then feels "ashamed" for thinking so. Since they cannot make love, they begin to fantasize.

"Let us talk of Madrid," Robert proposes. In doing so, he surrenders "to the luxury of going into unreality." In repeating the phrase a few paragraphs further on – "Then he surrendered again and let himself slip into it, feeling a voluptuousness of surrender into unreality" – Hemingway signals Robert's conscious awareness of entertaining a fiction as a fiction. Maria joins in, helping to imagine their hotel room and the buying of new clothes.

The surmise becomes qualified when Maria tells Robert that "the Pilar told me that we would all die tomorrow and that you know it as well as she does." After hearing this, "there was no slipping into make-believe again." Now Robert feels himself simply "lying to his girl." But he nevertheless once again starts surmising, and they begin to talk about Maria's hair growing long, like Garbo's at the cinema.

Robert's throat grows thick at the thought, and he surrenders again: "Now the making believe was coming back in a great rush and he would take it all to him. It had him now, and again he surrendered and went on." Added by hand to the typed manuscript, the sentences quoted indicate Hemingway's commitment to affirming the central place of surmise in a fully realized relationship. And it is out of these harmless and gentle surmises that the later painful and educating revelations will arise.

It is not so easy, as Robert Jordan does here, to engage in "a complete embracing of all that would not be." Making believe requires the continual vigilant awareness that the mind has committed itself to something made, contingent, and wholly dependent upon the faithfulness of the human spirit. The experience called "love" is the ultimate making believe, and, in chapter thirty-one, Hemingway allows two characters to create the possibility of an enduring love out of one last night of pillow talk.

While Maria wants "to learn to be a wife," the primary work being forwarded here is Robert's learning to be a husband. His education takes him somewhat unawares when Maria asks, "is there not some other thing that I can do for thee?" Robert demurs, but the issue of sexual doing has been broached, and so Maria follows her own train of thought, wondering if "I could tell thee of what was done to me if I ever began to think of it again." Despite Robert's saying "Do not tell it," and despite Maria's feeling "as though it had never happened since we were first together," she proceeds to tell her story.

Much of what she tells Robert was added in revision by Hemingway; he did not at first imagine the need to include so many detailed rememberings of Maria's story. All of page 351 in the novel was interpolated into an earlier draft. The added material begins near the bottom of page 350 with "After the shooting of the *matadero*" and ends at the top of page 352 with the words "feel the scar with thy finger." The interpolated material includes two key incidents: the death of Maria's parents at the hands of the Falangists and the shaving of her head.

Maria's parents die with dignity, and, in the last sentence of the chapter, Robert will say to her, "I'm very proud of your family." Part of his education involves imagining a partner's Family Romance as integral with his own. Even more important is the necessity for "a good man," as Pilar calls Robert, to accept the woman he loves as coming to him with prior sexual experience. While Maria holds off from describing the physical act of rape itself, the details leading up to it are hard enough to take. She is tied by the wrists in a long line of girls. Then she is lifted into a barber chair, her braids are cut off and stuffed into her mouth, and she is shaved with clippers while looking on at "the horror" in the mirror. Maria ends up being carried to her father's office. "And it was there that the bad things were done," Maria concludes. Robert listens and then signals having heard enough by saying, "Do not tell me any more."

Hemingway here reveals Robert as not quite up to the task of living out the consequences of the claim Faulkner had so much admired. The claim is made relatively early in *For Whom the Bell Tolls*: as we have seen, the passage Temple Drake remembers from Hemingway is found not in chapter thirty-one but only some seventy pages into the novel, in chapter seven. "She said that nothing is done to oneself that one does not accept and that if I loved some one it would take it all away." Maria repeats Pilar's words near the end of chapter seven, after Robert has already made the complementary claim: "No one has done anything to thee. Thee, they cannot touch."

In chapter thirty-one, on her last night with Robert, Maria takes the risk of sharing with him "something that ought to have remained hidden and secret, and yet comes to light." Her history shatters the fantasy at the heart of heterosexual marriage, that a woman can come to a man as virginal and intact. In mingling the story of her parent's marriage with the story of Maria's abuse at the hands of the fascists, Hemingway imposes upon Robert a strong sense of standing in as a replacement rather than allowing him to indulge the illusion of being Maria's unique and original love.

After Robert and Maria say good night, he continues to think about "the part she had not told him." He speculates on the Spanish character and on whether he truly understands it. "To understand is to forgive," he ventures. Robert then thinks against the thought just expressed: "That's not true. Forgiveness has been exaggerated." At the chapter's end, we see him beside himself in a sane sense, proposing wisdoms and also subjecting them to criticism. We see him thinking, at home in "his mind, that was his best companion."

Hemingway has prepared the way for this achievement by enacting a painful progression of thought in the preceding chapter. As he broods on the coming military offensive, six paragraphs into chapter thirty, Robert tells himself, "The orders on this are very clear." At this point in the text,

Hemingway interpolated twenty-one handwritten pages that eventually reduced down to five pages of print. Written in a strong, sure hand with only a few minor insertions and crossings out, the added pages begin with the words "Too very clear" and look to have been composed in one fell swoop. In them, Robert Jordan is granted a more detailed and emotion-laden family history than any other Hemingway character has been or will be granted.

In this famous passage, Robert remembers his father's suicide and being given the gun by the coroner. The next day, he rode up to the high country and to a deep lake where he "climbed out on a rock and leaned over and saw his face in the still water, and saw himself holding the gun." For Robert, the mirror-moment allows him to act out a symbolic suicide and so prepares him for his decision at the end of the novel not to repeat "that business that my father did." Only after remembering this moment, and in sharing the felt consequences of it with himself during his final reverie, as Maria shares her trauma with Robert in chapter thirty-one, can he become integrated again.

Robert goes on to remember his grandfather and his Indian relics, raises the question of whether "the good juice" might skip a generation, recalls the sick feeling of knowing for the first time that his father was a coward, judges that "if he wasn't a coward he would have stood up to that woman," and comes to rest on a question: "I wonder what I would have been like if he had married a different woman."

These memories circle around the lingering possibility of embarrassment. Robert imagines a meeting between himself, his father, and his grandfather. "Then, as he thought, he realized that if there was any such thing as ever meeting, he and his grandfather would be acutely embarrassed by the presence of his father." While Robert can bring many of the painful facts of his family past to light, he cannot resolve his relationship with them. He remains especially stuck on the question of the mother, a figure granted a power to shape the destinies of both a father and a son. In concluding his foray into the past, Robert engages in a qualified act of forgiveness: "He understood his father and he forgave him everything and he pitied him but he was ashamed of him."

"Who forgives?" Anselmo asks Robert Jordan early on – who forgives "since we do not have God here any more?" "It is thyself who will forgive thee," Robert Jordan answers. Here, he seems sure enough of the answer. But it is an answer Robert must continually relearn as he struggles not only with the morality of killing men but with the complexities of having a family history and an emotional life. What Robert Jordan cannot quite forgive when he thinks of his father is his own shame. In staging this insight, Hemingway again makes the case for the kind of forgiveness that matters most to him – self-forgiveness. The claim "nothing is done to oneself that one does not accept" refers above all to the emotions a self inflicts upon itself as it responds to the thing done. The not accepting is the self-forgiveness. A self can only begin to free itself of shame and guilt and embarrassment, as Hemingway demonstrates in the two extraordinary chapters dealing with Robert Jordan's last night on earth, by thinking hard about these feelings and by finding someone with whom they can be shared.

Hemingway asks Robert Jordan to confront his embarrassment about his father a second time, when, in saying good-by to Maria before the attack on the bridge, he remembers the farewell with his father at the train. His father had kissed him good-bye and offered a blessing and "his moustache had been moist and his eyes were damp with emotion and Robert Jordan had been so embarrassed by all of it . . . that he could hardly bear it." This is the old familiar Hemingway embarrassment over expressed emotion, and it is time that it be overcome. With Maria, "now, at this parting," he feels "as young again as he had felt before that train left." In this moment of awkward repetition, Robert is able to recall the earlier "awkwardness," to feel it again, to understand its source, and, in acknowledging the perpetual liability of a grown man to feel so young again, to find a way to forgive in his father what he must accept as alive in himself.

With the mother, it is more complicated. In the novel, Robert's mother forms the limit of contraction on his memories of his father. His thinking about his family ends with a speculation: "Maybe the bully in her helped to supply what was missing in the other." Beyond this, nothing more is conveyed about this unnamed "her." Hemingway will never make a direct and separate peace with this haunting figure. Instead, he approaches all that the mother has come to stand for through that diffused set of fantasies and apprehensions and behaviors I have called "the uncanny."

In learning to face the fact of and the history behind Maria's sexuality, Robert makes his own kind of peace with the experience of having originated from a female body. Nick Adams at Indian Camp is the first Hemingway character to experience the mother's body as the uncanny thing. That body, in turn, stands at the center of a complex set of recognitions that come to be understood by the Hemingway hero as constituting the facts of life. In implicating himself in "the crime of death and birth," as Yeats calls it – in loving a woman and in fathering a child – a man risks exposure to a mix of self-loss, anxiety, guilt, and responsibility. Given the weight of these burdens, the husband in "Indian Camp" deems it simpler to step aside.

"Let me see thy hand," Pilar says to Robert Jordan, during their first meeting. He has already raised the issue of fortune-telling when he talks to Anselmo about "looking into the future in English"; anticipating outcomes is, after all, to be expected in a story dealing with the proper timing of an explosion. With the introduction of Pilar, a seasoned hand-reader, the practice of divination becomes an explicit theme.

By being explicit, Hemingway is able to divest divination of its uncanny force. In chapter two, Pilar looks into Robert's hand, drops it, and stands up without saying anything. She performs this expressive series of gestures after Robert has had to deal with Pablo's accurately predictive question, "If you are wounded in such a thing as this bridge, you would be willing to be left behind?" Readers are required from the beginning of the novel, then, to live with a strong indication of how it will end. But this awareness works in a way quite different than does the sense of fatality conjured at the beginning of *A Farewell to Arms*. In *For Whom the Bell Tolls*, Hemingway makes it possible to read forward with hope and to "despise whatever bad ending there could be."

By filling rather than killing time, and by asking his reader to live through virtually every moment of Robert's seventy happy hours, including even his dreams, Hemingway negates the operative power of "a man seeing ahead what is to happen to him." Immersion dispels apprehension. Even Pilar will back away from her unspoken prediction, dismissing "that thing of the hand" as "gypsy nonsense." Somewhat earlier, in chapter nineteen, she insists, however, on defending the practice of divination one last time. It occurs during a discussion of being able to smell one's death in advance. Pilar issues explicit instructions for divining "death-to-come" through the senses. It is a passage marked by a bravery of style that is also a breaking of style:

> It is important that the day be in autumn with rain, or at least some fog, or early winter even and now thou shoudst continue to walk through the city and down the Calle de Salud smelling what thou wilt smell where they are sweeping out the *casas de putas* and emptying the slop jars into the drains and, with this odor of love's labor lost mixed sweetly with soapy water and cigarette butts only faintly reaching thy nostrils, thou shouldst go on to the Jardín Botánico where at night those girls who can no longer work in the houses do their work against the iron gates of the park and the iron picketed fences and upon the sidewalks. It is there in the shadow of the trees against

> the iron railings that they will perform all that a man wishes; from the simplest requests at a remuneration of ten centimos up to a peseta for that great act that we are born to and there, on a dead flower bed that has not yet been plucked out and replanted, and so serves to soften the earth that is so much softer than the sidewalk, thou wilt find an abandoned gunny sack with the odor of the wet earth, the dead flowers, and the doings of that night. In this sack will be contained the essence of it all, both the dead earth and the dead stalks of the flowers and their rotted blooms and the smell that is both the death and birth of man.

In this sack will be contained the essence of it all: in this astonishing passage, Hemingway offers his reader a grab bag filled with his obsessive subject matter.

Scribner's objected to Pilar's speech as "definitely horrifying" and pressured Hemingway to remove it. In a letter to Max Perkins, Hemingway admitted that the speech might "make an ugly noise when played alone." But it was necessary to retain it:

> The smell of death part (chapter 19) seems to me to be an integral and valid part of the whole thing. You remember there is a whole dark business about that from the very start ... the question about forebodeings.... It isn't dragged in.... The book is one whole thing; not just a lot of parts.

Hemingway had perhaps written better than he knew, since the passage was integral not only to *For Whom the Bell Tolls* but to a twenty-year struggle with the "mysterious and homelike."

The "whole dark business" alluded to in the letter to Perkins had been going on not only from the beginning of *For Whom the Bell Tolls* but from "the very start" of Hemingway's career. It is "integral"; it is "a valid part of the whole thing." "Death and birth," Pilar says, as if to remind us of the conflation of beginnings and ends experienced by Nick in "Indian Camp." Once again, life begins and ends in a "dead ... bed." And yet, even as Hemingway defends the centrality of this material to Max Perkins, his novel is bidding it farewell. Psychic material once approached with the utmost seriousness is reduced in "the smell of death part" of the novel to something in which Robert is having his nose rubbed. While he plays along in order to humor Pilar, he is clear in his refusal to accept her fantasy as anything more than debris from an unexcavated unconscious. And that is the brilliance of the passage – to take the elements that make up Hemingway's "uncanny complex" and to mix them together into such an absurd jumble as to divest them of their power and their force.

The sentence beginning "In this sack will be contained the essence of it all" was added by Hemingway in revision; it is one more instance of the workings of a second will. The word "revision" acknowledges the priority of the already-seen: it is a visioning again, a turning back rather than an original departure. Revision accepts the givenness of things even as it expresses the hope that they can be changed for the better. In acknowledging an insufficiency, and in seeking to correct it, revision operates throughout Hemingway's career as a kind of self-forgiveness. To cut from or to add to the text is to model through the act of composition the kind of self-scrutiny and self-amendment a character like Robert Jordan so courageously seeks.

These capacities are put to the test as Robert lies dying and resolves not to "do that business that my father did." He honors his place in a family line by refusing to repeat the patterns laid down by that line. Robert chooses not to kill himself, as his father had. But he does find himself thinking about doing so and is therefore required to enact a kind of temptation scene. As the pain in his crushed leg increases, he says to himself, "I will do it all right but I'd much prefer not to have to." In surviving the temptation, and in moving through embarrassment over his father to empathy with him, Robert ends in a loving refusal to emulate. In creating Robert Jordan, Hemingway displays his willingness to imagine characters who come to understand freedom as *the power to revise a story*.

"Farewell is about the best word I know in English," Hemingway wrote to Arnold Gingrich in 1932, and his longest novel contains his most satisfying farewell. On their last morning together, Robert and Maria stage a preliminary version of their leavetaking. Robert says "Good-by *guapa*, I will see thee soon." As he says this he has "an unreal feeling about all of this now as though he had said it all before or as though it were a train that were going, especially as though it were a train and he was standing on the platform of a railway station." It is at this point that Robert remembers his father's farewell at the train.

The Hemingway male has been afflicted by such reminiscences, as when Frederic experiences falling in love with Catherine as a game played before, "seeing it ahead like the moves in a chess game," or when Jake "felt as I felt once" as he crosses the square in Pamplona after being beaten up by Robert Cohn. In such moments, a character is visited by an "anxiety" that "can be shown to come from something repressed which *recurs*." The uncanny is always there, just out of sight, and Hemingway's habits of repetition operate at once to express and to repress it. In this way, it remains both mysterious and homelike. Such returnings of the repressed structure, in displaced forms, a good part of Frederic's and Jake's inner lives.

With Robert Jordan, it may look the same, but it is different. Like Frederic and Jake, he is sometimes visited by a sense of déjà vu. It first happens when he attempts to provoke Pablo, "knowing as he spoke that this had all been gone through before; having that feeling that he was playing a part from memory of something that he had read or had dreamed, feeling it all moving in a circle." And it happens in the initial good-bye with Maria, when he is carried back to the scene at the train:

> "Good-by, *guapa*," he said awkwardly.
>
> "*Salud*, Roberto."
>
> Robert Jordan had not felt this young since he had taken the train at Red Lodge to go down to Billings to get the train there to go away to school for the first time.

Able now to range around in time, Robert says good-bye to Maria, is reminded of the scene with his father at the train, restages the scene in his mind, and then returns to the present moment:

> It was only now, at this parting, that he ever felt as young again as he had felt before that train left. He felt very young now and very awkward and he was saying good-by as awkwardly as one can be when saying good-by to a young girl when you are a boy in school, saying good-by at the front porch, not knowing whether to kiss the girl or not. Then he knew that it was not the good-by he was being awkward about. It was the meeting he was going to. The good-by was only a part of the awkwardness he felt about the meeting.

The awkwardness Robert feels with his father at the train is about expressed emotion; his father's eyes are damp with it. Feeling awkwardness now, with Maria, Robert realizes it is not about feelings being felt and displayed but rather about "the meeting he was going to." Presumably the meeting being anticipated is with "the way all men end." Robert feels awkward because in saying "I will see thee soon," he is saying something that may not be true. He may not, in fact, see her soon. He may be killed. He is not feeling the awkwardness of something repressed that is recurring – he is freeing himself of that – but rather the awkwardness of whether his words can mean what they say. And this is important to him since the one thing he owes her at the end is accuracy. "Keep it accurate," he says to himself, "Quite accurate."

The final good-bye, which takes place almost sixty pages later, has been purged of all awkwardness. Robert has brought to light and forgiven in himself his embarrassed feelings about his father and is now, given his crushed leg and the agreement that he is to be left behind, quite sure he is going to die. The pain in his leg even becomes so severe that he finds himself considering suicide: "Listen, if I do that now you wouldn't misunderstand, would you? *Who are you talking to*?" he thinks to himself. "Grandfather, I guess," is the answer, but then he says "No," since the clear answer to the question is the word "father," a man whose "cowardice" Robert has been permitted to understand in a new and startling way. And he is able to come to such recognitions after having said, in perfect sincerity, the most true and beautiful thing one Hemingway character ever says to another: "I go with thee."

Like so many of the things said and done and remembered in *For Whom the Bell Tolls*, Robert's farewell is a repetition with a difference. A model of faithfulness has earlier been provided by Don Guillermo and his wife. In Pilar's story of the day of revolution in a small town, Don Guillermo is the fifth man to be brought out and made to walk between the lines of flails. He walks forward well and calmly. "He was a fascist, too, for the religiousness of his wife which he accepted as his own due to his love for her." As he stands looking at the double line, a woman begins to scream. "'Guillermo,' she cried. 'Guillermo. Wait and I will be with thee.'" He waves toward the sound. A drunkard yells out "Guillermo," in mockery, and Don Guillermo runs toward the man, "blindly, with tears now running down his cheeks." And then the lines begin to fill up with drunkards. "After Don Guillermo," Pilar says, "I felt a feeling of shame and distaste."

And so a wife of an enemy is allowed to voice the same words with which Robert will attempt to comfort Maria. "With thee," she cries, as in "I go with thee." It is this reaching across a political and emotional gap, this capacity to empathize with the enemy, and to grant her one's own fears and longings, that sets *For Whom the Bell Tolls* apart.

"Go," Robert keeps saying to Maria, "stand up and go and we both go." If you go, "I go with thee." In what sense can this possibly be true? In many of the ways that matter and perhaps in the way that matters most. Earlier, Robert has told himself that "What you have with Maria . . . is the most important thing that can happen to a human being. There will always be people who say it does not exist because they cannot have it." Love is an experience believed into being, and, as Robert argues, people can only experience what they believe to be possible. Love is a rumor kept alive by stories, stories like the one told in *For Whom the Bell Tolls*, and whether or not a reader assents to the offered fiction, despite all the awkwardnesses surrounding Robert's and Maria's three days together, will depend in part upon whether or not she believes she can have it, too.

"That we have had," Robert thinks to himself in chapter thirty-nine. "That cannot be taken away nor lost." He says this to himself as he and

Pablo set out with the ammunition that will blow the bridge. Two claims are being made here; that he has "had" love and that love, once had, cannot be taken away. Once brought into existence, love *exists*. It may be the truest thing about us, the warrant of our willingness to care and to give and to take in the face of our personal mortality.

Robert errs, however, in casting his experience of love into the past tense, and he will correct the tenses as he lies alone and waits for the riders to reach the sunlit place. "I hate to leave it very much and I hope I have done some good in it. I have tried to with what talent I had," he tells himself. Then he issues the correction, one Hemingway also issued to himself, since the two italicized sentences that follow were penciled in between the lines of Hemingway's manuscript: "*Have, you mean. All right, have.*" This is where Robert has learned to live, in the eternity of the "now." Having done so – having really lived – he has earned the privilege of saying what he says to Maria.

The truth of Robert's claim resides in part in the chosen tense: he does not say "I *will* go with thee." He says "I go with thee." This is not simply a comforting way of speaking; in saying these words, and in keeping it all in the present tense, Robert is making a literal claim about an imaginative truth. He invokes the continuous present in which their love lives. Maria goes and survives in order to keep the chain of loving and remembering alive. In saying what he says, Robert is being "accurate." He will always go with Maria in her heart, which is the only way, Hemingway has come to understand and accept, that any of us – in life or in death – ever really go with anyone.

CHAPTER 11

Befriending
The Old Man and the Sea

In May 1952, Hemingway accepted an offer to print the entirety of *The Old Man and the Sea* in a single issue of *Life* magazine for the sum of $40,000. When the magazine appeared in September, it sold 5,318,650 copies in two days. The novel won the Pulitzer Prize in 1953, and, a year later, was singled out for praise in Hemingway's Nobel Prize citation. Within five years of its publication, *The Old Man and the Sea* had been translated into twenty-six languages. Reviewing the novel in *Shenandoah*, William Faulkner began with a two-word sentence fragment: "His best."

Faulkner's words have an elegiac lilt, as if he were writing out of a moment in which it had become possible to single out the pre-eminent achievement of a now-finished career. As the 1950s wore on, and as no additional books by Hemingway came into print, the sentence might have been amended to read, "His last." And Santiago's story, to borrow a title from *In Our Time*, can be read as "The End of Something." Or, as Hemingway wrote in "Big Two-Hearted River," "It made a good ending to the story." It makes a good ending to the story of Hemingway's writing life because, in it, that which could be accomplished has been accomplished, and now the time has come to rest, and to dream of lions.

The Old Man and the Sea does not, however, conclude with a strong sense of an ending. Once back in his shack, Santiago falls asleep in exhaustion, and, when he wakes to find Manolin offering him hot coffee, he tells the boy that he is not "lucky" anymore. But Manolin soon has him talking about fishing together again and about the need to get a good killing lance and how to grind it. No more did Hemingway, after finishing his "best" book and receiving his prize, cease from his work. Given the number of books quarried posthumously out of the pages written by him during the 1950s, the almost ten years that remained to Hemingway after the publication of *The Old Man and the Sea* can be regarded as one of his most productive periods. A novel appearing to mark the end of something had in fact opened the way for a late-life flourishing.

The story of an old fisherman who catches a huge fish and then loses it to sharks was first told by Hemingway in a 1936 *Esquire* article called "On the Blue Water." Three years later, Max Perkins received a letter about some "very long" stories Hemingway intended to write, including one about "the old commercial fisherman who fought the swordfish." It was to contain "everything he does and everything he thinks in all that long fight with the boat out of sight of all the other boats all alone on the sea." Five years later, Hemingway again alluded to his desire to write a "novel – not war book. It should have the sea and the air and the ground in it."

It was not until January 1951, however, that Hemingway actually began writing *The Old Man and the Sea.* He worked at a furious pace, sometimes more than tripling his normal output of five hundred words a day. Completed in six weeks, the Santiago story was still being conceived of by Hemingway as Part 4 of the big "sea book" that had preoccupied him since the end of the Second World War.

In the eighteen months between the completion of the novel and its appearance in print, Hemingway suffered three incalculable losses. His mother Grace died in June 1951. Pauline Hemingway died that October, at the age of fifty-six. After a violent telephone conversation with Ernest about their wayward son Gregory, Pauline had gone to bed in tears. Awakened by a "horrendous scream" in the early morning hours, Virginia Pfeiffer rushed her sister to Los Angeles's St. Vincent's Hospital. The doctors, aware that Pauline's blood pressure had skyrocketed and then dropped precipitously, but unable to locate the source of her pain, watched her die of shock on the operating table. An autopsy revealed "a rare and unusual tumor of the adrenal medulla." The tumor could be stimulated to secrete an abnormal amount of adrenaline in response to "a sudden stressful incident."

In February, 1952, Charles Scribner, Jr. died of a heart attack. Scribner had replaced Max Perkins as a correspondent after Perkins's death in 1947 and had been intimately involved in helping to prepare *The Old Man and the Sea* for publication. Hemingway had written "Charlie" in the summer of 1951, reassuring him that "if anything happened to him, Scribner could safely publish 'the old man and the sea' as one small book." "I was very happy you liked what you read," Hemingway wrote to Scribner in March 1951, "but I would have thought you a certifiable fool if you had not (he says cheerfully)."

Michael Reynolds speculates that the losses suffered by Hemingway during this period gave him access to memories and feelings that made it possible for him to begin *The Garden of Eden*, a story deeply rooted in his honeymoon with Pauline. Here is what Hemingway wrote to Scribner on the day after Pauline had died: "The wave of remembering has finally risen so that it has broken over the jetty that I built to protect the open roadstead of my heart and I have the full sorrow of Pauline's death with all the harbour scum of what caused it. I loved her very much for many years and the hell with her faults."

If there is a rupture in the Hemingway story, a collapse of the defenses he had built to protect himself from a tsunami of regret, it appears to have occurred in the months after the completion and before the publication of *The Old Man and the Sea*. It was time, as it is for David Bourne in writing the elephant story in *The Garden of Eden*, to begin "attacking each thing that for years he had put off facing." While this act of facing would make many things possible, including *The Garden of Eden* and *A Moveable Feast*, it marked the end of something as well. That ending was at once a culmination and a departure, a work of summation that stands wonderfully and terribly alone. It occurred in *The Old Man and the Sea*, and it could only have happened there because the novel was completed *before* a wave of remembering broke through the roadstead of its author's heart.

Hemingway's work can be read as a continual search for an ever-elusive home, one expressive of a longing that achieves temporary satisfaction in *The Old Man and the Sea*. "Let us take the stuff home," Manolin says in the opening pages, as he picks up the gear from Santiago's boat. They walk up the road together to the old man's shack and "through its open door." There is a bed, a table, a chair, and a place on the dirt floor for cooking with charcoal. On the walls are "relics of his wife," a picture of the Sacred Heart of Jesus and another of the Virgin of Cobre. "Once there had been a tinted photograph of his wife on the wall but he had taken it down because it made him too lonely to see it and it was on the shelf in the corner under his clean shirt."

After Santiago goes out "too far" and loses the marlin to the sharks, he will turn back toward "the glow of Havana" and head home to his "good town." He finds the current and "knew where he was now and it was nothing to get home." He thinks about "bed" as "a great thing" and, once in it, falls asleep with his arms out straight and his palms up. In the morning Manolin comes to the shack, and, when he sees the old man's cut and battered hands, he begins to cry. When Santiago wakes up, Manolin brings him coffee and the old man notices "how pleasant it was to have someone to talk to instead of speaking only to himself and to the sea."

In the easeful and caring give-and-take between Manolin and Santiago, Hemingway creates an indelible "fiction" of adoption. "If you were my boy," Santiago says to Manolin early on. "But you are your father's," he continues, as if to chasten a wish so openly expressed. Manolin never uses the word "father," although he does once refer to "papa." Otherwise, he speaks only of his father as a "he": "He is almost blind"; "I do not like for him to waken me. It is as though I were inferior"; "He never wants anyone to carry anything." Santiago responds, "We're different . . . . I let you carry things when you were five years old." As Carlos Baker writes, Manolin's love for Santiago is "the love of a son for an adopted father."

Hemingway was never very big on blood ties. The primary bonds in his fictions are affiliative rather than filial. In *The Old Man and the Sea*, this activity of reaching out in a horizontal rather than a vertical way reaches its extreme limit. The imagination of the book, which speaks for Santiago even when he himself is not speaking, engages in a continual act of *befriending.*

Given the pervasive *heimlich* mood, it is surprising to discover how often Santiago uses the word "strange." To Manolin he says, "I am a strange old man," and the claim is repeated after the marlin has sounded and he vows to kill him in all his greatness and glory. "'I told the boy I was a strange old man,' he said. 'Now is when I must prove it.'"

But this strangeness has nothing to do with estrangement. It is in fact a quality Santiago shares with the fish he must kill: "'If you're not tired fish,' he said aloud, 'you must be very strange.'" Once the fish has been lashed to the skiff, Santiago recalls him hanging "motionless in the sky before he fell" and is "sure there was some great strangeness." The turtles, too, are "strange in their love-making," as is the water in "the strange undulation of the calm."

Hemingway's use of the word "strange" provides a small example of the controlling pattern of the book: the continual finding of likeness. This work is forwarded most obviously by the use of simile. What makes this act of finding likeness strange is that a hallmark of the early Hemingway style had been its avoidance of figurative language. A marked change is being announced when Hemingway chooses to end the opening paragraph of his novel with a simile: "The sail was patched with flour sacks and, furled, it looked like the flag of permanent defeat."

A more relaxed approach to figuration is accompanied by an easing of the strictures on what can or should be voiced. While vestiges of the old superstitions remain – "he knew that if you said a good thing it might not happen" – Santiago nevertheless talks a considerable amount. This speaking aloud allows Hemingway to externalize a drama largely interior. Santiago thinks about the fish and the sharks, of course, but also about Joe DiMaggio and the lions on the beach in Africa and about the time he won "the hand game." "Now he said his thoughts aloud," Hemingway writes. The point is to bring what is in the mind into the light by giving it the shape and sound of spoken words. As Santiago performs this work, he remembers, wishes, regrets, and, above all, ventures comparisons.

As early as December 1926, a reviewer of *The Sun Also Rises* had noted "that neither in his short stories nor in this novel does Hemingway make use of a single simile. To him things are not 'like' other things." Years later, as Max Perkins wrestled with Scribner's over the use of four-letter words in *A Farewell to Arms*, he expressed an awareness that "any circumlocutions . . . would be inconsistent with the way you write. . . . I pointed out as an instance that you almost never even used a simile."

Of course, similes and metaphors can be found along the way, as when in "The End of Something" Marjorie refers to the abandoned mill as "our old ruin." She then pushes her impulse toward comparison a little further by way of an overt simile: "It seems more like a castle." The sentence that follows – "Nick said nothing" – indicates his impatience with this mode of responding to the world and may form part of the basis for his feeling that love "isn't fun anymore." As if to demonstrate his own expertise, Hemingway follows Marjorie's lazy comparisons with an audacious one. A trout's back comes up out of the water and makes the minnows jump wildly. "They sprinkled the surface like a handful of shot thrown into the water."

So, yes, I can play this game, too, Hemingway's lovely simile suggests. I, too, can bring to the surface the mind's continual seeking after similitude in dissimilitude. That I will not continue to do so after this one instance of showing that I can arises from my desire to leave such work to the reader, who, in being asked to move through a verbal terrain where everything seems so carefully noticed as to have to mean something, is to be left on his or her own in the figuring out of what these meanings might be.

The pervasive sense of an overwhelming symbolic logic hovering just below the level of the literal is a feeling Hemingway's early style at once arouses and suppresses. The uncanny mood of a story like "Indian Camp" depends upon the way in which it insinuates without actually spelling out the fact that something more is going on than meets the eye. From the perspective of rhetorical decorum, Hemingway's investment in "the uncanny" thus acquires a stylistic as well as a psychological dimension. In a metaphoric prose, a tenor (the subject) is accompanied by its vehicle (the metaphorical term itself). The abandoned mill is the tenor; "our old ruin" is the vehicle. When he is operating on the iceberg principle, the surface of Hemingway's prose presents itself to us as the vehicle of an unnamed tenor. In refusing overt figuration, Hemingway creates the sensation that even the smallest detail in his prose may, in fact, be figurative. When Hemingway turns to metaphor, or to the even more obvious comparisons enforced by the "like" or "as" of a simile, he makes explicit that implicit tension between the literal and the figurative that had given his early work its air of suspicious calm.

In *The Old Man and the Sea*, the sail "like a flag of permanent defeat" is followed by scars in the hand "as erosions in a fishless desert" and by eyes "the same color as the sea." There are clouds "like mountains" and clouds "like friendly piles of ice cream." As the first night falls, Santiago passes "a great island of Sargasso weed that heaved and swung in the light sea as though the ocean were making love with something under a yellow blanket." When he lashes the fish to his boat, Santiago notices that "the fish's eye looked as detached as the mirrors in a periscope or as a saint in a procession." The shark's teeth also earn a double comparison: "They were shaped like a man's fingers when they are crisped like claws."

Metaphors and similes extend human consciousness out into the universe of things. Under their power, the disparate is brought close; our figurations attempt to make a home out of the world. In so reading the sea and the sky, the narrative voice of *The Old Man and the Sea* continuously expands the territory that can be included in the good place. This ongoing act of figuration forwards a work of befriending that allows Philip Young to read the novel in his 1966 "Reconsideration" as issuing from "a writer who is at long last completely at home in this life and world."

It is perhaps more accurate to say that the novel forwards a *fiction* of so being at home. Early on, Manolin asks Santiago, "May I take the cast net?" He asks the question even though he knows "there was no cast net and the boy remembered when they had sold it. But they went through this fiction every day." In this offhand and seemingly inconsequential moment, Hemingway signals to his reader that the way ahead will involve going through a fiction together.

Santiago likes "to think about all things that he was involved in," and these relations appear to stop nowhere. Engaging in an ongoing and unforced perception of linkages and family resemblances, Santiago's fiction of belonging expresses itself most openly through his repeated use of the words "brother" and "friend."

In *Concealments in Hemingway's Works* (1983), Gerry Brenner attempts to read Santiago "antithetically." He proceeds to question "why *brother* dominates Santiago's word-hoard" and reminds us of Santiago's claim: "There are three things that are brothers: the fish and my two hands." And he discovers a telling pun, arguing that "Santiago's wishes for Manolin to be with him are wishes for a brother, since a *mano*(lin) is literally a little hand, figuratively a small brother."

Bridling against the "halo" that seems to surround Santiago's skiff, Brenner proceeds: "An antithetical reading of Santiago's fraternal ethic finds it self-serving. It grants Santiago and any who embrace that brotherly ideal a measure of irresponsibility not available to people who must fulfill the role of parent, spouse, or child. Quite simply, a brother's responsibilities have only the force of religious commandment; psychologically self-imposed, they are not obligatory. A brother can honor fraternal responsibilities and bask, modestly or immodestly, in the self-satisfaction of his supererogation. Or a brother can ignore those responsibilities without feeling guilty."

Hemingway was himself a master at making and breaking friendships, and it is a question as to whether the fraternal relation was not his most cherished human tie. He spent so little time with his three sons as to make it difficult to conceive of him as serving as more than a fantasy father figure, despite the idealizations that may have occurred after the fact. With both friends and wives he was given to dramas of replacement, and it is sad and moving to see him at the end of his life accompanied by so few of the people he had loved along the way. Seeking always for continuity in his writing life, Hemingway's experience of human relationships appears to have called forth in him, as Fitzgerald wrote, an intensity so powerful as often to burn itself out. Still, and despite the ill treatment at which he was so expert, Hemingway drew people to him. As Hadley was to remember, "men loved him, women loved him, children loved him, even dogs loved him."

We can perhaps lessen the harshness of Brenner's judgment of Santiago by returning to the word "fiction." Any saintliness Santiago possesses is being offered up by Hemingway not as an achievable identity but as an aspirational ideal, just as the natural world's responsiveness to Santiago's promptings is meant to indicate that we have once again entered into a romance. To object to Santiago's goodness or holiness or his conviction of belonging is to object not to a failure of representation but to Hemingway's choice of literary mode.

"Wasn't his lifelong subject *saintliness*?" Reynolds Price asks in his essay on Hemingway. "His search was not for survival and the techniques of survival but for goodness, thus victory." If such a search was in fact Hemingway's, it is an effort made all the more poignant given the honest admissions of the fallings short. Santiago, in Faulkner's words, is "*a might-have-been which is more true than truth*" – a supreme fiction – and it is against his achieved saintliness that Hemingway is asking us to measure both the deficiencies in our characters and in his own.

If there is a saintly model here, it is Saint Francis. Santiago feels "sorry for the birds" he sees "always flying and looking and almost never finding." The porpoises are called "brothers," and "the wind is our friend." Cosmic distance itself is abolished when Santiago calls the stars his "distant friends."

The old man even finds a way to collapse an aboriginal distinction on which Hemingway exerts an ever-increasing pressure as his career unfolds: the distinction between the slayer and the slain. "You are killing me, fish," he thinks to himself, as his hands begin to cramp and his back starts to ache. "I do not care who kills who," he goes on to admit. As he does so often, Santiago then turns upon his thought. "Now you are getting confused in the head, he thought. You must keep your head clear. Keep your head clear and know how to suffer like a man. Or a fish, he thought." In this thought, two animals are seen as comparable by way of a shared capacity for suffering.

Santiago imagines that he can talk to the world. After the sun has risen on the second day with the fish, "a small bird came toward the skiff from the north." "How old are you," he asks the bird. He plays with the surmise of affinity for a few more sentences, noting that "the bird looked at him when he spoke." Then his mind turns to thoughts of the hawks that come out to meet sea birds. "But he said nothing of this to the bird who could not understand him anyway and who would learn about the hawks soon enough." Once again, Hemingway allows a character to extend and then to retract a surmise. In doing so, he represents Santiago's perceptions of affinity as self-critical rather than sentimental.

While Hemingway fills his novel with open and embraced comparisons, he is less invested in the truth value of these affirmations than in the activity of making them. Perceiving likeness is Santiago's way of entertaining the fiction of the world as a sufficient home. The emphasis falls upon the act of the mind, not upon the objects of thought. Yet a number of readings of *The Old Man and the Sea* have attempted to convert perceived likenesses into fixed symbols: the sea is a careless goddess, the sharks are critics, Santiago is Christ.

In the closing paragraphs of his novel, Hemingway anticipated the readings to which his novel would be subjected. A tourist sees the marlin skeleton affixed to Santiago's skiff and mistakes it for a shark. As Thomas Strychacz argues, the "several different groups of spectators" at the end "restore the act of interpretation as an element of plot. And, retrospectively, they invite readers to compare their experience of the text with those offered within the fictive world of the novella."

Carlos Baker initiated symbol-hunting in Hemingway when he isolated the images of mountain and plain in *A Farewell to Arms*. "Once the reader has become aware of what Hemingway is doing in those parts of his work which lie below the surface," Baker maintains, "he is likely to find symbols operating everywhere." Hemingway was in any case opposed to any such reading of *The Old Man and the Sea*. Writing to Bernard Berenson in the month of the book's publication, he maintained: "there isn't any symbolysm (mis-spelled). The sea is the sea. The old man is an old man. The boy is a boy and the fish is a fish. The shark are all sharks no better and no worse."

But when is a hand only a hand? Santiago worries a great deal about the condition of his hands, and his continual references to them gather into a powerful structure of imagery. In order to understand all that Santiago's hands can and cannot do for him, as well as to appreciate Hemingway's deft refusal to convert one of his recurring images into a definable symbol, it may be useful to trace the history of his writing about hands.

The image of the hand surfaces as early as "Indian Camp," where "Nick watched his father's hands scrubbing each other with the soap." The hands do not *mean* something here; what is meaning-bearing is Nick's falling back on synecdoche so as to bracket off a manageable part of what is happening from the unmanageable whole. The image resurfaces in "In Another Country" (1927), where a man who has lost the use of a key body part proves able to rise above, through moral or physical compensation, men in the book who are much more whole. Before the war, the major had been the greatest fencer in Italy; now he brings his "withered" hand to a hospital for treatments in which he has no confidence. The deeper injury, however, is internal and surfaces as a kind of postscript, when the major tells Nick, "A man must not marry," and leaves the room. He returns, apologizes, and says, "I would not be rude. My wife has just died. You must forgive me." The major then begins to cry. He cries openly and unashamedly, "his head up looking at nothing, carrying himself straight and soldierly." Few of Hemingway's characters are at once so dignified and so undefended.

The "thing of the hand" haunts *For Whom the Bell Tolls*, where it refers to reading the future in one's palm. Like many of Hemingway's heroes, Robert Jordan spends his time trying to see ahead. At first, he is open to Anselmo's question, "Can you read in the palm of the hand?"

> "No," Robert Jordan said and he dipped another cup of wine.
> "But if thou canst I wish thee would read in the palm of my hand and tell me what is going to pass in the next three days."

Anselmo recommends Pilar, she reads the palm, and, correctly foreseeing Robert's end, refuses to speak of what she sees. While its ending has been effectively given away, the novel settles into a debate over whether a man truly carries his fortune in his hand. This debate expands to cover all forms of divination and culminates in chapter nineteen. To the question "Do you believe in the possibility of a man seeing ahead what is to happen to him?" Robert replies that such forebodings are "evil visions," projections of what one fears, and therefore need not be accepted. "Seeing bad signs, one, with fear, imagines an end for himself and one thinks that imagining comes by divination." While Pilar marshals counter examples, she will, under the pressure of the attack on the bridge, finally renounce them: "In regard to that thing of the hand. That is all gypsy nonsense."

Robert's father has killed himself with a hand gun. Afterward, Robert throws the Smith and Wesson into the deepest lake he can find. He sees the reflection of himself "holding the gun" as he does so, sees himself pointing a gun at himself in the moment of disposing of it, and so has a premonition that he will repeat his father's act. It is against this "evil vision" that Robert's resistance to divination is meant above all to defend. And the novel upholds him in his resolve. Lying wounded at the end, Robert will refuse "to do that business that my father did." On the contrary: one of Robert's last acts is to touch "the palm of his hand against the pine needles where he lay." He uses his hand to extend his life. The novel literalizes the metaphor of the hand as fortune in order to reject it.

Writing is also a business of the hand. As we watch Robert sketching the bridge, "glad at last to have the problem under his hand," we encounter the sense of relief Hemingway may well have felt in 1939 in finally starting to write *For Whom the Bell Tolls*. There was no such gladness in writing *Across the River and into the Trees*. Hemingway's blustering denials of doubt in the project ("for Christ sake have some confidence," he wrote Charles Scribner, Jr. after receiving page proofs) are enough to suggest diminished confidence in his creative power.

More striking is the way in which this anxiety finds an objective correlative in a part of Colonel Cantwell's body. He makes love with his "big, long, strong, spatular fingered hand." The need for such dexterity has been contrived by Renata's indisposition, and the Colonel's hand proves useful despite having "been shot through twice":

> The wind was very cold and lashed their faces but under the blanket there was no wind nor nothing; only his ruined hand that searched for the island in the great river with the high steep banks.
>
> "That's it," she said.

The Colonel searches and finds twice more on the gondola ride. The injured man's prowess has been anticipated in *To Have and Have Not*, where Harry Morgan makes love to Marie with an arm from which the hand has been amputated. "Go ahead," Marie says. "Go ahead now. Put the stump there. Hold it there. Hold it. Hold it now. Hold it."

In *Across the River and into the Trees*, a gathering anxiety about what the hand can still do leads Hemingway to convert it into an object of fantastic power. While the Colonel downplays its sensitivity, Renata assures him, "There is very much sensation in that hand." It has become the stuff of her dreams: "last week, every night, or I think nearly every night, I dreamed about it, and it was a strange mixed-up dream and I dreamed it was the hand of Our Lord." Renata may confound the Colonel's hand with that of the Creator, but creation is the one thing the Colonel refuses to do with it:

> "But you got your hand honorably?"
>
> "Yes. Very honorably. On a rocky, bare assed-hill."
>
> "Please let me feel it," she said.
>
> "Just be careful around the center," the Colonel said. "It's split there and it still cracks open."
>
> "You ought to write," the girl said. "I mean it truly. So someone would know about such things."
>
> "No," the Colonel disagreed. "I have not the talent for it and I know too much."

The Colonel is more comfortable using his hand for sex than for writing. In his last memory of Renata, he beats up two sailors with a fist possessed of its own miraculous refractory period. "There is nothing broken in it and that sort of swelling always goes down." Attention here is displaced from one kind of tumescence to another: "I love you with two moderately swollen hands and all my heart." Hemingway thus asks a character to act out a fantasy that the hand can both stand in for and prove more resilient than the penis. Writing for the Colonel is at best a terminal occupation: "He reached into his pocket and found a pad and pencil. He put on the map reading light, and with his bad hand, printed a short message in block letters." Almost the last thing the Colonel does is to write something, in a sort of child's hand, and it is his will.

In *The Old Man and the Sea*, Santiago worries about nothing so much as the "treachery" of a hand. "If he cramps again let the line cut him off." Amputation is here a melodramatic extension of a deeper threat: a man who brings up things from the depths feels in danger of losing control of "the working part of his hand." Santiago's struggle is less against the marlin or the sharks than against his hands. So, when he addresses his hands as his brothers, it may be less an act of befriending than a token of the looming possibility of self-alienation. "There are three things that are brothers: the fish and my two hands." In the logic of the metaphor, Santiago can be seen as standing outside this announced brotherhood, one in which his hands seem to side with the very opponent they are meant to master. "'How do you feel, hand?' he asked the cramped hand that was almost as stiff as rigor mortis. 'I'll eat some more for you.'" The "you" is here reduced to the body part by way of which a man makes his living. Having no appetite himself, Santiago has become the feeder of his hands and keeps himself alive in the hope that they will return to his control.

Almost all we know of Santiago's past comes from his one extended memory of the hand game:

> They had gone one day and one night with their elbows on a chalk line on the table and their forearms straight up and their hands gripped tight. Each one was trying to force the other's hand down onto the table .... They changed the referees every four hours after the first eight so that the referees could sleep. Blood came out from under the fingernails of both his and the negro's hands and they looked each other in the eye and at their hands and forearms and the bettors went in and out of the room and sat on high chairs against the wall and watched .... And at daylight when the bettors were asking that it be called a draw and the referee was shaking his head, he had unleashed his effort and forced the hand of the negro down and down until it rested on the wood.

The prose here evokes a time when the power of a man's hand held him "dead even" or better with his competitors. And it raises the question of how long a man can remain willing or able to "sweat blood" over the labor of his hands.

Until he is dead, perhaps. "I'll stay with you until I am dead," Santiago says to the fish. He then imagines the fish to have answered: "He'll stay with me too, I suppose." In saying these things, Santiago not only reconfigures the marriage ceremony but reminds us of the experience on offer – one of staying with something.

"Stay with them," Santiago tells Manolin only a page in. He can allow his adopted son to stay with the lucky boat because he knows he can carry him with him in his heart. After Santiago cuts the working part of his hand and considers eating the bonito, he extends the reach of his promise to the fish: "you can stay with him forever." And, later, if the fish "stays down forever," "then I will stay down with him forever."

The drama of fidelity here being invoked has already been enacted in a scene where Santiago remembers hooking one of a pair of marlin. The panic-stricken female makes a wild, despairing fight and "all the time the male had stayed with her." Then the refrain begins: "He had stayed so close that the old man was afraid he would cut the line with his tail . . . the male fish had stayed by the side of the boat . . . the male fish jumped high in the air beside the boat to see where the female was and then went down deep, his lavender wings, that were his pectoral fins, spread wide and all his wide lavender stripes showing. He was beautiful, the old man remembered, and he had stayed."

He was beautiful, the old man remembered, and he had stayed. On re-reading *The Old Man and the Sea*, this was the sentence that stayed with me. My admiration for it only increased when on inspecting the manuscript I saw that it had been added by hand to Hemingway's typescript as one more evidence of the workings of a second will (See JK/EH 190, pages 26–42).

Of course, the old man's wife has not stayed. All we know of her is that she is gone and that looking at her photograph makes him feel too lonely so he keeps it on a shelf under his one clean shirt. The loneliness is the token of having kept her in memory. Near the end, Manolin says to Santiago, "I will bring you your clean shirt." If he carries through on the promise, it will involve an uncovering of loss.

Manuscript evidence suggests that Santiago may have lost his wife before she left him. As he approaches the little harbor, he finds himself thinking about various kinds of friends. "The wind is our friend, anyway, he thought. Then he added, sometimes. And the great sea with our friends and our enemies. And bed, he thought. Bed is my friend. Just bed, he thought."

Hemingway had originally allowed Santiago another thought, one taking the form of a question. It came after "Bed is my friend." In Item 190, the manuscript of *The Old Man and the Sea*, the question reads as follows: "Why did I never love bed when I had her? You did, he thought. But then you loved too many beds. But beds were all the same and the sea is a greater whore than all." After writing these sentences, Hemingway decided to cross them out. This was not the book in which to explore the plight of a husband who has loved too many beds.

Santiago's work is what there is left to stay with. All his other attachments are a kind of "fiction," a poem of the act of the mind. But his work is what he has, and, at the end, it is easy for Manolin to talk him into acquiring a new good killing lance as a replacement for his broken knife.

After the first shark hits, Santiago talks to himself. "But I must think, he thought. Because it is all I have left. That and baseball. I wonder how the great DiMaggio would have liked the way I hit him in the brain?" All the talk about baseball in the novel comes round to the great DiMaggio and his bone spurs. After his hand begins to cramp, Santiago tells himself to "be worthy of the great DiMaggio who does all things perfectly even with the pain of the bone spur in his heel." Santiago persists in the comparison despite his ignorance of the nature of the ailment. "What is a bone spur?" he goes on to ask himself. He thus acknowledges the power of a pain of which he cannot conceive. And he and DiMaggio are linked in another way, since Santiago will be required to swing at the sharks with any weapon that comes to hand, until all are lost or broken. "If I could have used a bat with two hands I could have killed the first one surely," he will be driven to say.

While working through pain makes the two men comparable, there is a difference involved: unlike DiMaggio, Santiago will not be forced by his pain into early retirement. Bone spurs were foremost among the injuries and ailments compelling DiMaggio to leave the game of baseball in the year in which *The Old Man and the Sea* was written. Hemingway saw baseball, like writing, as a game being played for mortal stakes, and his invocation of a great artist no longer able to finish out his stint because of inconceivable pain was to have for him a premonitory force.

But Santiago is finally not that done-for artist. For all his pains and losses, he is working and planning to work up until the end. And the promise of continuous creation is made fully present to the reader in the moment of first seeing the fish:

> The line rose slowly and steadily and then the surface of the ocean bulged ahead of the boat and the fish came out. He came out unendingly and water poured from his sides. He was bright in the sun and his head and back were dark purple and in the sun the stripes on his sides showed wide and a light lavender. His sword was as long as a baseball bat and tapered like a rapier

> and he rose his full length from the water and then re-entered it, smoothly, like a diver and the old man saw the great scythe-blade of his tail go under and the line commenced to race out.

When the fish finally rises, it is as if the motion of a career has been completed – and re-begun. At the beginning, dignity had demanded that seven-eighths of the iceberg be kept under the surface. Then, as Hemingway opened himself to the task of making the dark things plain, the contours of the iceberg began to be revealed. Here, in *The Old Man and the Sea*, the prolongation of the moment through a series of "and's" and prepositional phrases is familiar enough. There is the old joy in looking and the descriptions it enjoins. "In the sun," Hemingway writes, "in the sun": he is still a master of repetition. The casual and compounding comparisons – a sword like a baseball bat and a rapier, a fish "like a diver" – are, however, new. The fish himself is the possessor, through simile, of the humanly fashioned tool Santiago will later come to wish for: so the process of identification begins. *Unendingly*, however, is the truly astonishing touch. This act of surfacing, like the effort to bring the iceberg to light, is one expressed as being without end. In one prophetic utterance, and against all the upwelling exhaustions and anxieties, Hemingway sums up the history of his life-work and foresees the fate to which it would be consigned, as those of us who continue the attempt to catch his meanings find ourselves participants in the making of an unending career.

PART IV

Remorse

CHAPTER 12

Replacement and Remorse

The Garden of Eden and *A Moveable Feast*

As Hemingway neared the end of his writing life he returned to his beginnings, as a husband and as a writer. *A Moveable Feast* deals openly with the days of awe in Paris and with the replacement of a first wife with a second. *The Garden of Eden* encodes these beginnings in a novel about a honeymoon in the south of France. David and Catherine Bourne look like a version of Ernest and Hadley, with a similar replacement of the wife occurring in the person of Marita. But there is a problem with this reading of the novel, since the woman Ernest honeymooned with in the Camargue was not Hadley, but Pauline.

The Garden of Eden can be read as a sequel to *A Moveable Feast*; in the memoir, Hemingway savors and then loses his first marriage, whereas in the novel, he gives us a fictional version of the beginning and the end of his second one. In each book, a writer replaces one woman with a "new" one. The romance of beginnings must therefore compete with an emotion that has been accumulating since the end of Paris, with remorse.

The available textual history of the two books makes a case for reading them as complementary efforts, just as Hemingway's inability to finish either project originated in a set of recognitions each book worked to enforce.

Hemingway never finished work on *The Garden of Eden*, but, when, in fact, did he begin it? Rose Marie Burwell argues for 1948; Michael Reynolds for 1952. Reynolds bases his claim on his belief that Hemingway could not have accessed the material in his story until after Grace and Pauline were dead. It is a compelling argument, one in which I would like to believe. But Burwell's account of the postwar writings is so meticulously researched and so sympathetically imagined as to give any conclusions made by her considerable weight.

Burwell's *Hemingway: The Postwar Years and the Posthumous Novels* is a book with the force and the economy of a novel itself. Burwell gathers her arguments around a grand surmise: the four "unfinished novels"

Hemingway left behind at his death – books later published as *A Moveable Feast, Islands in the Stream, The Garden of Eden*, and *True at First Light/ Under Kilimanjaro* – "form a tetralogy that is Hemingway's portrait of the artist as writer and painter, and as son, husband and father." In Burwell's estimation, the discoveries Hemingway made about himself while writing this vast and interconnected ur-text made him unable to finish it. In William Blake's words, Hemingway subjected himself to a Last Judgment. "Whenever any Individual Rejects Error & Embraces Truth," Blake wrote, "a Last Judgment passes upon that Individual."

The Garden of Eden appears to have been the piece of this tetralogy on which Hemingway worked the hardest and the longest. While Hemingway had embarked on writing about "sexual experimentation" as early as 1946, Burwell argues that he had not fully differentiated *Eden* as a story of its own until the spring of 1948. She bases this conjecture on letters written to Carlos Baker and to Mary Hemingway, as well as on the short haircut prescribed for Mary in the summer of 1948. "The first of the two documentable periods of concentration on *Eden*" did not begin, Burwell allows, until 1950, when Hemingway, "anticipating that he might not live to finish *Eden* . . . wrote a provisional ending." "The second period of concentrated work on *Eden*," Burwell continues, "began in late 1957."

Hemingway started another book in 1957, *A Moveable Feast*. From this point on, the novel and the memoir evolved in complementary fashion. John Leonard has, in fact, established that most of *Eden* was written during what Burwell calls "the second period of concentrated work," during the years in which Hemingway was giving shape to memories of his young life in Paris.

Leonard bases his findings on "an internal series of dates" written on the manuscript of *The Garden of Eden* in Hemingway's hand. Chapters thirteen through thirty-five of the manuscript, he determines, as well as the provisional ending, were written in 1957 and 1958. From these chapters, Tom Jenks quarried chapters seven through thirty of the published novel.

Burwell dates the writing of the provisional ending to May 1950. Leonard argues that "her conclusion seems based on a misreading of the date (May '58) she found in the manuscript." He proceeds to demonstrate that "the '8' in 'May '58'" – a date added in Hemingway's hand – "is written in such a way that the upper loop is significantly oversized when compared with the lower loop. At first glance it appears to be an '0,' but closer inspection shows it to be an '8.'"

Leonard's findings support the view that most of *The Garden of Eden* was written in 1957 and 1958, years in which Hemingway was also working on *A Moveable Feast*. In fact, as J. Gerald Kennedy has shown, "during the late fifties he moved back and forth between the manuscripts" of *Eden* and *Feast*, "on one occasion, at least, jotting ideas for both works on the same sheet of paper."

I found such a piece of paper while looking through a folder labeled "Chapter 20. Schruns. Version Two." It is an unnumbered page of scribblings, lists, and crossings-out and things written on the slant. One of the notes reads, "I have called both of these women Catherine because . . . ." Then, at the other end of the page – you have to turn it around in order to read it – Hemingway has written: "Poverty in Paris an illness" and "the rich who collect people as some other people do pictures." The first note refers to the heroine of *The Garden of Eden* and the second to the arrival of the rich in *A Moveable Feast*. Hemingway's two most distinctive posthumous publications were thus linked enterprises arising out of an intense and final period of revaluation, and they need to be read together for their full significance to emerge.

With incantatory force, *The Garden of Eden* immerses a reader in a world of seductive repetitions playing upon the theme of pleasure and how to keep it from ending. We hook a big fish and pull it in before an admiring crowd. We stare at the grains of pepper sprinkled into the cup and stir the pat of butter into the boiled eggs. There is wine, always wine, and a bar in the hotel where we can mix our own drinks. At the nearby beach, we swim in only our skin and deepen our tans. There is talk, lots of talk, often talk about how happy we are and how long it will last. In the nights and in the mornings and in the afternoons, we make love, and it seems as if it will all go on forever.

But the young woman feels compelled to vary the routine. First, she tries something new in bed. Then, she cuts her hair. The young man plays along and has his hair cut and lightened, too. But he holds back a part of himself. As her will to change accelerates, he sees that they have moved out of the beginning and through the middle and may be rapidly approaching the end.

Then, instead of the two, there are three of them: the wife brings another young woman into their lives. The husband, a writer, begins to withdraw to the room where he works on stories about his past. As he does so, he stops work on the writing that has made his wife so happy, the narrative of their honeymoon.

The triangle soon becomes a sexual one. The two women sleep together, and then the new girl sleeps with the husband. The wife becomes as jealous of the new arrangement as she has been jealous of her husband's work. He has success in the work, finishes two stories, and shares the finished stories with the new girl. The wife, seeing this, burns the husband's papers. She leaves, and writes a letter of apology. The husband tries and fails to rewrite the lost stories. Then, on his second try, and in the last scene in the book, he finds the lost sentences coming back to him complete and entire.

In *The Garden of Eden*, Hemingway explores the tension inherent in any marriage between the generic and the specific. The title of the novel announces a re-enactment of the first fall in which we sinned all. And the couple is familiar – even a little clichéd – in its belief in the possibility of a unique happiness. Yet, like people in any human couple, they are unique, burdened by natures and habits and inheritances that make them strange to each other and to themselves. So, there is perhaps a hope that they can avoid acting out once again the old script.

The tension between the generic and the specific is on display in the novel's very first word: "They were living at le Grau du Roi then and the hotel was on a canal that ran from the walled city of Aigues Mortes straight down to the sea." Places here get named, but people do not. It is somehow more important that we know ourselves to be in the Camargue, in the south of France, than to know who we are with. The place is described as "pleasant," "cheerful," and "friendly." The story promises to be one of "interesting adjectives," marked by words like "handsome" and "wonderful." The young man, David Bourne, is not named until page seven; the young woman, Catherine Bourne, until page seventeen. Meanwhile, the unnamed couple spends its time fishing, swimming, looking, bicycling, drinking, making love, and, above all, eating. "They were always hungry but they ate very well."

The fall out of the generic and into the specific occurs in the novel's fourth paragraph: "On this morning there was . . . ." Hemingway's "this" signals a move out of fantasy and into existential time. The experience of fall will continue to repeat itself until the couple has worn out its love.

The specific action of the novel begins with a question; an instability is being expressed, an inability to abide a particular silence:

> "What are you thinking?" the girl asked.
> "Nothing."
> "You have to think something."
> "I was just feeling."
> "How?"
> "Happy."
> "But I get so hungry," she said.

The man is content to feel and not to think or to talk; he is trying to live "in it." But the girl finds herself thrown beyond the moment by appetite. "I'm getting hungry already," she says, "and we haven't finished breakfast." And then, in an offhand way, she tells her husband, "I'm going to destroy you."

Once again, Hemingway gives away an ending at the start. But this plot is so familiar that the warnings may go unheeded – or unneeded. It is the plot anyone who marries lives out in some way, the story of how we attempt to "know" each other and in doing so also come upon ourselves.

The Garden of Eden begins with an implicit question: how do you live out a plenitude? How, when you have everything, can you even know that you are happy? By finding something lacking in it. In *Paradise Lost*, the work that founds the novel of marriage in English, Adam begins by asking for something. He tells God he is lonely: "With mee / I see not who partakes." His world may be filled with "living creatures," but with none of these can he enjoy "conversation." So God consents to make a woman, and marriage is born.

This second plenitude proves no more stable than the first since Eve finds herself without enough to do. She proposes gardening alone, Adam reluctantly consents, and she returns from her work day with the bitten apple.

In *The Garden of Eden*, history also begins with a woman's wish. Her name for the forbidden fruit is "surprise."

> He poured her another small glass of the wine and filled his own.
> "I have a big surprise. I didn't tell you, did I?" the girl said.

Catherine's appetite for surprise expresses a longing to break the plenitude and to replace it with a world of uncertainty and risk where anything can happen. Against the perfection of our first home, she chooses *story*.

David may be the writer in the family, but Catherine's "actions," as Kathy Willingham points out, "provide the bulk of the novel's plot." She is, like Shakespeare's dark designers, a free artist of herself, or, as novelist E. L. Doctorow writes, "a brilliant woman trapped into a vicarious participation in someone else's creativity." While Catherine's "jealousy of the work" is made obvious enough, it is not the emotion from which she departs, nor is the burning of the clippings the act that finally distinguishes her.

Mark Spilka reads "the conversational artist Catherine Bourne" as "Hemingway's finest female creation," just as he reads Marita as "the perfect adjunct wife that Catherine has heroically refused to become." It is like claiming Eve to be the true hero of *Paradise Lost*, a claim with which I am in sympathy. Blake thought Milton was of Satan's party without knowing it, but I would say the case is even stronger for his Eve. She, after all, has dreams and remembers them, she has the artist's natural curiosity, the will to violate the rules, she insists on her right to both pleasure and knowledge, and she, as a result, commits the first creative act.

That act makes something possible by breaking something else. A fantasy of oneness is traded in for the possibility of loss, differentiation, suffering, and growth. Like Eve, Catherine will also be assigned the blame: as Adam hems and haws when Christ comes down to visit in Book Ten of Milton's story, Eve meets their judge with a simple admission: "The Serpent me beguil'd and I did eat." In her letter of self-judgment, Catherine is also candid: "I did it and I knew I did it and I can't undo it."

It is perhaps natural enough for readers to identify Hemingway with writer David Bourne and to assume that in creating Catherine he is working out some residual resentment about his second wife. It was Pauline who seduced him into a "betrayal" of Hadley, and it was Pauline he honeymooned with in the Camargue. Read in this way, Pauline-Catherine gets what is coming to her: she will pay for having made her husband fall in love with her by being replaced by the perfect adjunct wife.

This allegory stylizes what happened between Ernest and Pauline. It also relies for its logic upon a set of conservative identifications within the logic of gender (David = Ernest and Catherine = Pauline) that the novel is at pains to push beyond. What if Hemingway actually "identified," to use that shopworn term, as much with Catherine as with David? He is, after all, very much like her. He was an experimenter; he had unappeasable hungers; he liked the feel and look of a woman's short hair; he was, in many ways, in a word applied to Catherine Bourne, a "Devil."

The point to be made is that in any re-enactment of the Fall – in any marriage worth the name – each of us is Adam and each of us is Eve. Her unappeasable curiosities and appetites play themselves off against his awareness that there are limits – or that there need to be limits – to both desire and imagination.

Just as the plenitude of Adam's solitude is broken up and fulfilled by marriage, so the plenitude of marriage can be broken up and redeemed by divorce. In each case, there is a fortunate fall out of states that have come to feel oppressive in some way. In the myth of the Fortunate Fall, mankind pays for its curiosity and disobedience by falling into a world of labor and labor pains and death, even while it gains a compensating knowledge. What is gained is awareness itself and, with it, the capacity for experience. Nothing happens in the Garden of Eden, and it is this unending and static "happiness" against which Catherine, like Eve, lodges her protest. Marriage itself – or at least a first, innocent marriage – is here represented, to use Hemingway's own words, as "the happiness of the Garden that a man must lose." *Must lose*, he writes, as if divorce were a necessary component of growth.

But what if you marry not only a second but a third and even a fourth time? How to think about all that was paid and learned in the exercising of a second will more wise? It is one thing to be given the freedom to fall, but it is quite another to *keep on* being given it. "Should God create another Eve," Adam says, when confronted with the choice between his wife and God, "loss of thee / Would never from my heart." At this point in human history, the worst thing Adam can imagine is a replacement, "another Eve." Adam has in some sense divorced God in order to stay with Eve, and there can be no going back on that fortunate fall without rendering its high emotions both trivial and absurd.

In 1916, Sherwood Anderson divorced his first wife, Cornelia Lane, and married Tennessee Mitchell. In 1924, he divorced Tennessee and married Elizabeth Prall. Six years later, he divorced Prall and married Eleanor Copenhaver. It was the second act of replacement that arrested Hemingway, as he records in a January 1925 letter to Bill Smith:

> Tennessee as I remember was a swell woman. I didn't know her long but felt as though I knew her well. Sherwood was never as good as when he was with her and he'd be with her yet if he didn't have this idea that life is a sort of pony express where he travels the fastest that changes women the oftenest.

One of the most melancholy lines in Hemingway is voiced by Harry Walden to himself, as he lies dying in "The Snows of Kilimanjaro": "If it had not been she it would have been another." He means to say that any number of other women could have accompanied him on the road to self-ruin. He says as much in order to absolve his wife Helen of any "fault" in the matter. But Harry's modestly charitable gesture also articulates a sense of female partners as being interchangeable. As the practice of finding "another Eve" is repeated, the freedom conferred by the right to divorce can deliver a man up to a sense of deadening inconsequence. Near the end of his life, in a sentence published in *Under Kilimanjaro*, Hemingway wrote, "I wondered about how many true loves to which you were faithful, until you were unfaithful, a man could have." And, in one of the last letters he ever wrote, in April 1961, Hemingway informed Charles Scribner, IV that he wished to withdraw *A Moveable Feast* from publication. The letter was not mailed and was finally sent by Mary Hemingway to Scribner's editor Harry Brague on July 18, 1963. In the letter, Hemingway wrote of fears of being "unfair" to the women he had loved and of being appalled by the pattern revealed by the story: "Then I had a chapter about Pauline coming into our life, deceiving Hadley, that Hadley doesn't even know and how the pattern is repeated (in Miss Martha again)."

"I'm going to be changed," Catherine says, a few pages into *The Garden of Eden*, and so she cuts her hair. "It was cut with no compromises," cropped as short "as a boy's." What comes with the surprise is a fantasized escape from the prescriptions of gender. "I'm a girl. But now I'm a boy too and I can do anything and anything and anything."

The chapter culminates in the scene where this girl/boy sodomizes her husband:

> He had shut his eyes and he could feel the long light weight of her on him and her breasts pressing against him and her lips on his. He lay there and felt something and then her hand holding him and searching lower and he helped with his hands and then lay back in the dark and did not think at all and only felt the weight and the strangeness inside and she said, "Now you can't tell who is who can you?"

Never explicit in his sex scenes, Hemingway once again falls back on words like "something" and "strangeness." The Publisher's Note at the head of the volume has already informed readers that "beyond a very small number of minor interpolations for clarity and consistency, nothing has been added." Editor Tom Jenks has nevertheless added two words to this passage. "Searching *lower*" and "strangeness *inside*" are phrases guiding our gaze, and the italicized words have been invented by Jenks.

"At the end they were both dead and empty but it was not over." How quickly the fall completes itself here: in the last sentence of chapter one, only a few paragraphs further on, David is already saying farewell. "Goodbye Catherine goodbye my lovely girl goodbye and good luck and goodbye."

Since the publication of *The Garden of Eden*, transgressive sexuality has become a hot subject in the Hemingway industry. He is increasingly credited with possessing a more complex understanding of "gender" than had heretofore been acknowledged. It is easy to see how the 1986 novel might well have shaken things up and redirected attention toward Hemingway's sense of gender as performative. But I am hard pressed to find in the sodomy scene anything stranger than in the scene between Brett and Jake in chapter VII of *The Sun Also Rises*. Brett has left Jake's room in order to deal with the Count and comes back to find Jake lying on the bed with his face away from her:

> I did not want to see her.
> "Sent him for champagne. He loves to go for champagne."
> Then later: "Do you feel better, darling? Is the head any better?"
> "It's better."

Whatever form of solace has been offered here, it is difficult to imagine it as any less inventive than Catherine's probing with her hand.

In *The Garden of Eden*, the pattern of experimentation followed by remorse repeats itself and accelerates until it finally burns itself out. David is obviously titillated and unsettled by the sexual experimenting and responds to it after the fact in fairly conventional and defensive ways. But it is not the sex that threatens him as much as it is the rate of change. "What can there be that will not burn out in a fire that rages like that?" he asks himself in chapter two, thus linking Catherine's ever-increasing love of speed with her burning of the manuscripts at the story's end. It is as if she wants to do something that cannot be forgiven or foresworn, a "destructive" act that might rival David's "inventive" ones.

Catherine's story can be read as a version of the revenge against time. Her impatience, her love of speed, her insatiability – all this can be understood as a protest against the way in which the immediacy of any one moment is consumed by the arrival of the next. It is a fair enough reading, one reinforced by the frequent appearance of the time markers "back" and "ahead." Another way in which to read the novel, however, might be as a canny inquiry into gender as the product and prisoner of the division of labor.

Throughout *The Garden of Eden*, Catherine is represented as competitive with and finally destructive of David's work. But what if the emphasis were shifted a little, and the question is asked: How supportive is her husband of Catherine's need to create? Looked at under the cover of this question, Catherine's restlessness is the offspring of a marriage that left her with not enough to do.

"The posthumous novels return repeatedly," Rose Marie Burwell argues, "to the threat that families and women pose to the creative artist." Hemingway's "distrust of women's entry into the creative process," she continues, is typically rendered "in terms of Hadley's loss of his manuscripts in 1922." Hence the decision, at the end of *Eden*, to have Catherine admit to having "Burned the clippings."

As Part Two opens, David and Catherine have left le Grau du Roi and driven to Hendaye. From there, they will move to Madrid and then back to France. Once in Spain, David looks back at le Grau du Roi as simple and asks himself whether that "time was all simple because you could write a little of it simply?" What made that time simple is not the quality of David's writing but the fact that the activity of writing has not been allowed to compete with the honeymoon narrative for the reader's attention. The headlong descent into divorce does not begin until the division of labor in the marriage is made more apparent by David's withdrawing into his room in order to write his African stories.

Catherine, it turns out, had wanted to be a painter but, as she says, "I can't paint at all and never could . . . it's just like being hungry all the time and there's nothing you can ever do about it." Hers can be read as the tragedy of an ambition with no talent. And, like anyone else, she is responsible for finding something to do in the world. Catherine fears she will make nothing that lasts: "I don't want to die and it be gone." David tries to console her by suggesting she view herself as an artist of experience: "You know what you saw and what you felt and it's yours." Beyond her gifts as a conversationalist, she does have a talent for creating "a text," as Kathy Willingham observes, "not with language, with her body."

Despite her obvious talents, Catherine finds herself up against a social apparatus that supports a man in his work and assumes a woman's role as the primary element in that support. Asked early on by a waiter, "Is Madame also a writer?" "No," Catherine replies, "Madame is a housewife."

Things only begin to get really bad between Catherine and David once he begins to leave "to work in the room." He is working on the ongoing narrative of the honeymoon, a project begun at Catherine's request. It is not until chapter eleven that David turns aside from this kind of writing in order to begin work on the first of his two African stories, "the story which he believed he must write now or lose."

After putting down his pencil on his first day of writing, David joins Catherine at a café, makes her an absinthe, and is met with a bile that seems to come out of nowhere:

> "So make your own, you clipping reader," she said.
> "What was that?" the young man said to her.
> "I didn't say it."
> But she had said it and he said to her, "Why don't you just shut up about the clippings."

David receives a letter "fat with clippings" on the morning after Catherine imposes her first surprise. The clippings are reviews of his recently published novel. He shares them with her and she is "frightened by them . . . . How can we be us and have the things we have and do what we do and you be this that's in the clippings?" She goes on to compare the clippings to "somebody's ashes in a jar."

When Catherine calls David a "clipping reader," she is reducing him to a man who writes for praise. He meets her with "Shut up"; it is their first real fight. In the earlier clipping scene, she had said, "Please let's not fight," and, when the fight does arrive, it follows upon David's "being the only one who had worked."

This is the set-up. Catherine questions it, but David does not. He simply suggests that she become an epicure of duration, an artist of memory. Hemingway set *The Garden of Eden* in the 1920s, but he wrote it in the late 1940s and the late 1950s. In the process, he was somehow able to tap into "a yearning," in Betty Friedan's words, "that women suffered in the middle of the twentieth century in the United States." Friedan calls it The Problem That Has No Name.

Without a name for the problem, without a working discourse in which the dynamic between men and women might receive an accurate description, it is perhaps inevitable for David and even for his author to fall back upon Catherine's motive for burning the papers as "jealousy of the work." Catherine is without words with which to disagree. In a manuscript passage cut from the published novel, one that might have appeared in her letter of apology, she wrote: "We were partners but I didn't know enough to love what I didn't understand." But she does understand, at some level beyond the available words, that life to him would be death to her and that she has to burn her way out.

One of the major reassessments enforced by my summer of reading Hemingway was in my judgment of Pauline. I had always accepted the characterization of her in the 1964 *A Moveable Feast* as the "unmarried young woman" who befriended Hadley Hemingway and who "then unknowingly, innocently and unrelentingly" set out to marry her husband. Having lived by the sword, Pauline eventually died of it, betrayed herself by Martha Gellhorn as Hadley had originally been betrayed.

Yet Pauline, of all the wives, appears to have been the most devoted to Hemingway's success. "She has the best judgement of all," Hemingway wrote to Max Perkins, as he found himself on "the stretch" in writing *For Whom the Bell Tolls*. Pauline was one of the few readers who found *The Torrents of Spring* funny; she served as the inspiration for Catherine Barkley in *A Farewell to Arms*; she read Henry James aloud to her husband; it was her uncle Gus Pfeiffer who helped to finance the first safari; she created his first permanent home; she was the one person "whose word I take on grammar."

If there is an iceberg continually surfacing in the pages of manuscript Hemingway left behind, it is Pauline. When I use the name "Pauline," I mean to refer to that complex of memories, misunderstandings, lingering resentments and regrets, and self-judgments that swirl around Hemingway's experience of replacing one wife with another. *A Moveable Feast* has established the myth that his great remorse was over the betrayal of Hadley, although the sentences containing the word "remorse," a word appearing at least six times in the manuscript pages describing Hemingway's first experience of being in love with two women at once, were all cut from the 1964 edition. Still, the very fact that Hemingway was able to inscribe much of that story on the page argues for a more resolved relationship with his betrayal of Hadley than with his betrayal of Pauline.

A Moveable Feast was first edited into print by Mary Hemingway and Harry Brague in 1964. After the appearance in 2009 of the Restored Edition of *A Moveable Feast*, edited by Seán Hemingway, it became possible to discover how willfully that earlier act of shaping had suppressed the figure of Pauline. Not only did the 1964 edition cut out whole sections of text dealing with Hemingway's feelings about Pauline, it went so far as to entirely eliminate her name from any of the edition's pages. Pauline had, in fact, been named in the scene where Ernest visits the bicycle racing track near Auteil, "where Pauline and I saw" – not "where we saw" – the great rider Ganay fall and heard his skull crumple under the crash helmet as you crack an hard-boiled egg.

"There is no ~~mention~~ account of Pauline in this book on purpose," Hemingway wrote, on the back of one of the pages in which he struggled to find an ending for his Paris book. But his ambivalence over whether or not to include Pauline resulted in repeated mention of her. "I left out when it started with Pauline," he wrote, in one of the "Fragments" published at the end of the Restored Edition. "That part, the part with Pauline, I have not eliminated," he wrote in another fragment. Hemingway had long since demonstrated, as in the final chapter of *Death in the Afternoon*, that to mention what will not be written about is to write about it.

While the Restored Edition does elect to print much of this material, it also chooses to omit a number of very powerful mentions of Pauline that can be found in the surviving manuscripts. After Hadley had married "a much finer man than I ever was," Hemingway was to find, by his own account, an equivalent happiness with Pauline. A telling sentence appears in the JFK Folder titled "Chapter 20. Schruns. Version Three." "Then I was happy and without any remorse and I never worked better nor was I happier and I loved the girl truly and she loved me truly and well and we had as good a life together for many years as early Paris had been."

This lovely sentence, inserted in Hemingway's hand into a page of typescript, ought to appear on page 219 of the Restored Edition, after the paragraph in which Hemingway describes Hadley marrying a finer man. For some reason, it has been omitted from that text.

As good a life ... as early Paris had been, Hemingway writes. In the published versions of *A Moveable Feast*, the word "good" is usually reserved for memories of Hadley, as when Hemingway describes her second marriage as "one good and lasting thing that came of that year." But in the manuscripts that do survive, as in the sentence quoted here, Hemingway retrospectively applies the adjective "good" to memories of Pauline. While these usages have been omitted from the Restored Edition, they do exist and are an essential part of the complex record Hemingway left behind.

Again, in a folder labeled "Schruns. Version Two," Hemingway wrote that "the destruction of two people's happiness and making and the forgeing of a new happiness and the good work that came out of it is not part of this book." In a sentence published on page 235 of the Restored Edition, he wrote of "the part with Pauline" he was saving for another book: "It could be a good book because it tells many things that no one knows or can ever know and it has love, remorse, contrition, and unbelievable happiness *and the story of truly good work* and final sorrow." The italicized words have been omitted from the sentence as printed in the Restored Edition.

So goodness, when associated with Pauline, does not qualify for inclusion in even a grandson's final cut.

Hemingway did then in fact attempt, near the end, to give Pauline a little of the simple acknowledgment due to her. He worked at this task on two fronts and at the same time, in the directly confessional pages of *A Moveable Feast*, and through the displacements of *The Garden of Eden*, where a story about a second marriage is disguised as being about a first one. It was the making and breaking of a life with Pauline, I have come to believe, that occasioned in Hemingway the deepest feelings of remorse.

The obvious happiness of Hadley's second marriage clearly worked to allay Hemingway's feelings of remorse about his treatment of his first wife. Out of his bad behavior had come a good thing. But with Pauline, it was different. She never remarried, and she stayed on in the home she had made for her husband in Key West. She never resumed her journalistic career, and she died far too young. Whatever might have been Pauline's feelings about herself after the end of her marriage – and she insisted on burning most of her letters to and from her husband – it must have been difficult for Hemingway not to wonder if he had committed what is in marriage an unforgivable sin: using up a partner's chance.

And then there was the "unbelievable wrenching, kicking happiness" of the life with Pauline that also had been betrayed. It was a feeling for which Hemingway had sacrificed "everything," as he admitted in a letter written to Pauline during the period of their enforced separation, when she had retreated to her family home in Piggott, Arkansas, and he had remained in Paris. The letter is dated November 12, 1926:

> All I can think is that you that are all I have and that I love more than all that is and have given up everything for and betrayed everything for and killed off everything for are being destroyed and your nerves and your spirit broken all the time day and night and that I can't do anything about it because you won't let me.

The core sentence here is "you . . . are being destroyed." But there are more "I's" than "you's" in the entire sentence; it is the writer's own experience of separation that is the center of concern, feelings and actions that interpose themselves between the subject of the core sentence and its predicate. Read as prediction, the sentence anticipates the full range of emotions Ernest will live out with Pauline as he moves, after a desperate declaration of love, to a sense of self-sacrifice and resentment, to self-judgment, to sympathy, and finally to a kind of blame.

At the time Ernest left Hadley for Pauline, he could not have known he was entering into a "pattern" that was to be "repeated." In looking back from the late 1950s, it was the "re" that arrested him – the *againness* of it all. An outright statement of the point can be found in "The Pilot Fish and the Rich," one of the Additional Paris Sketches grouped together at the back of the Restored Edition:

> It wasn't that the decisions were wrong although they all turned out badly finally from the same fault of character that made them. If you deceive and lie with one person against another you will eventually do it again. If some person is able to do it to you once another person will do it again.

These sentences achieve a striking compression of time. When Hemingway writes, "It wasn't that the decisions were wrong," he is affirming the fundamental rightness of choosing to go with Pauline. They were, for a time, dreadfully happy. Then – only a few words later in the same sentence – he finds himself writing that it "all turned out badly." The marriage to Pauline failed – or, rather, Hemingway chose to end it. When he writes, "If you deceive and lie with one person you will eventually do it again," he appears to be referring to something done by Pauline. A little further down the page, Hemingway adds, "For the girl to deceive her friend was a terrible thing." But, of course, the person who was to "do it again" was Ernest, not Pauline.

The "you" in the "If you deceive" sentence appears to project blame while actually accepting it. It is another example of Hemingway using the second person in order to reveal a painful truth about the "I" hiding behind the "you."

But the following sentence is the one carrying the most emotional weight. In it, the word "you" is surrounded by the words "some" and "another." "If some person is able to do it to you once another person will do it again." Here, Hemingway identifies not with the deceiving but with the deceived "you." The victimizer becomes the victim in a chain of deceivings happening "again" and "again."

Hemingway's remorse stems from the original betrayal of Hadley, surely, but, in looking back, another warrant for the feeling lies in the recognition that he had thereby entered a dynamic without end. The deceivings and the replacings were not to stop. The pain and grief of this recognition was necessarily delayed; it could only become Hemingway's portion once those original decisions – which *were not wrong* – themselves "turned out badly." This second and more chastening remorse could only have come, that is, after he had deceived and betrayed Pauline.

The word "remorse" derives from the Latin *remordere*, "to bite again." Hemingway's remorse arises out of his awareness that once a certain course of action is initiated, the self will "do it again." So there is nothing freeing about feeling remorse. It manifests itself as an addiction, as Balzac understood: "Remorse is impotence; it will sin again. Only repentance is strong; it can end everything." Remorse gnaws at the self, and, in this sensation, the self can take a kind of fierce pleasure. Repentance frees the self of the bite – and the pleasure – and the reason Hemingway could not submit to it was because it would have required him to commit to the dispersal of what he most valued, along with his work: his experience. Repentance could have freed Hemingway, but it would have left him with nothing. Between remorse and nothing, Hemingway chose remorse.

CHAPTER 13

How to End It

The Garden of Eden and *A Moveable Feast*

The Garden of Eden and *A Moveable Feast* each contain Scenes of Writing in which an aging Hemingway conjures versions of his younger writing self. In these scenes, Hemingway returns to the "*start of all he was to do*" and also demonstrates where, as a writer, he has ended up. As these acts of self-appraisal shade into self-judgment, Hemingway embraces a crucial emotional task even as he proves unable to finish the actual work at hand.

The Paris memoir begins with a young man coming in out of the cold into a pleasant café, taking out a notebook, and beginning to write:

> I was writing about up in Michigan and since it was a wild, cold, blowing day it was that sort of day in the story. I had already seen the end of fall come through boyhood, youth and young manhood, and in one place you could write about it better than in another. That was called transplanting yourself, I thought, and it could be as necessary with people as with other sorts of growing things.

Transplanting occurs when either a writer or a reader, face to face with a literary work, is made to feel "in it." There is a sense of stepping out of the present moment of writing and into the scene being imagined in a seamless way. Acts of transplanting occur again in *Feast*, when Hemingway finds that he does "not want to leave the river where I could see the trout in the pool" and when it "went so well you could make the country so that you could walk through it." Each act of transplanting celebrates the physical intensities and immediacies made possible by Hemingway's early style.

David Bourne experiences transplanting as he writes the elephant story: "He did not think that he could go on with the story that morning and for a long time he could not. But he knew that he must and finally he had started and they were following the spoor of the elephant on an old elephant trail . . . ." Within the space of a single sentence, Hemingway's prose transplants David out of a difficult moment of writing and into the space he has not been able to imagine.

The Scenes of Writing in the novel differ from those in the memoir, however, in being rendered in the third person. As a result, the reader is less inclined to identify the writer in *The Garden of Eden* with the author of it. There is a distance involved and a distinction being drawn. David is seen to be writing about the elephant story in one way, while the third-person narrator constructed by Hemingway *writes about David's writing* in quite another way. The difference between the two kinds of writing is meant to register the distance Hemingway has traveled since he, too, honeymooned in the Camargue.

David begins writing the elephant story in chapter eighteen:

> He did not sleep for a long time. When he did he had dreams of Africa. They were good dreams until the one that woke him. He got up then and went direct from that dream to work. He was well into the new story before the sun came up out of the sea and he did not look up from where he was to see how red the sun was. In the story he was waiting for the moon to rise and he felt his dog's hair rise under his hand as he stroked him to be quiet and they both watched and listened as the moon came up and gave them shadows.

Once again, Hemingway achieves a seemingly effortless segue between the scene of writing the story and the sensation of being in it. The sun not being looked at in the "now" of the writing room becomes the moon being waited for in the "then" of the story being recovered. Encountering such a passage "whoever read it . . . would find what was there and have it always."

Such a scene accomplishes a fusion of writer, reader, and text, an experience often on offer in early Hemingway. But the author of *The Garden of Eden* turns out to be invested in another effect as well: he is after the experience of standing off. As the reader of the novel watches David Bourne compose the elephant story and sometimes finds himself transplanted into it, he is also distanced from that activity by way of the commentary provided by the narrative voice.

Of course, Hemingway himself never participated in an elephant hunt as a boy, just as Nick Adams had never seen an Indian woman having a baby. Hemingway could have chosen any number of situations as the vehicle for his allegory about his own beginnings as a writer. But the elephant story serves his purposes well, touching as it does upon territory with which Hemingway's readers have long become familiar: the education of the son, friendship and its betrayals, the acquisition and keeping of a secret, the imminence of violence and death. The story also adds something crucial to the list – the onset of remorse.

Just as Hemingway is writing a story about a character who practices a style he no longer employs, so the boy in the elephant story is being asked by his father to participate in an activity in which he no longer believes. Yet it is Davey, as his father calls him, who has in fact set in motion the final capture of the elephant: "he had found the elephant at night and followed him to see that he had both of his tusks and then returned to find the two men and put them on the trail." Davey knows that his father and Juma are "proud of that," but, in the course of the hunt, Davey comes to wish "that he had never betrayed the elephant and in the afternoon he remembered wishing that he had never seen him. Awake in the moonlight he knew that was not true."

In this moment of self-correction, the boy Davey refrains from laying claim to a feeling not yet his. And the mature David, looking back, is careful to note the reticence of his younger self. The problem now, for the writer, parallels the problem then, for the boy: "his feeling about the elephant had been the hardest part and he knew he would have to get away from it and then come back to it to be certain it was as it had been, not later, but on that day. He knew the feeling had begun to form but he had been too exhausted to remember it exactly."

When feelings come to us is one of Hemingway's great subjects. There is often a deferral involved. "I did not know that then," Frederic Henry says near the beginning of *A Farewell to Arms*, "although I learned it later." The habit of "getting something for nothing" – of not paying for experience by feeling it as it happens – "only delayed the presentation of the bill." But, as Jake Barnes says, "the bill always came." Jake tries and fails to pay as he goes and so is led to conclude: "That was morality; things that made you disgusted afterward." For David Bourne, and for the Hemingway of *A Moveable Feast*, delayed payment takes the form of remorse.

David Bourne's confrontation with the issues of memory and feeling comprise one of Hemingway's most moving depictions of the demands he placed upon his capacities for emotional honesty, demands that David honors most, perhaps, when he fails to meet them. Thus, in chapter twenty-two, David does not at first "think that he could go on with the story," and, when he does, he stops writing once he begins to feel "he did not have it right yet." David may have stopped writing, but the narrator of *The Garden of Eden* continues on nevertheless:

> That was where he stopped in the hunt that morning. He knew he did not have it right yet. He had not yet gotten the enormity of the skull as they had come onto it in the forest nor the tunnels underneath it in the earth that the

> beetles had made and that had been revealed like deserted galleries or catacombs when the elephant had moved the skull. He had not made the great length of the whitened bones nor how the elephant's tracks had moved around the scene of the killing and how following them he had been able to see the elephant as he had moved and then had been able to see what the elephant had seen. He had not gotten the great width of the one elephant trail that was a perfect road through the forest nor the worn smooth rubbing trees nor the way other trails intersected so that they were like the map of the Métro in Paris. He had not made the light in the forest where the trees came together at their tops and he had not clarified certain things that he must make as they were then, not as he recalled them now.

"He had not," the narrator says, again and again, in sentences proceeding to describe in beautiful detail the very thing that David has "not gotten" or "not made." As an old friend says to Hemingway in one of the sketches for *A Moveable Feast*, "you have to put in now." The thickness of the description in this passage, with its relaxed intermingling of figurative language and empathy with a doomed animal, is surely one of the loveliest things Hemingway ever wrote.

Just who is to be credited with these acts of making? Is it the boy Davey, who first sees the enormity and the length and the width and the light? Is it the man David, who cannot yet get these things "right" and yet who so clearly remembers them? Is it the narrator who, despite all the "not's," goes on to fill out each sentence in precise detail? Or is it Hemingway, who, in one last act of *praeteritio*, creates a passage as self-reflexive as it is indicative of a change in both stance and style?

As the paragraph about not getting and making continues to unfold, David Bourne's failure becomes difficult to distinguish from success:

> The distances did not matter since all distances changed and how you remembered them was how they were. But his change of feeling toward Juma and toward his father and toward the elephant was complicated by the exhaustion that had bred it. Tiredness brought the beginning of understanding. The understanding was beginning and he was realizing it as he wrote. But the dreadful true understanding was all to come and he must not show it by arbitrary statements of rhetoric but by remembering the actual things that had brought it. Tomorrow he would get things right and then go on.

Davey's understanding began, we are told, out of the tiredness felt during the hunt. The following sentence begins by appearing to repeat the point: "The understanding was beginning . . . ." As the sentence unfolds, however, a reader is made to see that the understanding that "was beginning" *then*, for Davey, is also an understanding beginning *now*, under the pressure of another kind of tiredness, and that David Bourne, the mature writer, is "realizing it" as he writes.

"But the dreadful true understanding was all to come." It is to come for Davey, during the climax of the hunt, and it is to come for David, as he recalls and writes about that event. Of course, Davey's experience of understanding has in fact already happened and belongs to the past. But it has not yet been represented as happening in the time of the novel and so belongs to what might be called the future of the narrative. This is why the narrator can speak of it as yet "to come."

Feelings are something we have to wait for; their abruption into our lives cannot be forced. For a writer, it is important to honor the gap between the *then* and the *now*. "He did not know it then," Hemingway wrote in *A Moveable Feast*; "I do not know about that now," he wrote a few pages later.

"They were getting close to him," the narrator reports, in the climactic chapter twenty-four. "He tried to remember how he had felt. He had no love for the elephant yet. He must remember that. He had only a sorrow that had come from his own tiredness that had brought an understanding of age. Through being too young, he had learned how it must be to be too old." Just which "he" is being referenced in these repeated pronouns? The ambiguity of reference achieves a rich confusion between the "young" Davey and the "old" David Bourne. "David tried to remember how Davey had felt," Hemingway might also have written. "Davey had no love for the elephant yet. David must remember that," he could have continued. By not doing so Hemingway draws his reader into the difficult work of tracking a self across time.

David Bourne more than once tells himself that the "now" of the moment of writing cannot be allowed to contaminate the "then" of the story as it happened: "The hardest to make truly," David thinks to himself, "was how he had felt and keep it untinctured by how he had felt later." The young self and the old self are to be kept distinct. Yet the question of when feelings arise is one failing to yield a stable or a single answer as the years accumulate and as the recalling imagination finds itself drawn back ceaselessly into the past.

When the elephant moves into thick cover, Juma and the father go in after him. Davey hears a high squealing and smashing and the reports of two guns. He finds Juma bleeding from the face and his father white and angry. They follow the blood spoor and find the elephant "anchored, in such suffering and despair that he could no longer move." The father shoots again and the elephant goes down with his shoulder broken.

> He did not move but his eye was alive and looked at David. He had very long eyelashes and his eye was the most alive thing David had ever seen.
> "Shoot him in the ear with the three oh three," his father said. "Go on."
> "You shoot him," David had said.

"You shoot him," Davey says. In the face of his refusal, Juma takes Davey's rifle, pushes its muzzle into the elephant's ear hole, and fires angrily. The eye of the elephant opens wide and then glazes over as the blood runs in bright streams down the wrinkled gray hide. The father acknowledges his son's part in the kill – "Well we got him, Davey, thanks to you" – and begins talking about patching up the wounded Juma. "We have to get the packs before it's dark," he says to Davey. "Let's go."

The paragraph that follows displays the suppleness and expressiveness of Hemingway's late style:

> His father had known how he had felt about the elephant and that night and in the next few days he had tried if not to convert him to bring him back to the boy he had been before he had come to the knowledge that he hated elephant hunting. David had put no statement of his father's intention, which had never been stated, in the story but had only used the happenings, the disgusts, the events and feelings of the butchering, and the work of chopping out the tusks and the rough surgery on Juma disguised by mockery and railery to keep the pain in contempt and reduce its stature since there were no drugs. The added responsibility David was given and the trust that was offered him and not accepted he had put in the story without pointing their significance. He had tried to make the elephant alive beneath the tree anchored in his final anguish and drowning in the blood that had flowed so many times before but always staunched and now was rising in him so he could not breathe, the great heart pumping it to drown him as he watched the man who came to finish him.

How he had felt about the elephant: this allusion to David's inner life leaves marvelously open-ended the question of what is being felt. As the narrator here makes plain, in the story David Bourne is writing he has "put no statement of his father's intention, which had not been stated, in the story." He has relied instead on detailing happenings and disgusts and events and feelings. Themes like responsibility and trust have been "put in the story without pointing their significance."

Yet to mention leaving out things like statement and intention and significance is, of course, to put them in. It is to include rather than to omit. The story David Bourne is writing about the elephant hunt, Hemingway indicates, is not at all like the story he is writing about David Bourne's writing. David Bourne's way of writing belongs to

Hemingway's early style. But the elephant story works in the way it does because it has been invaded by Hemingway's reflective and inclusive late style, a style more willing to put things in instead of leaving them out.

In the aftermath of the elephant hunt, Hemingway completes his allegory of the birth of his own youthful writing self. Davey approaches the elephant carcass and scrapes some of the dried blood off the tusks with his thumbnail. "That was all he took from the elephant except the beginning of the knowledge of loneliness."

This knowledge is imposed upon Davey by the nature of an exchange with his father after the hunt. "He was a murderer you know, Davey," the father says. "They were all trying to kill him weren't they?" Davey responds. "I'm sorry you got so mixed up about him," the father answers. Then Davey says, "I wish he'd killed Juma." Later, after the drunken party back at the camp, the father asks, "Do you want to make peace Davey?" Davey gives a kind of answer: "'All right,' he said because he knew this was the start of the never telling that he had decided on."

The start of the never telling marks the fall into Hemingway's early style. What never telling protects from view is feeling, although for readers willing to attend to the omissions, and as Hemingway wrote in "Hunger Was Good Discipline," "the omitted part would strengthen the story and make people feel something more than they understood."

"This was the start of the never telling," Hemingway writes in the climactic scene. But, once again, it proves difficult to pinpoint a moment of resolve. Despite what is claimed in chapter twenty-four, the start of the never telling had begun even earlier. It arises out of a complex meditation on friendship in chapter twenty-two. Juma and his father have tracked the bull to where he has come to see his dead friend, and Davey leads them to the place. "How long do you suppose he and his friend had been together?" Davey asks his father. The father replies that he does not know and that Juma neither knows nor cares. "I care, David thought."

It is the bull's friendship with another bull that has given him away. It has, we might say, "betrayed" him. But the real betrayal is Davey's, and he now knows it: "It's my fault. I betrayed him."

For Hemingway, *betrayed* is a word reverberating throughout his postwar writing with an intensifying force.

"I should have kept him secret," Davey thinks to himself. "I'm going to keep everything a secret always." He decides at this moment to "never tell anyone anything again."

In this account, the genesis of secrecy lies in the discovery of one's capacity for betrayal. The resolution to never tell is not a simple act of negation; it is an embrace of a certain style of imagination. Davey's father may try to reverse this fall; he may try to bring his son back to the boy he had been before he had come to the knowledge that he hated elephant hunting. But the only way open is forward, into a writing life in which Davey's defensive decision never to tell anyone anything again is transformed into David Bourne's resolve "only to remember accurately and the form came by what he would choose to leave out."

It is striking to realize that Hemingway's art of omission is supplied with its genesis story in a novel and in a memoir written at the end of the career. In conceiving of the elephant story, David Bourne may set out to omit "statement" and "intention" and "significance" and thereby remain faithful to the style of "never tell," just as in writing "Big Two-Hearted River" a young American in Paris chose to write a story about the war with no mention of the war in it. But in writing about two young writers in *The Garden of Eden* and in *A Moveable Feast,* the nearly sixty-year-old veteran of the writing table admitted statement and intention and significance, as he had chosen to do long since. In imagining these two young writers and in inviting his readers to share in their Scenes of Writing in such an intimate way, Hemingway at once pays tribute to the birth of his early style and affirms, once again, how fully he has moved beyond it.

As he worked on the elephant story, Hemingway was also writing his Paris memoir. This work, too, involved an acknowledgment of remorse. There is plenty of remorse in *A Moveable Feast,* and yet what is striking about the published versions of the book is how each suppresses the appearance of the very word. These cuts indicate a will to have the text of the memoir conform to the strictures of Hemingway's early art of the omitted rather than to allow it to deploy the more expansive, meditative, and self-accusing quality of the later work.

In *A Moveable Feast,* Hemingway did at times maintain that he was still trying "to write by the old rule that how good a book is should be judged, by the man who writes it, by the excellence of the material that he eliminates." In such a formulation, cutting is embraced as part of the writing rather than the editorial process. It is an act committed by a writer *as he writes,* not by an editor after the fact. Hemingway continues:

> I cut ruthlessly and I hope it makes what is in stronger. I left out when it started with Pauline. That would have been a good way to end this book except that it was a beginning not an ending. Anyway I wrote it and left it out. It is intact and it starts another book.

These sentences can be found in The Restored Edition in a final section called "Fragments."

By 1957, when Hemingway embarked on *A Moveable Feast*, his story was all behind him. Was it a series of stops and starts, of ruptures and cuttings off, or was it a set of repetitions and continuities? How was he to cut into the past so as to remain true to what had happened and to be true as well to the old rule that a book is judged by the excellence of the material it eliminates?

By ignoring "the old rule." Hemingway's repeated claims about cutting ruthlessly and about things left out are the best evidence that the rule was in suspension, as it had been long since. To write about what had been eliminated was to include it. The more Hemingway worried the issue of "the part with Pauline," the more sentences he generated about her. That these sentences did not become part of the 1964 edition of *A Moveable Feast* was a decision made by Mary Hemingway and Harry Brague, not by Hemingway himself.

As Hemingway continued to work on his memoir, the ethical problem of how to give each character her due became inseparable from the formal question of how to end the story. Hemingway found himself facing an impasse, and one way out lay in not finishing. "Finishing is what you have to do," David Bourne tells himself. "If you don't finish, nothing is worth a damn." But, as Hemingway opened "the *remises* or storage places" where his memories had been locked away, and as the stories poured out, it became difficult to distinguish an ending from a beginning or to determine just where the "finish" might lie. A great writer found himself at the last face to face with the overwhelming integrity of the life. There was a longing to see it steadily and to see it whole. "There is nothing cut that means anything," Santiago says about his cut hands, and, by the time Hemingway came to write *The Garden of Eden* and *A Moveable Feast*, he had come to feel that no part of his life could be cut away without the whole losing its meaning.

One emotion Hemingway did not eliminate was remorse. As time went on, he came to feel more and more of it. A sense of having betrayed himself and many of the people he loved runs deep in the work of the postwar years. The Thomas Hudson of *Islands in the Stream* is "a man of big remorses." It is not an emotion he can keep down. "He could feel it all coming up; everything he had not thought about; all the grief he had put away and walled out."

Hemingway did not cast out remorse, but his editors did. In *The Garden of Eden*, reference to remorse has been fiercely suppressed by Tom Jenks's cuts. In the novel as published, the word "remorse" surfaces only in chapter eight, where it appears four times. During my reading of the thirty-seven folders comprising the EH Typescript/Pencil Manuscript of *The Garden of Eden*, I discovered fifteen additional places where Hemingway used the word. Six examples are provided below; the italicized passages are those Jenks has cut. I indicate as well the approximate locations in the published novel where this material might have been included:

- in chapter seven, David gets up after Catherine has been "a boy" again and walks out into "the high plateau air." In the manuscript passage, the narrator says that David "*felt no remorse.*"
- in chapter nine, David and Catherine talk about cutting and lightening their hair. When he hesitates, Catherine says, "*Don't get remorse even before you've done it.*"
- in chapter thirteen, Catherine looks dead and toneless. David says a drink will do her good. "*I had true remorse once and it did,*" he adds.
- in chapter seventeen, in a conversation between Catherine and Marita cut by Jenks, Catherine says about the lovemaking in Madrid: "*He really wanted to do that too but he had that terrible remorse.*"
- in chapter twenty, after David has stopped his work for the day on the elephant story, he thinks about everything he and Catherine have done together: "*I loved Madrid too except that I had remorse and nothing could be right for me to do that gave that remorse.*"
- in chapter twenty-nine, Marita and David talk about Madrid, and David says, "*I had remorse too. Black remorse.*" Marita answers: "*I promise you about remorse. David I* know *about remorse.*" He answers back, "*Nobody knows about another person's remorse.*"

Whatever David's pervasive remorse may be about, Jenks's editing has radically reduced its presence in the book.

"Remorse" was also cut from "There Is Never Any End to Paris," the chapter with which Mary Hemingway decided to end *A Moveable Feast.* But the word appears at least six times in the pages of manuscript edited down in order to create this final chapter. Most of these elided passages can be found in The Restored Edition, in a chapter called "The Pilot Fish and the Rich."

"The new and strange girl" – Hemingway is writing about Pauline – "undervalued the power of remorse." Having decided "to move steadily and relentlessly toward marriage," this new girl views the breaking up of the Hemingway marriage as only "a necessary step." Being with her "gave me such happiness and un-killable dreadful happiness so that the black remorse came and hatred of the sin and no contrition, only a terrible remorse." Then comes the moment when Hemingway sees Hadley standing by the train tracks and wishes he had died before he had loved anyone but her.

But, back in Paris, the other thing starts again. "Remorse was a fine good thing and with a little luck and if I'd been a better man it might have saved me for something worse probably instead of being my true and constant companion for the next three years." Hemingway proceeds to consider the wages of deceit. "If you deceive and lie with one person against another you will eventually do it again." For "the girl to deceive her friend was a terrible thing but . . . being in love I accepted all the blame for it myself and lived with the remorse." And, finally, "the remorse was never away day or night until my wife had married a much finer man than I ever was or ever could be and I knew that she was happy."

In passages only made widely available with the publication of The Restored Edition, a reader witnesses Hemingway's assumption of blame. For a man so given to projecting blame, it is a remarkable achievement.

How to end *A Moveable Feast* was the last writing problem on which Ernest Hemingway worked before taking his own life. On April 18, 1961, Hemingway detailed his struggle to finish the book in a letter addressed to Charles Scribner, IV. The letter was never mailed and only came to light in July 1963, when Mary sent it along with her edited version of the Paris book to Harry Brague, the editor she was working with at Scribner's.

In the letter, Hemingway wondered whether his book could be published "without a final chapter." For a month, he had been attempting to write it, and he had not been able to do it. As he confessed to Scribner, he had "tried as many as fifty times to end properly." The attempts at an ending were later edited down by Mary Hemingway into "There Is Never Any End to Paris," the final chapter in the 1964 text. As Jacqueline Tavernier-Courbin demonstrates in *Ernest Hemingway's* A Moveable Feast (1991), the "many rewrites" of these pages indicate them as having given Hemingway the most trouble and left behind the most complicated section of the entire manuscript. Given the difficulties he was having in finishing, and given his concerns about offending a number of persons depicted in his memoir, Hemingway went on to tell Scribner that he wished to withdraw the manuscript from publication.

The Restored Edition of *A Moveable Feast* reduces its number of chapters from twenty to nineteen and bases these changes on "a typed manuscript with original notations in Hemingway's hand." It also reorders Mary's chosen sequence of chapters and therefore undoes her sense of an ending. In *How It Was*, Mary admitted to "switching about some chapters for continuity's sake." As a result, her version culminates in the scene where Hemingway sees his wife standing by the train tracks and wishes "I had died before I ever loved anyone but her." Seán Hemingway's version culminates in the scene where Hemingway reassures Fitzgerald that in his proportions as a man he is "perfectly fine." The one ordering places the emphasis on marriage and its betrayals, the other on friendship and its competitions.

In Rose Marie Burwell's judgment, Hemingway was unable to finish *A Moveable Feast* as he approached the climax of his story because he was becoming "tormented by what was becoming clear" about his treatment of Hadley and Pauline and because he was facing "truths that resulted in his letter of withdrawal." "I failed to complete the pieces," the letter to Scribner's began. In it, Hemingway worried over lawsuits and about being "unfair" to Hadley and to Paul Mowrer. The writing about Pauline, he conceded, was "wonderful but awful." He had made too much of Hadley, "making her out to be the only person I ever loved. I loved Pauline, of course, but no one has any idea what went on in those days." With unlimited time, perhaps, he might be able to finish the book, but "very bad worries" and "the Rochester bout" – he is referring to his recent hospitalizations and shock treatments in Minnesota – have broken him down. "I am very sorry. It is not to be published the way it is now and it has no end."

Given the ambivalences and sorrows out of which Hemingway found himself writing near the end, and given the complexity of the manuscript material he left behind, there can be no definitive edition of *A Moveable Feast*. "The Restored Edition" simply provides another take on how to organize a set of literary remains first organized into print forty-five years earlier by Hemingway's fourth wife. Anyone who has examined Items 121-189D in the Kennedy Library will quickly discover that the 2009 edition in no way conforms to the "original manuscript text" of *A Moveable Feast*: that text is filled with deletions and insertions and marginal scribblings and breakings off that only a photographic facsimile could hope to reproduce. Moreover, The Restored Edition elects to omit – or inadvertently overlooks – words and phrases and even entire sentences from a number of manuscript pages it has chosen to reproduce. Since Hemingway stopped working on this material before he had a chance to edit it into its final form, and since he often continued editing his work even after it had been set in galleys, there is simply no way of knowing what would have made his final cut.

So, which ending to prefer? In his Introduction to The Restored Edition Seán Hemingway admits that after trying "to write an ending for over a month," his grandfather suggested to Charlie Scribner that the book be published without a final chapter. We know that the ending Hemingway was trying to write consisted of pages that became "There Is Never Any End to Paris"; we know that this material comprised a good part of "the final chapter" Hemingway could not finish. As Jacqueline Tavernier-Corbin has shown, the drafts comprising this file date from the winter and spring of 1961: "Still work on it Feb. 16"; "March 28, 29, 30, April 1"; and "Continued 27th, March 27." Seán Hemingway even goes so far as to admit that his grandfather's "betrayal of Hadley with Pauline . . . would have been a logical ending to the book." This being the case, it is a question as to why the grandson did not choose to make the story of the betrayal the final chapter of his edition of *A Moveable Feast.*

He was, for one thing, being true to a list. The list is printed in Burwell on pages 161–62, where she describes it as Hemingway's "arrangement for the nineteen chapters he intended to use." The following sequence of chapters is based on JFK Item 188, seven folders of typescript with very occasional corrections in Hemingway's hand:

(1) "A Good Café on the Place St.-Michel"
(2) "Miss Stein Instructs"
(3) "Shakespeare and Company"
(4) "People of the Seine"
(5) "A False Spring"
(6) "The End of an Avocation"
(7) "*Une Génération Perdue*"
(8) "Hunger Was Good Discipline"
(9) "Ford Madox Ford and the Devil's Disciple"
(10) "With Pascin at the Dome"
(11) "Ezra Pound and His Bel Esprit"
(12) "A Strange Enough Ending"
(13) "The Man Who Was Marked for Death"
(14) "Evan Shipman at the Lilas"
(15) "An Agent of Evil"
(16) "There Is Never Any End to Paris"
(17) "Scott Fitzgerald"
(18) "Hawks Do Not Share"
(19) "A Matter of Measurements"

Mary Hemingway rearranged this chapter order in a number of ways, but her most considerable choices involved adding "Birth of a New School" as chapter ten and moving chapter 16 to the final position, as chapter twenty. According to Robert Trogdon, she also made another choice: "all references to Hemingway's second wife, Pauline Pfeiffer, were eliminated." But Pauline *is* referred to in Mary's version, as "an unmarried young woman" and as "the girl I was in love with." What Trogdon might rather have said is that Pauline is not *named.*

Both editions of *A Moveable Feast* do agree about where the book should begin. It opens as Hemingway makes his way out of the bad weather into a pleasant café, begins to write about up in Michigan, notices a girl who comes into the café, is "disturbed" and "excited" by her, takes possession of her – "you belong to me now" – returns to his work, closes the notebook to see that the girl has gone, orders a dozen *portugaises* and a half-carafe of white wine, starts to make plans for leaving Paris, and then returns to his flat, where his wife says "I think it would be wonderful" in response to his suggestion of traveling to Austria for the winter.

The scene in the good café is a beautiful episode about coming in from the cold into a clean, well-lighted place where a young man who does not yet know who he will become finds food and drink and work and even a kind of love. Like Nick Adams, he is "in his home where he had made it." He is "there, in the good place." But the measure of how far this character has moved beyond the seekings and findings offered in *In Our Time* lies in the ease of accomplishment:

> The story was writing itself and I was having a hard time keeping up with it. I ordered another rum St. James and I watched the girl whenever I looked up, or when I sharpened the pencil with a pencil sharpener with the shavings curling into the saucer under my drink.
>
> I've seen you, beauty, and you belong to me now, whoever you are waiting for and if I never see you again, I thought. You belong to me and all Paris belongs to me and I belong to this notebook and this pencil.

For the young man in the scene, the future lies all ahead. But the older man writing about that younger man does know what he will become, as does any reader familiar with Hemingway's life and work. That reader knows that everything here being celebrated as so dear will be dismantled; she knows how it ended. The continuing and complex act of the mind enjoined by *A Moveable Feast* could therefore be described as *remembering the future*: what is up ahead for the young man in the café is really behind us, and we read forward into the volume in possession of a chastening awareness of all that lies in store for him. The "plenty of days coming" that Nick imagines as available to him at the end of "Big Two-Hearted River" have, for Hemingway, come and gone.

Looking back while moving ahead had been the Hemingway predicament. His sense of how we spend our life in time works, therefore, to create a longing for an experience of the present moment. The perspective granted the knowing reader of *A Moveable Feast* allows her to re-enact this sense of thrownness in an excruciating way. So a reader is perhaps grateful when a vignette succeeds in creating a feeling of being present to warmth, and food, and a pretty girl, and a story that writes itself. Beyond that, there is a moment in which the young man enters fully into his talent:

> Then I went back to writing and I entered far into the story and was lost in it. I was writing it now and it was not writing itself and I did not look up nor know anything about the time nor think where I was nor order any more rum St. James. I was tired of rum St. James without thinking about it. Then the story was finished and I was very tired. I read the last paragraph and then I looked up and looked for the girl and she had gone. I hope she's gone with a good man, I thought.

It is fair to say that Hemingway here does succeed in creating an act of presence. But it is also necessary to admit that the scene in the good café also looks ahead. In the 1964 edition, the structure of the first chapter anticipates the structure of the final one: in each, a triangle is set up in which another woman comes between Hadley and her husband. The pattern laid down in chapter one will be fulfilled in chapter twenty when Ernest decides to stay in Paris with "the girl I was in love with" instead of catching the first train to Austria in order to return to his wife. And the fantasy in which the young writer sends the girl off with "a good man" is also re-enacted in the final sentence of The Restored Edition's "Winters in Shruns": "The only one, Hadley, who had no possible blame, ever, came well out of it finally and married a much finer man than I ever was or could hope to be and is happy and deserves it and that was one good and lasting thing that came out of that year."

"When there were the three of us instead of just the two," the final chapter of *A Moveable Feast* begins. Once again, an innocent triangle is set up; the threesome here being referred to is comprised of Hadley, her husband, and her son. But the word "three" reverberates ominously forward to anticipate the arrival of the unmarried young woman who "becomes the temporary best friend of another young woman who is married, goes to live with the husband and wife and then unknowingly, innocently and unrelentingly sets out to marry the husband .... Then, instead of the two of them and their child, there are three of them."

David Bourne is another Hemingway character who finds himself "in love with both of them." We are mid-way through *The Garden of Eden* now, Catherine has introduced Marita into the twosome, and David finds himself trying to think his way through the situation:

> He looked down into the sea and tried to think clearly what the situation was and it did not work out. The worst was what had happened to Catherine. The next worse was that he had begun to care for the other girl. He did not have to examine his conscience to know that he loved Catherine nor that it was wrong to love two women and that no good could ever come of it. He did not yet know how terrible it could be. He only knew that it had started. The three of you are already enmeshed like three gears that turn a wheel, he told himself and also told himself one gear had been stripped or, at least, badly damaged. He dove deep down into the clear cold water where he missed no one and then came up and shook his head and swam out further and then turned to swim back to the beach.

The paragraph offers itself as the fictional encoding of the hard thinking about the past Hemingway engages in at the end of his memoir. But David is *in it*; he does not have the advantage of retrospect afforded the narrator of *A Moveable Feast*. His act of the mind is more immediate and more desperate and is prefaced by an imperative directed at the thinking self: "Do not start blaming who you love nor apportioning blame. It will all be apportioned in due time and not by you."

David looks down into the sea and tries to think *clearly*. After having his thoughts, he dives deep into the cold *clear* water. These acts of looking and diving body forth his act of the mind. David's thoughts may not be as clear as the water, but they are accurate enough. They attempt a precise calculation of harm done, a distinguishing between "the worst" and "the next worse." They own up to having done wrong. And they also admit to a limit on what can be known by confessing that how terrible it could be is a discovery still awaiting him. The "situation" cannot possibly "work out"; this much becomes clear. What does work out is David's thinking. He has begun the essential work of seeing a situation, and his part in it, for what it is.

David proves remarkably prescient in his instructions to himself about blame and in his prediction about how and when knowledge will come. The knowledge he knows he does not yet possess arrives in *A Moveable*

Feast, a book written concurrently with *The Garden of Eden*. And the blame is apportioned not by the "you" who narrates these sentences but by the man who authored them. The question remains: will that author also dive deep?

In the 1964 edition of *A Moveable Feast*, the one that casts out remorse, the Hemingway character represents the "situation" as befalling him. Somehow, two have become three. "The husband has two attractive girls around when he has finished work. One is new and strange and if he has bad luck he gets to love them both." With the publication of The Restored Edition, readers have been supplied with a version of these events in which the Hemingway character admits agency and accepts blame. His eventual divorce and remarriage is revealed as a willful act of transplanting expressive of a desire to change his life.

That desire is indirectly acknowledged earlier in "A False Spring." It is a chapter filled with premonitions: "When spring came, even the false spring," the chapter begins, as if to herald another bad season, the "nightmare winter" with Pauline. The young couple is happy but engages in a continual "fight against poverty." Even so, they agree to spend money at the track and to stop at Pruniers after having had some luck for a meal of oysters and *crabe Mexicaine*. On a walk afterward, they engage in a game of "Do you remember," talking like an old couple looking back. In their tone of preemptive nostalgia, these rememberings herald an eventual loss.

"We should live in this time now and have every minute of it," Hadley says, as she stands with her husband on the bridge near the Louvre. All the talking and walking has made them hungry again, so they decide to buy an expensive meal at Michaud's. As they gaze in at the restaurant window, Hemingway wonders "how much of what we had felt on the bridge was just hunger. I asked my wife and she said, 'I don't know, Tatie. There are so many sorts of hunger. In the spring there are more. But that's gone now. Memory is hunger.'" Then they go in and have a wonderful meal:

> It was a wonderful meal at Michaud's after we got in; but when we had finished and there was no question of hunger any more the feeling that had been like hunger when we were on the bridge was still there when we caught the bus home. It was there when we came in the room and after we had gone to bed and made love in the dark it was there. When I woke with the windows open and the moonlight on the roofs of the tall houses, it was there.

A feeling like hunger persists even after the speaker has eaten two big meals and has made love. Lying there in the dark, the young husband feels it important "to try to think it out" the way David Bourne "tried to think clearly" about his situation, but he finds himself to be "too stupid." It is the second time he has applied the word "stupid" to himself in the chapter.

"Stupid" is a somewhat stupid word. It permits the narrator to at once hide and to confess. He knows something is wrong; he knows that he has hungers that are unappeased. What he has felt on the bridge is certainly not "just hunger"; it is an apprehending that desire is full of endless distances. He may say to himself that "I was hungry in a simple way," but he is in fact discovering what Catherine Bourne discovers – the urge to drive "beyond what they had for something new."

In the opening sentences of "A False Spring," Hemingway writes that "the only thing that could spoil a day was people and if you could keep from making engagements, each day had no limits." But it is toward the arrival of new people and especially of an attractive girl who "is new" that the sixty-year-old writer, looking back on his twenty-five-year-old self, knows that younger self to be heading. "During our last year in the mountains new people came deep into our lives and nothing was ever the same again." It is the anticipation of this ending that causes Hemingway to end a chapter filled with so many satisfactions on a discordant note:

> But Paris was a very old city and we were young and nothing was simple there, not even poverty, nor sudden money, nor the moonlight, nor right and wrong, nor the breathing of someone who lay beside you in the moonlight.

In "A False Spring," the narrator does, however, manage a graceful integration of love and work. "In the spring mornings," he tells us, "I would work early while my wife still slept." He works at home; he has no need of a café. On the particular day being remembered, he decides to go downstairs to buy a morning racing paper and then walks "back fast to climb the stairs and get my work done." But before he starts to work again, he looks at the paper and sees they are running at Enghien. "So that day after I had finished work we would go racing." If they win, they can perhaps even afford to buy a nice dinner.

In chapter one, on the other hand, the worlds of work and love may intersect, but the second world is experienced as subordinate to the first. The girl Hemingway sees in the café may "belong to me now," but he closes out the passage about who belongs to whom by adding, "and I belong to this notebook and this pencil." Once he puts his pencil down, he also confesses to having the familiar feeling of being "empty and both sad and happy, as though I had made love."

A Moveable Feast's opening Scene of Writing offers a premonitory view of the tensions between love and work – and between one woman and another – that will generate its remorse-filled ending. In "A Good Café on the Place St.-Michel," the worlds of work and love both feed and compete with each other, with the victory going to the work. How to reconcile these worlds, and these experiences, the opening chapter appears to be asking, and how to begin the transplanting from one relationship to another after becoming root-bound, when the pot has come to feel too small? Plants cannot transplant themselves, but people can, and it is as "necessary with people as with other sorts of living things."

Hemingway's beginnings are bound to his endings with an almost terrifying narrative logic and emotional force: in "Big Two-Hearted River," Nick Adams returns to the landscape of "Indian Camp" to find that even the surface of the earth has been burned away, and in *For Whom the Bell Tolls*, despite everything having changed in the story's seventy hours, Robert Jordan finds himself still alive and in the world and in the same place where he began, lying on the pine-needled floor of the forest. These repetitions-with-a-difference *mean* something; they enlist the imagination of the reader in the work of understanding how we earn our endings. No ending is more earned than the ending of *A Moveable Feast*, and the character who earns it is named Ernest Hemingway. And that ending is implicit in the beginning and even determined by it; the set-up of "A Good Café on the Place St.-Michel" is an act of self-editing on the part of an author who knows exactly where his story means to end. What I am saying then is this: given the deft handling of the experiences of transplanting and triangulation in its opening chapter, it is only fitting that *A Moveable Feast* ends with Hemingway's painful and self-indicting refiguration of these themes and these experiences. The book has to end with Hadley and Pauline.

Hemingway did something remarkable as he worked away in his final days on his Paris book: he created an ending that is also a beginning. I quote again the passage about when it started with Pauline:

> I cut ruthlessly and I hope it makes what is in stronger. I left out when it started with Pauline. That would have been a good way to end this book except that it was a beginning not an ending. Anyway I wrote it and left it out. It is intact and it starts another book. You can only write it in fiction of course. It has the most happiness in it and it is the saddest book I know. But it comes later.

A little later in the draft, he writes of "the part with Pauline" as "a start rather than an ending."

For the Restored Edition to have relegated this material to an Appendix instead of incorporating it into a final chapter is a missed opportunity. Seán Hemingway justifies such decisions by claiming to have taken his grandfather at his word: "Hemingway had decided against including this material in the book because he thought of his relationship with Pauline as a beginning, not an ending." But the richness of "the part with Pauline" deserves to be included in a composite chapter that would also act as a final one. Hemingway understood the part to be played by the "authority of editing," and, if Max Perkins had not predeceased him, one can well imagine Perkins insisting on this material being so combined and so positioned.

Mary's edition has the advantage of creating a book with an end commensurate with its beginning. It has the disadvantage of having eliminated most of the candid assumption of blame and admission of remorse. All this has been made available in The Restored Edition, although the material is scattered throughout. The engaged reader is now in a position to collate this material, to imagine how it might be integrated into "There Is Never Any End to Paris," and to compose the ending that Hemingway left so radically open.

What then would we have? It would be an unusual if not a unique ending for Hemingway, one in which he allowed himself to end with a sense of beginning. Having once believed that "it is not fair to start a new story at the end of an old one," he did at the last permit himself to contemplate breaking his old rule. These promptings have as much authority as do any of the other attitudes and feelings Hemingway was also to record.

In practicing the art of omission, Hemingway had come to understand the power of the thing left out to make the reader feel more. At the end, a part of him persisted in this writing practice: "The bulldozing of three people's hearts to destroy one happiness and build another and the love and the good work and all that came out of it is not part of this book. I wrote it and left it out. It is a complicated, valuable and instructive story. How it all ended, finally, has nothing to do with this either. Any blame in that was mine to take and possess and understand."

These sentences were not included in the 1964 edition and can be found in the "Winters in Schruns" chapter in The Restored Edition. They are an admission masquerading as an omission: here, as elsewhere in Hemingway's work, to talk about what is being "left out" is most emphatically to include it. So, at the end, a part of Hemingway was still cleaving to the early practice of leaving things out and of keeping endings and beginnings distinct. At the same time, another part of Hemingway sought to make allowance for the sense that life may admit of more continuities and of a greater interpenetration between the phases lived and the choices made than can be accommodated by the stringent punctuations of his early art. It was time to acknowledge "my own part" in the destroying of happiness and in the consequent feelings of remorse. There were, as he wrote at the end of *Death in the Afternoon*, a few practical things to be said.

For Hemingway to admit rather than to omit was to recommit himself to a notion of integrity first fully articulated in *For Whom the Bell Tolls*. The truly "integrated" self – it is a word Hemingway applies to Robert Jordan at the end of his story – is no longer satisfied to separate the things that can be talked about from the things that cannot. To write "I left out when it started with Pauline" was in fact a way of letting her in, and the gentle irony of Hemingway's doing the very thing he claims not to be doing will not be lost upon the attentive reader. Pauline found her way in not because she was the most loved or the most reviled of the Hemingway women. Not because she was anything in particular – although she surely was extraordinary. It is simply that Pauline was an inextricable part of an ongoing story that could be cut into and edited in the telling but that had been experienced as "complete and entire" in the living. That experience, like any life, had a definite end. But the writing that came out of it proved to be unending, although Hemingway, having ensured this outcome by way of his very inability to finish, could not have known this. What he did know and sought to make clear in pages among the last he was to write is that we can accord the people we have loved no higher dignity than to call them by their living names.

Scattered Papers

"There was always much paper about the dead," Nick Adams says to himself, in the opening paragraphs of "A Way You'll Never Be." He has returned by bicycle to see where the attack had gone across the field. The dead lie "alone or in clumps in the high grass of the field and along the road, their pockets out, and over them were flies and around each body or group of bodies were the scattered papers." There is much material as well, bayonets and entrenching tools and empty gas mask cans, but Nick's gaze is drawn to the prayer books, group postcards, propaganda postcards, small photographs of village girls, and "the letters, letters, letters."

Nick has been here before, in an earlier attack. Now, the town and the road and the bank of the river are "very lush and over-green since he had seen it last and becoming historical."

The story begins with Nick going back to a place where he was wounded. But the activity of returning has long since begun during his sleepless nights. Nick has a recurring dream: "Outside of Fossalta there was a low house painted yellow with willows all around it and a low stable and there was a canal, and he had been there a thousand times and never seen it, but it was there every night as plain as the hill, only it frightened him. That house meant more than anything and every night he had it."

In words like these, the invitation to interpretation begins. The house means more than anything, but just what it means Hemingway does not specify. We are free to go back to Fossalta as he himself once did and to discover the limits of physical return. Meanwhile, all about us, and ever-available, are the papers, the scattered papers.

They are not so scattered as they used to be. The Cambridge Letters Project has already managed to locate hundreds of pages of previously unknown correspondence and is bringing more than six thousand letters into print in superbly edited volumes. At the Hemingway Room in Boston, copies of the manuscripts of the novels and stories have been placed within an arm's reach. And the books and writings still left behind at the Finca

Vigía are becoming available to anyone able to get into Cuba, if he or she has the right papers.

Hemingway was a great saver of paper. He took care with his manuscripts, making daily word counts, revising in legible ways, giving them to a friend or relative, depositing them in bank vaults. "Becoming historical," he knew, came not from living large but from putting words down on a page.

But he did live large and traveled so passionately that he laid down pilgrim trails. Towns were transformed into tourist sites by the words he left behind. Life for him was an affair of places, and, in honor of his love of them, the members of the Hemingway Society gather one year in Petosky, or in Key West, or in a city in Spain.

Nick's return to the stricken field is both forensic and therapeutic: he wants to find out something, and he wants to fix something in himself. He is a kind of autobiographer. The more telling and unending work of self-encounter takes place, however, in his nightly dreams, although the images recurring in them mean more than any one excavation project can determine.

A librarian unlocks the door to the Hemingway Room and I walk in. I lay out my papers on one of the cherry tables and begin the work for the day. Perhaps it is as simple as checking the spelling of a single word. Did Hemingway write *bitter* or *better*, in that ending for *A Farewell to Arms*? An answer awaits me on the shelf, tucked away in one of the blue-green boxes. The suggestiveness of the work he did finish and the seductiveness of the work he did not complete ensures that Hemingway will continue to surface, like Santiago's marlin, "unendingly." For those of us who love the work, it is a matter of bringing something into the light. I will spend the hours like this, jumping up, locating a box, carrying it to the table, leafing through its folders, writing down a word. Here is where I find him, and soon I am in it again and surrounded by paper, the scattered papers.

Notes

Hemingway's published works are referred to using the abbreviations provided in the first volume of *The Letters of Ernest Hemingway* (Cambridge 2011). A complete list of the abbreviations can be found in Works Cited.

Items in the Hemingway Collection, John F. Kennedy Library, Boston, are referred to by file number or name, folder number, and page number (where page and folder numbers are available), e.g., JK/EH 422.1/21, 4, where 422.1 is the file number, 21 the folder number, and 4 the page number.

Items from the Ernest Hemingway Papers in the Clifton Waller Barrett Library, Albert and Shirley Small Special Collections Library, University of Virginia, Charlottesville, VA, are cited as UVA 6250.

INTRODUCTION: HEMINGWAY UNBOUND

"IMPORTANT To Be Opened": Mary Hemingway, *How It Was*, 504.

"letters written by me": *SL*, xxiii.

"the worthy from the": *How It Was*, 506.

"Read ALL of somebody": Bishop, *One Art*, 596.

"I see me dead": *FTA*, 126.

"very embarrassed": *SS*, 32.

"terrible remorse": JK/EH, 422.1/19, 22.

"People are not as": JK/EH 83. For Whom the Bell Tolls, Manuscript / EH Typescript, manuscript fragment.

"theory . . . feel more": *MF*, 75.

"Hemingway had a hard": Wyatt, "Hemingway's Uncanny Beginnings," 476.

"the motion through the": Warren, *All the King's Men*, 407.

"all stories, if continued": *DIA*, 122.

"growth after middle age": Cowley, *A Second Flowering*, 252.

"The first right that": *BL*, xi.

"Hemingway's life was becoming": Reynolds, *Hemingway: The Final Years*, 114.

"sizable component of melancholy": Rovit and Brenner, 169.

"you write with the": JK/EH, 422.1/21, 4.

"alternative endings": *A Farewell to Arms: The Hemingway Library Edition*, 303.

"unfinished": Burwell, 1.

"a complete reading text": *UK*, ix.

"closure": Ibid., 456.

"'That's too bad,' I": JK/EH 223A/34, 850.

"something that was going": *SAR*, 167.

"*the start of all*": Ibid., 70.

CHAPTER 1: AT THE BEGINNING

"At the lake shore": *In Our Time*, 1925 edition, 15. Subsequent quotations are from the 1930 edition of *In Our Time* (*IOT*).

"Over to the Indian": *IOT*, 15.

"the word 'and' consciously": Ross, 279.

"so that when you": *LEH*, Vol. 2, 286.

"a participating witness": Reynolds, *Hemingway: The 1930s*, 4.

"not important": Ibid., 16.

"several things": Ibid., 17.

"you could omit anything": *MF*, 75.

"interne": Ibid., 17.

"You'll lose it if": *SAR*, 245.

"customarily presents itself as": Fiedler, 317.

"*a woman having a*": *IOT*, 21.

"very hard to have": Ibid., 85.

"everything behind": Ibid., 134.

"There isn't any good": Ibid., 112.

"having babies": Ibid., 12.

"The scenes of childbirth": Comley and Scholes, 27.

"that ought to have": Freud, "The 'Uncanny,'" 130.

"home where he had": *IOT*, 139.

"undoubtedly belongs to all": Freud, "The 'Uncanny,'" 122.

"that class of the": Ibid., 123–24.

"mysterious and homelike": *IOT*, 139.

"*Oh, we call it*": Freud, "The 'Uncanny,'" 127.

"What interests us most": Ibid., 129.

"which develops toward an": Ibid., 131.

"In the early morning": *IOT*, 19.

"What's all this irony": *SAR*, 113.

"Nick, standing in the": *IOT*, 18.

"She is the most": *BL*, 460.

"No, I think it's": *IOT*, 19.

"three days before": Ibid., 16.

"Why did . . . I don't": Ibid., 19.

"I see": Ibid., 16.

"Damn squaw bitch!": *IOT*, 17.

"Is dying hard, Daddy?": Ibid., 19.

"*The only writing that*": *NAS*, 246.

"mental conversation": *LEH*, Vol. 2, 170.

"*Nick in the stories*": *NAS*, 246.

"mind-forg'd manacles": Blake, 27.

"How good a book": *MF-RE*, 234.

"is done to oneself": *FWBT*, 73.

"incision": *IOT*, 17.

"*Just a few weeks*": *NAS*, 4.

"The cord was caught": *FTA*, 327.

"Caesars form of childbirth": *SL*, 346.

"I do . . . the wound": *FTA*, 325.

"the paragraph describing Catherine's": *Reynolds, Hemingway's First War*, 45.

"thick-edged . . . high welted": *FTA*, 325.

"I always cut a": Bruccoli, *Conversations with Ernest Hemingway*, 49.

"would be greatly improved": *MAW*, xvii.

"slitting": *IOT*, 155.

"That's one for the": Ibid., 18.

"to him . . . intact": *GOE*, 247.

"one true sentence": *MF*, 12.

"*a cinematograph film*": *IOT*, 131.

CHAPTER 2: A SECOND WILL

"as though they were": JK/EH 422.1/37, 2.

"Memory is the best": Mellow, 210.

"series of short prose": Baker, *Hemingway: A Life Story*, 108.

"there was any controlling": Reynolds, *Hemingway: The Paris Years*, 140.

"It has form all": *LEH*, Vol. 2, 41.

"chapter headings": *LEH*, Vol. 2, 154.

"I am writing some": *LEH*, Vol. 2, 103.

"not even in his": Smith, 35.

"Oh, it's so big": *SS*, 85.

"*inaccrochable*": *MF*, 15.

"like looking with your": *LEH*, Vol. 2, 166.

"What will I have": Ibid., 259.

"All the . . . The first": Ibid., 154.

"about the best I've": Ibid., 295.

"negro": *IOT*, 57.

"I like to be": Ibid., 61.

"The new story makes": *LEH*, Vol. 2, 295.

"its rightful place as": Smith, 36.

"But sometimes when I": *MF*, 12.

"At the lake shore there / was": JK/EH 493, 9.

"At the lake shore there was another / row-boat": JK/ EH 96, Typescript of *In Our Time*. The folder contains a photocopy of page 230 of *The Transatlantic Review*.

"excisions": *LEH*, Vol. 2, 295.

"*ashamed*": *NAS*, 3.

"*He was afraid of*": Ibid., 4.

"*that was what . . . Maybe*": Ibid., 3.

"*deleting*": Smith, 35.

"mental conversation": *LEH*, Vol. 2, 170.

"usual method of arriving": Oldsey, *Ernest Hemingway: The Papers of a Writer*, 38.

"reading": *IOT*, 27.

"reading a . . . It was": Ibid., 72.

"wished he had brought": Ibid., 155.

"He was going back": Ibid., 156.

"He was going back to camp to read": JK/EH 277, 10 and JK/EH 278, unnumbered page.

"a second Will more": Wordsworth, "Ode to Duty" in *Wordsworth: Poetical Works*, 385.

"everything hangs on": *LEH*, Vol. 2, 322.

"behind": *IOT*, 134.

"ahead": Ibid., 15.

"the parts held together": Wilson, "Hemingway: Gauge of Morale" in Bloom, *Ernest Hemingway: Bloom's Modern Critical Views*, 7.

"hell": *IOT*, 111.

"there is a line": *TOTTC*, 267.

"It is a short": Lawrence, 311.

"chronologically": *NAS*, v.

"over-all narrative": Ibid., vii.

"Book is called In": *LEH*, Vol. 2, 277.

"Max *please believe* me": Reynolds, *Hemingway: The 1930s*, 49.
"frozen moments": Reynolds, *Hemingway: The Paris Years*, 140.
"Dear Ezra, I will": *LEH*, Vol. 2, 41–42.
"Chapters from In Our Time": JK/EH 97A.
"*They hanged Sam Cardinella*": *IOT*, 143.
"humiliation is intensified by": Strychacz, 222.
"postulates the existence of": Ibid., 223.
"to sleep": *IOT*, 142.
"In the morning the": Ibid., 145.
"He felt he had": Ibid., 134.
"*He was not thinking*": *NAS*, 249.
"plenty of days": *IOT*, 156.
"even the surface had": Ibid., 133.
"loose": Lawrence, 312.
"The train went on": *IOT*, 133.
"We got off the": JK/EH 279, 1.
"They": Oldsey, *Ernest Hemingway: The Papers of a Writer*, 43.
"The story was about": *MF*, 76.
"He did not need": *IOT*, 135.
"Sharp at the edge": Ibid., 137.
"That house meant more": *SS*, 408.
"Inside the tent the": *IOT*, 139.
"Each sentence refuses to": Sartre, 116.
"*querencia*": *DIA*, 150.
"This place is pretty": *SS*, 368.
"It seemed like a": *FTA*, 216.
"There were still good": *GHOA*, 285.
"It's a good place": *IIS*, 25.
"daughter": *CSS*, 609.
"father": Ibid., 628.
"in the dark he": Ibid., 615.
"This *unheimlich* place": Freud, "The 'Uncanny,'" 152–53.
"smoothed out": *IOT*, 138.
"It's a symbol": Ibid., 42.
"hallucinated urgency": Hovey, 33.
"the sequence of motion": *DIA*, 2.
"You would have to": *IOT*, 155.
"He looked back. The": Ibid., 156.
"When I stopped writing": *MF*, 76–77.
"Ahead the river narrowed": *IOT*, 154.
"finished a swell story": *LEH*, Vol. 2, 140.
"trying to do the": Ibid., 141.
"*He, Nick, wanted to*": *NAS*, 247.
"starting to . . . choke it": *IOT*, 142.
"*writing that was any*": *NAS*, 246.
"*started with . . . broke the*": Ibid., 247.
"meditations . . . Hemingway, remarks are": Stein, *Stein: Writings 1903–1932*, 875.
"that the last eleven": *LEH*, Vol. 2, 172.
"Wouldn't it be funny": Ibid., 171.
"mental conversation . . . just the": Ibid., 170.
"If a writer of": *DIA*, 192.
"*Cezanne would. . . moving in*": *NAS*, 248.
"*the old boy was*": Ibid., 249.
"a mallard drake in": *ARIT*, 297.
"We'll keep him for": Ibid., 298.
"There is no end": *A Farewell to Arms, The Hemingway Library Edition*, 305.
"beating": *FWBT*, 471.

CHAPTER 3: THE END OF PLEASURE

"against time": *FTA*, 208.
"the demand to survive": Price, 141.
"hum": *SAR*, 161.
"We all got in": Ibid., 93.
"It felt good to": Ibid., 111.
"It was a long": Ibid., 118.
"this Brett business": Ibid., 123.
"the road into the": Ibid., 125.
"One morning I went": Ibid., 126.
"healthful interlude": Jane E. Wilson in Nagel, *Critical Essays on Ernest Hemingway's* The Sun Also Rises, 185.
"pleasure": *SAR*, 129.
"badly marked": Ibid., 212.
"low as hell": Ibid., 222.
"the water directly into": Ibid., 223.
"at the table, and": Ibid., 224.
"In the morning it": Ibid., 227.
"epicure of duration": Nabokov, 185–86.
"Then later: 'Do you'": *SAR*, 55.
"After supper we went": Ibid., 111.
"*the greatest pleasure*": *NAS*, 247.
"Why don't they start?": *SAR*, 138.
"A look of eager, deserving": Ibid., 22.
"my life is going": Ibid., 10.
"incapacity to enjoy": Ibid., 42.
"As the bull came": *DS*, 204.
"not as he had": *SAR*, 220.
"the most difficult, dangerous and": *DIA*, Glossary.
"The bull charged and": *SAR*, 220.
"He made the three": Svoboda, 72.
"the narrator's expertise is": Ibid., 76.
"Your Englishman on the": JK/EH 77.
"caught by time": *GHOA*, 12.
"drinking this, the first": Ibid., 6.
"of drinking the whiskey": manuscript of *Green Hills of Africa*, UVA 6250, 5.
"Don't go back": *DLT*, 176.
"Walking across the square": *SAR*, 192–93.
"It is a mannerism": Ashley, 39.
"a feeling of things": *SAR.*, 146.
"feeling of going through": Ibid., 64.
"little friend, Zizi": Ibid., 63.
"Oh darling, I'm so": Ibid., 64.
"I walked . . . I read": Ibid., 35–36.
"I just talk around": Ibid., 245.
"you could omit anything": *MF*, 75.
"paid": *SAR*, 148.
"This hum went on": Ibid., 161.
"to see him hurt": Ibid., 148.
"made me disgusted at": Ibid., 149.
"I sat beside Brett": Ibid., 167.
"I like it very": Ibid., 174.
"she saw why she": Ibid., 167.
"purity of line": Ibid., 168.
"I've lost my self-respect": Ibid., 183.
"sentimental": Ibid., 101.
"pimp": Ibid., 190.
"Don't we pay for": Ibid., 26.
"smiling in his embarrassed": Ibid., 130.
"a very special secret": Ibid., 131.
"the pleasure of discovering": Ibid., 132.
"his embarrassed smile": Ibid., 171.
"Montoya stood embarrassed": Ibid., 172.

"not even nod": Ibid., 177.
"Montoya did not come": Ibid., 228.
"hurt in the war": Ibid., 17.
"Che mala fortuna!": Ibid., 31.
"impotent": Ibid., 115.
"steer": Ibid., 141.
"joystick": Ibid., 116.
"by page 39": Svoboda, 9.
"I just had an": *SAR*, 115.
"eunuch": Quoted in Nagel, *Critical Essays on Ernest Hemingway's* The Sun Also Rises, 37.
"unmanned": Ibid., 38.
"sexually incapacitated": Quoted in Nagel, 38.
"on the Importance of": *LEH*, Vol. 2, 446.
"we have only Hemingway's": Spilka, 201.
"I wondered what a": *SL*, 745.
"had been wounded in": Bruccoli, *Conversations with Ernest Hemingway*, 120.
"thinking about Brett and": *SAR*, 31.
"It's funny to write": *SL*, 225–26.
"*was the greatest pleasure*": *NAS*, 247.
"I had learned already": *MF*, 26.
"by then I knew": Ibid., 62.
"I learned not to": Ibid., 13.
"to get . . . to make": Ibid., 25.
"This is a novel": typescript of *The Sun Also Rises*, UVA 6250, 1A.
"much too expensive": Ibid., 1A.
"grand vitality": Ibid., 5.
"very good at being": Ibid., 6.
"I did not want": Ibid., 7.
"novel will have that": Ibid., 9.
"a feeling of condescending": *F. Scott Fitzgerald: A Life in Letters*, ed. Matthew J. Bruccoli, 142.
"of no importance": Ibid., 144.
"sententious preliminaries": Ibid., 142.
"Ernest I can't tell": Ibid., 144.
"Robert Cohn was once": *SAR*, 3.
"snotty": JK/EH, *The Sun Also Rises* 194. Notebooks: Book I, 15.
"I've read his Great": *LEH*, Vol. 2, 348.
"an unaffected scorn": *The Great Gatsby*, 6.
"permanently flattened": *SAR*, 3.
"maybe his mother had": Ibid., 4.
"Why I felt that": Ibid., 99.
"I have commenced with": *SL*, 213.
"I believe that the": Ibid., 215.
"the best looking kid": Svoboda, 6.
"until after the completed": *MF*, 184.
"Please do what you": *F. Scott Fitzgerald: A Life in Letters*, 144.
"I'd like to see": Ibid., 279.
"something very important to": *MF*, 189.
"the way I was": Ibid., 190.
"rotten habit of picturing": *SAR*, 13.
"dreadful bore": Fleming, "Second Thoughts" in Nagel, *Critical Essays on Ernest Hemingway's* The Sun Also Rises, 164.
"as a character in": Ibid., 164–65.
"as an attempt to": Ibid., 165.
"to get rid of friends": *SAR*, 11.
"Hi, Hem. What are": *MF*, 91.
"to make a stand": Ibid., 92.
"keep the hell away": Ibid., 94.
"I worked better than": Ibid., 96.

CHAPTER 4: FALSE SURMISE

"In *A Farewell to Arms*": *Reynolds, Hemingway's First War*, 238.
"she will make you": *FTA*, 99.
"in the late summer": Ibid., 3.
"dictates *A Farewell to Arms*": Burwell, 71.
"I could . . . I cannot": *FTA*, 13.
"It has only happened": Ibid., 249.
"Why not end the": *F. Scott Fitzgerald: A Life in Letters*, 167.
"kills the very good": *FTA*, 249.
"burst of eloquence": *F. Scott Fitzgerald: A Life in Letters*, 264.
"one of the most": Ibid., 167.
"a movement without hope": *ARIT*, 297.
"there is no end": JK/EH 70, the page is numbered "7" in a librarian's hand.
"lying with Catherine on": *FTA*, 231.
"hard floor for a": Ibid., 232.
"a separate peace": Ibid., 243.
"You were out of": Ibid., 232.
"lied . . . game": Ibid., 30.
"I wished we had": Ibid., 36.
"I wish she were": Ibid., 37.
"Maybe she would pretend": Ibid., 37–38.
"is always built upon": Price, 138.
"against time": *FTA*, 208.
"the nights were cool": *FTA*, 3.
"It came very fast": Ibid., 6.
"Their rifles were wet": Ibid., 4.
"had not wanted to": Ibid., 93.
"embarrassed": Ibid., 184.
"sacred, glorious, and sacrifice": Ibid., 184.
"There isn't any me": Ibid., 115.
"We really are the": Ibid., 139.
"I'll say just what": Ibid., 105.
"and it would all": Ibid., 114.
"*Do* we have to": Ibid., 18.
"Have you ever loved": Ibid., 19.
"Catherine is believable, as": Spilka, 220.
"the rains": *FTA*, 4.
"I'm afraid of the": Ibid., 126.
"a study in apprehension": *DIA*, 56.
"Well, we were in": *FTA*, 197.
"inner life": *THHN*, 177.
"O western wind, when": *SL*, 189.
"When I came back": *FTA*, 10.
"when I got home": Ibid., 28.
"We'll be back": Ibid., 267.
"Ahead the road turned": Ibid., 208.
"Ahead across the wet": Ibid., 210.
"Ahead across the plain": Ibid., 212.
"angry and yet certain": Ibid., 26.
"God knows I had": Ibid., 93.
"when I saw her": Ibid., 91.
"I had wanted to": Ibid., 13.
"he had always known": Ibid., 14.
"That was what you": Ibid., 327.
"The hay smelled good": Ibid., 216.
"all strange": *SAR*, 192.
"in a little time": *FTA*, 153.
"feeling that we had": Ibid., 249.
"like our home": Ibid., 309.
"heavy timber": Ibid., 226.
"a good place": Ibid., 216.

"*perishable*": Reynolds, *Hemingway's First War*, 41.

"*the kingdom of heaven*": Ibid., 40.

"*you were born loving*": Ibid., 41.

"Don't touch a thing": Reynolds, *Hemingway: The 1930s*, 9.

"But after I had": *FTA*, 332.

"Hemingway made an even": Oldsey, *Hemingway's Hidden Craft*, 58.

"six months gone with": JK/EH 71, 2.

"the original ending . . . inferior": Grebstein, 215.

"Nothing was changed then": JK/EH 70, 41.

"All of the alternative": *FTA-HLE*, XVII.

"Please go out and": *FTA*, 314.

"The waiter brought a": Ibid., 318.

"*Give it to me*": Ibid., 319.

"This was . . . This was": Ibid., 320.

"a freshly skinned rabbit": Ibid., 324.

"I had . . . He did": Ibid., 325.

"He looks like a": Ibid., 326.

"Poor little kid. I": Ibid., 327.

"all right . . . go and": Ibid., 328.

"I remembered . . . you took": Ibid., 329.

"Everything was gone inside": Ibid., 330.

"do our things with": Ibid., 331.

"I was not made": Ibid., 233.

"I do not think": Ibid., 325.

"parental devotion, filial return": Price, 139.

"You will die and": *FTA-HLE*, 303.

"You can stop a": JK/EH 64. The quotation can be found in a folder labeled "Manuscript, pages 642–652," on the second of two pages numbered "652."

"It goes on": *FTA-HLE*, 318.

"going on with everything": Ibid., 316.

"false ending with child": Reynolds, *Hemingway's First War*, 293.

"killed his mother": *FTA*, 325.

"He did not seem": *FTA-HLE*, 305.

CHAPTER 5: MAKING A WOUND

"It is still too": Young, *Ernest Hemingway: A Reconsideration*, 246.

"Actually I think we": *SL*, 545.

"small war on the": Lowell, *Collected Poems*, 386.

"I don't . . . I don't": *CSS*, 20.

"Ever since I had": *SL*, 608.

"We, in games . . . are": *DIA*, 22.

"One finds it in": James, "Henry James's First Interview."

"Hemingway's novel is an": Reynolds, *Hemingway's First War*, 60–61.

"There were many words": *FTA*, 185.

"not experienced the military": Reynolds, *Hemingway's First War*, 5.

"located accurate topographic maps": Ibid., 281.

"to the silk-worms eating": *SS*, 363.

"one of which got": Reynolds, *The Young Hemingway*, 19.

"The surgical chart of": Ibid., 18.

"I ate the end": *FTA*, 54.

"My legs felt warm": Ibid., 55.

"all that was happening": Ibid., 60.

"Did you do any": Ibid., 63.

"Suffering severe shrapnel wounds": Reynolds, *Hemingway's First War*, 170.

"carrying another wounded man": Oldsey, *Hemingway's Hidden Craft*, 43.

"alleged heroism": Robert W. Lewis, "Hemingway in Italy," 218.

"wounded by the explosion": Ibid., 215.

"bogus": Ibid., 218.

"The two . . . and notably": Ibid., 219.

"EH's wounding: the": Baker, *Hemingway: A Life Story*, 571.

"The machine gun bullet": *LEH*, Vol. 1, 131.

"Not a lie exactly": Reynolds, *The Young Hemingway*, 18.

"I picked up the": Bruccoli, *Conversations with Ernest Hemingway*, 4.

"In the *Sun* interview": Reynolds, *The Young Hemingway*, 21.

"His lies were quite": *IOT*, 70.

"atrocity stories": Ibid., 69.

"he lost everything": Ibid., 70.

"sideways as he pivoted": Svoboda, 62.

"and pulled his horse": *SAR*, 216.

"conception of superior strength": Ibid., 215.

"the hero with the": Wilson, *The Wound and the Bow*, 237.

"trauma theory of literature": Bruccoli, *Conversations with Ernest Hemingway*, 115.

"haunted . . . the first clue": Cowley, "Hemingway's Wound," 224.

"The experience of the": Hoffman, "The Secret Wound" in Gellens, 108.

"From here on the": Young, *Ernest Hemingway*, 12.

"two arguments": Young, *Ernest Hemingway: A Reconsideration*, 5.

"First, the notion that": Ibid., 5–6.

"Second, the one fact": Ibid., 6.

"if the 'wound' is": Spilka, 219.

"masculinity . . . the very anxiety": Moddelmog, 130.

"password": *MF-RE*, 182.

"something repeated": *SAR*, 64.

"remembering back": *SS*, 365.

"been blown up at": Ibid., 363.

"Sometimes I would fish": Ibid., 364.

"to the earliest thing": Ibid., 365.

"About the new house": Ibid., 365–66.

"What's this?": Ibid., 366.

"I've been cleaning out": JK/EH 168, Now I Lay Me /Manuscript Fragments, unnumbered page.

"I can recall no": Smith, 173.

"it is art that": Henry James, *Selected Letters*, 431.

"nothing is done to": *FWBT*, 73.

"the big wound": *MAW*, xvi.

"Bunny Wilson writing about": *SL*, 694.

"first war . . . I now": Cowley, "Hemingway's Wound," 229–30.

"'No,' I said. 'I'": *SAR*, 115.

"Well . . . A plane is": Ibid., 116.

"obscure hurt": James, *Notes of a Son and Brother*, 298.

"As for the Henry": *SL*, 208–09.

"lay off the Biography": Ibid., 247.

"*the only writing that*": *NAS*, 246.

"If I write about": *SL*, 400.

"When I hear from": Ibid., 744.

"Every writer is in": Ibid., 745.

"In Italy when I": *MF-RE*, 182.

"the experiences and knowledge": Ibid., 181.

"Some days it went": *MF*, 91.

"If you make it": *BL*, 216.

"You don't put your": Bennett, 101.

CHAPTER 6: AWKWARDNESS AND APPRECIATION

"the eye of a": *DIA*, 193.

"at this point it": Ibid., 63.

"At the first bullfight": Ibid., 1.

"I'm at work on": *LEH*, Vol. 2, 273.

"I'm going to write": Ibid., 276.

"In the afternoon fight": Ibid., 274–75.

"Bulls kill for fun": Ibid., 357.

"thing which it is": *DIA*, 63.

"It is impossible to": Ibid., 207.

"it is much more": Wilde, 359.

"I was too old": *DIA*, 171.

"Wine offers a greater": Ibid., 10.

"capable of transmitting constantly": Ibid., 10–11.

"capable of appreciation": Ibid., 10.

"study": Ibid., 3.

"preconceived opinions": Ibid., 33.

"the greatest difficulty, aside": Ibid., 2.

"effect": Ibid., 11.

"awkward sights": Ibid., 12.

"kept from being one": Ibid., 14.

"exists only in the": Ibid., 99.

"was working very hard": Ibid., 2.

"I believe I saw": Ibid., 234.

"and as he charged": *DLT*, 343.

"but it was not": Ibid., 344.

"all sorts of complicated": Ibid., 345.

"obsolete": Ibid., 346.

"at the first bullfight": *DIA*, 234–35.

"taken many people": Ibid., 4.

"those that were affected": Ibid., 5.

"a preliminary stage of": Freud, "Mourning and Melancholia" in *The Freud Reader*, 587.

"The Poor Horses": Robert W. Lewis, "The Making of *Death in the Afternoon*" in Nagel, *Ernest Hemingway: The Writer in Context*, 42.

"furnishes . . . emotion": *DIA*, 233.

"We owe God a death": *SS*, 32.

"Men search consciously or": Stanton, 96.

"is performing a work": *DIA*, 213.

"tragedy": Ibid., 6.

"Krebs looked at the": *IOT*, 75.

"subjective feelings were the": Lamb, *Art Matters*, 77.

"I am trying, always": *SL*, 380.

"certain plain words": Ibid., 381.

"This was omitted on": *MF*, 75.

"If a writer of": *DIA*, 192.

"I always try to": Bruccoli, *Conversations with Ernest Hemingway*, 125.

"find the scheme behind": Griffin, 212–13.

"Erudition shouldn't show . . . Ideally": Brasch, 222–23.

"You make something through": Bruccoli, *Conversations with Ernest Hemingway*, 129.

"the profundity of unseen": *DIA*, 203.

"it easily in all": Ibid., 193.

"horn knowledge": Ibid., 127.

"It is useless to": Stanton, 98.

"tests of the reader's": Ibid., 106.

"overemphasis on the personalities": Ibid., 110.

"Let it all change": *DIA*, 278.

"I believe that the": Ibid., 8.

"Where are we going": *IOT*, 15.

"the effect of the": *DIA*, 33.

"It is not enough": Ibid., 278.

"remain firm and erect": Broer, 61.

"grace under pressure": *SL*, 200.

"I had compromised myself": *DIA*, 172.

"*Villalta became one with*": *IOT*, 105.

"to fits of cowardice": *DIA*, 13.

"control the nervousness of": Ibid., 17.

"his feet jumped away": Ibid., 18.

"At the moment of": Ibid., 19.

"fear": Ibid., 157.

"awkwardness": Ibid., 217.

"does a great faena": Ibid., 221.

"Technique ... is always most": Ibid., 17.

"What they call your": JK/EH 123, Chapter 20.Schruns. Version Two; page is dated March 26.

"disembowellings": *DIA*, 7.

"extraordinary attempts at bravery": James, *Literary Criticism*, Volume Two, 1013.

"rules": *DIA*, 21.

"suertes": Ibid., 16.

"the conduct of a": Ibid., 13.

"uses everything that has": Ibid., 100.

"the really new ... the": Eliot, *Selected Prose*, 38.

"All right, I'll be": *DIA*, 78.

"dignity and passion": Ibid., 79.

"had trouble with his": Ibid, 80.

"on the sixth time": Ibid., 81.

"He was made out": Ibid., 82.

"He gave emotion always": Ibid., 79.

"decadence": Ibid., 68.

"to stumble and recover": Bouchard, 73.

"Hemingway's most distinctive and": Ibid., 168.

"inferior": Rovit and Brenner, 11.

"nine paragraphs that originally": Beegel, *Hemingway's Craft of Omission*, 51.

"an ending richer than": Reynolds, *Hemingway: The 1930s*, 79.

"If I could have": *DIA*, 270.

"ironic device": Beegel, *Hemingway's Craft of Omission*, 62.

"appears in many works": Ibid., 109.

"It is nice, every": *LEH*, Vol. 2, 334.

"*goes without saying*": Barthes, *Mythologies*, 59.

"You'll lose it if": *SAR*, 245.

"Am glad you liked": *SL*, 378.

"No. It is not": *DIA*, 278.

CHAPTER 7: HUNTING SHAME

"the edge of the": *GHOA*, 2.

"the best buff, the": Ibid, 153.

"A belle epoque of": *SL*, 443.

"constructed for himself according": Gordimer, 571.

"The way to hunt": *GHOA*, 12.

"Unlike many novels, none": Ibid., Foreword.

"It is not enough": *DIA*, 278.

"failed": Ibid., 176.

"The literary discussion, though": DeVoto quoted in *Hemingway in Context*, Ed. Moddelmog and del Gizzo, 385.

"Politics, women, drink, money": *GHOA*, 28.

"The most literary hunting": Quoted in Reynolds, *Hemingway: The 1930s*, 214.

"verbal dysentery": *GHOA*, 29.

"All modern American literature": Ibid., 22.

"Hemingway is writing a": Reynolds, *Hemingway: The 1930s*, 184.

"*Green Hills of Africa* is a book": Bouchard, 96.

"poisoned with envy": *GHOA*, 291.

"the steps in how": Ibid., 272.

"a smugly righteous bastard": Ibid., 132.

"I had gotten excited": Ibid., 259.

"the evening braggies": Ibid., 240.

"Lion, lion, rhino, buffalo": Ibid., 241.

"Tomorrow, sable": Ibid., 243.

"I had never seen": Ibid., 255.

"hard to see well": Ibid., 252.

"Terrain is what remains": *ARIT*, 123.

"Where's the bull?": *GHOA*, 252.

"the biggest": Ibid., 257.

"and I knew I": Ibid., 258.

"excited shooting": Ibid., 259.

"big bull": Ibid., 260.

"another sable": Ibid., 261.

"They all look like": Ibid., 105.

"For a minute I": Ibid., 263.

"something serious by now": Ibid., 264.

"old man": Ibid., 265.

"pounding ache": Ibid., 268.

"immeasurably the better man": Ibid., 269.

"killed it cleanly": Ibid., 272.

"all cows": Ibid., 273.

"That damned . . . I should": Ibid., 281.

"I do not like": *FWBT*, 39.

"I'd see the buffalo": *GHOA*, 282.

"the truth of Imagination": Keats, 54.

"For a minute I": *GHOA*, 263.

"For we have been where": manuscript of *Green Hills of Africa*, UVA 6250, 148 insert 2.

"Here I could shoot": *GHOA*, 285.

"Here I could shoot": manuscript of *Green Hills of Africa*, UVA 6250, 474.

"large trees": *GHOA*, 107.

"living in that Russia": Ibid., 108.

"I was thinking": *GHOA*, 108; manuscript of *Green Hills of Africa*, UVA 6250, 148.

"in the different seasons": *GHOA*, 109.

"Then Sevastopol made me": Ibid., 70.

"Hemingway attempts as unremittingly": Price, 152.

"I'm trying in all": *LEH*, Vol. 2, 286.
"sees everything, throws nothing": Beegel, *Hemingway's Craft of Omission*, 92.
"the empty condoms of": *GHOA*, 150.
"sack . . . the essence of": *FWBT*, 256.
"learn . . . as I go": *GHOA*, 25.
"the man who lived": Wolff, 97.
"The People in the": *Scribner's Magazine*, May 1935, Vol. 97, No. 5, p. 259.
"Quite deliberately, Hemingway was": Reynolds, *Hemingway: The 1930s*, 182.
"have not been admitted": *DIA*, 7.
"This ability to . . . distance": Comley and Scholes, 129.
"highly-righteous": *GHOA*, 94.
"me ashamed at having": Ibid., 95.
"irritable, righteous, pompous": Ibid., 120.
"new openness to the": Spilka, 234.
"ideal of how a": *GHOA*, 64.
"ashamed": Ibid., 259.
"ashamed": Ibid., 113.
"I'm afraid I gut": Ibid., 102.
"Every damned thing is": Ibid., 281.
"primitive emotions": Ibid., 291.
"But I was bitter": Ibid., 293.
"the recognition of the": Frye, 212.
"Tragedy seems to move": Ibid., 213.
"wheel of fortune": *FWBT*, 225.
"making me dizzy": Ibid., 227.
"'Happiness' is, after all": Didion, 210.
"I'd lie behind a": *GHOA*, 282.
"Here I could shoot": Ibid., 285.
"A continent ages quickly": Ibid., 284.
"Our people went to": Ibid., 285.
"that exploding, clanking sound": Ibid., 5.
"gotten brave, awfully suddenly": SS, 34.
"everything you do, you": Ibid., 73.
"It is finished": *GHOA*., 2.
"Wait a little": Ibid., 3.
"altogether happy": Ibid., 6.
"back to the time": Ibid., 46.
"estimations were only from": Ibid., 44.
"Take your time": Ibid., 230.
"That all seemed a": Ibid., 176.
"Oh, Jake, we could": *SAR*, 247.
"It was nice to": *GHOA*., 71.
"All I wanted to": Ibid., 72–73.
"I loved the damned": manuscript of *Green Hills of Africa*, UVA 6250, 94.
"have it *now*": *FWBT*, 169.
"Not for me": *SS*, 34.

CHAPTER 8: EMPATHY AND CANDOR

"white hunter": *SS*, 4.
"hate": Ibid., 25.
"a wild unreasonable happiness": Ibid., 32.
"solid . . . Mrs. Macomber": Ibid., 36.
"Every damned thing is": *GHOA*, 281.
"we understand . . . because we": Williams, 69.
"swishing rush in the": *SS*, 20.
"It was there exactly": Ibid., 11.
"It is an agent's": Williams, 70.
"some acknowledged": Ibid., 2.
"we are, in our": Ibid., 166.

"one another's eyes": *SS*, 6.
"the basic experience connected": Williams, 78.
"just shown himself, very": *SS*, 4.
"founded on values that": Williams, 73.
"merely some exaggerated sense": Ibid., 73–74.
"the notion of losing": Ibid., 77.
"internalized other": Ibid., 84.
"The source of the": Ibid., 103.
"It's not very pleasant": *SS*, 11.
"It was now lunch": Ibid., 3.
"red": Ibid., 5.
"before": Ibid., 11.
"It was now about": Ibid., 22.
"Now what in hell": Ibid., 8.
"I bolted like a": Ibid., 7.
"Maybe I can fix": Ibid., 8.
"I mean no one": Ibid., 7.
"Perhaps he had been": Ibid., 8.
"fear . . . elation": Ibid., 31.
"red": Ibid., 5.
"white": Ibid., 29.
"red neck": Ibid., 35.
"a ruddy fire eater": Ibid., 31.
"He was about middle": Ibid., 4.
"You know you have": Ibid., 5.
"miserably ashamed": Ibid., 11.
"redder": Ibid., 20.
"Which would you rather": Ibid., 6.
"Damned fine, eh?": Ibid., 32.
"I'm just scared, you": Ibid., 18.
"I don't want to": Ibid., 17.
"the way to take it": Ibid., 8.
"You know I don't": Ibid., 32.
"feeling of happiness about": Ibid., 33.
"You'll lose it if": *SAR*, 245.
"you're both talking rot": *SS*, 33.
"What's in her heart": Ibid., 27.
"Of course by the": JK/EH 689, 11.
"an admiring assistant introducing": Smith, 15.
"The lion still stood": *SS*, 15.
"I can think inside": Benson, 7.
"The bull had light": *SS*, 257.
"thought suddenly how a": *GHOA*, 148.
"I knew that I": manuscript of *Green Hills of Africa*, UVA 6250, 93.
"Macomber did not know": *SS*, 21.
"female cruelty": Ibid., 9.
"the hardest in the": Ibid., 8.
"When she left, Wilson": Ibid., 9.
"You've gotten awfully brave": Ibid., 34.
"There was no change": Ibid., 33.
"Something happened in me": Ibid., 32.
"It had taken a": Ibid., 33.
"The Coming Man . . . Through": Smith, 329–30.
"the one issue that": Smith, 335.
"Please stop it": *SS*, 37.
"She is begging the": Lamb, *Art Matters*, 146.
"It was neither all": *SS*, 11.
"whether we can or": Smith, 344.

CHAPTER 9: TAKING TIME

"Have had a very": *SL*, 499–500.
"the day of revolution": *FWBT*, 106.
"I wish there was": Ibid., 380.

"misfortune": Faulkner, *Faulkner: Novels 1926–1929*, 956.

"against": *FTA*, 208.

"He lay flat on": *FWBT*, 1.

"We lay there on": JK/EH 83, *For Whom the Bell Tolls.* Manuscript / EH Typescript, page 1.

"He lay flat on": JK/EH 83, 2.

"Christ I am tired": *TOTTC*, 281.

"how the other felt": *FWBT*, 324.

"pattern of tragedy": Ibid., 393.

"faked . . . broaden and fill": Woolf quoted in Mellow, 356.

"and for her everything": *FWBT*, 159.

"You can't remember sex": Doctorow, 226.

"This, that they were": *FWBT*, 379.

"What amateurs call a": Bruccoli, *Conversations with Ernest Hemingway*, 121.

"The cultivation of deliberate": Peterson, 22.

"sudden-ended always": *GHOA*, 72.

"not nearly as graphic": Gould, "A Tiny Operation with Great Effect" in Sanderson, 71.

"Robert Jordan knew then": Ibid., 72.

"slow up the time": *FWBT*, 431.

"on that same night": Ibid., 356.

"that reprieved feeling": Ibid., 368.

"How We Killed the": JK/EH 83, *For Whom the Bell Tolls*, Manuscript / EH Typescript, 326–350.

"hands down, the most": Stoneback, "The Priest Did Not Answer" in Sanderson, 106.

"Show us how to": *FWBT*, 101.

"I am an old": Ibid., 16.

"That is the way we": Ibid., 14.

"true regret": Ibid., 462.

"I would not have": Ibid., 208.

"I would restore them": Ibid., 209.

"fascists": Ibid., 103.

"All of his style": Ibid., 113.

"What we did. Not": Ibid., 134.

"*Vaya*, a day that": Ibid., 102.

"Dying was nothing and": Ibid., 312–13.

"*Now, ahora, maintenant, heute*": Ibid., 166.

"*He had already learned*": *NAS*, 122.

"Hemingway tended to think": Balassi, "The Writing of the Manuscript of *The Sun Also Rises*" in Nagel, *Critical Essays on Ernest Hemingway's* The Sun Also Rises, 106.

"You read what you": Bruccoli, *Conversations with Ernest Hemingway*, 112.

"You write until you": Ibid., 112–13.

"A problem which I": Ibid., 123.

"certain notions about the": *FWBT*, 168.

"life a life in": Ibid., 169.

"So if you love": Ibid., 168.

"Inside the sawmill one": Ibid., 194.

"This was how they": Ibid., 196.

"over the blued steel": Ibid., 280.

"I hate these pistol": Ibid., 318.

"the back of the": Ibid., 322.

"the sharp clarity": Ibid., 325.

"He was thinking: taking": Ibid., 326.

"It is hardly possible to": Frye, 319.

"Lieutenant Berrendo, watching the": *FWBT*, 471.

"twice-born": William James, *Writings 1902–1910*, 155.

"too late": *FWBT*, 94.

"Thou wilt blow no": Ibid., 53.

"approve of the moment": Ibid., 60.

"rendered useless by his": Ibid., 94.

"forced to a change": Ibid., 95.

"I had a moment": Ibid., 389.

"broken the pattern of": Ibid., 393.

"I was full of": Ibid., 127.

"He has shifted like": Ibid., 222.

"It will be quite": Ibid., 135.

"We are born with": *FTA*, 171.

"You died. You did": Ibid., 327.

"instruction": *FWBT*, 324.

"intelligent": Ibid., 230.

"You taught me a": Ibid., 380.

"I know . . . You only": Ibid., 381.

"Robert Jordan waved and": Ibid., 465–66.

"good life": Ibid., 467.

"Think about them being": Ibid., 470.

"just over the hills": Ibid., 467.

"People are not as": JK/EH 83, manuscript fragment.

"I hated to have": *SL*, 506.

"He could feel his": *FWBT*, 471.

"He lay on the": Ibid., 1.

"Two short chapters, amounting": *TOTTC*, 285.

"There in an old": Berg, "The Hunt for Hemingway" in *Vanity Fair*, October 2011, 284.

"Epilogue It was night": JK/EH 357, Manuscripts Book, *For Whom the Bell Tolls*.

"What do you think": *SL*, 514–15.

"She thought it was": *TOTTC*, 294.

"But it really stops": *FWBT*, 514.

CHAPTER 10: FORGIVENESS

"ex-dope-fiend nigger whore": Faulkner, *Faulkner: Novels 1942–1954*, 579.

"something even better, stronger": Ibid., 577.

"Because suddenly it could": Ibid., 576–77.

"Hast thou loved others?": *FWBT*, 71.

"not sick": Ibid., 73.

"what we did": Ibid., 134.

"dodged the *Thinking*": Hovey, 211.

"Nowhere in Hemingway's work": Evans in Waldhorn, 118.

"Hemingway creates Men of": Cirino, "The Persistence of Memory and the Denial of Self in *A Farewell to Arms*" in Cirino and Ott, 152.

"He felt he had": *IOT*, 134.

"If he looked too": Ibid., 135.

"mental conversation": *LEH*, Vol. 2, 170.

"Black River Manuscript": JK/EH 281, unnumbered page.

"true father-as-artist of": Ellison, 141.

"knew the difference between": Ibid., 140.

"there seems to be": Quoted in Warren, *Talking with Robert Penn Warren*, 41.

"coffee according to Hopkins": *IOT*, 142.

"You . . . have given more": *SAR*, 31.
"the head was mine": *FTA*, 231.
"hard floor for a": Ibid., 232.
"I was not made": Ibid., 233.
"*Who are you talking*": *FWBT*, 469.
"Listen, he told himself": Ibid., 304.
"But you were pretty": Ibid., 393–94.
"the greatest gift that": Ibid., 393.
"So do not think": Ibid., 394.
"He was completely integrated now": Ibid., 471.
"He was completely integrated again": JK/EH 83, Chapter 43, 129–130.
"soreness": *FWBT*, 341.
"Let us talk of": Ibid., 342.
"the Pilar told me": Ibid., 345.
"Now the making believe": Ibid., 346; sentence added to JK/EH 83, pages 699, 2–24.
"a complete embracing of": *FWBT*, 348.
"is there not something": Ibid., 342.
"I could tell thee": Ibid., 350.
"After the . . . feel the": JK/EH 83, pages 699, 2–24.
"I'm very proud": *FWBT*, 355.
"a good man": Ibid., 350.
"the horror": Ibid., 352.
"And it was there": Ibid., 353.
"No one has done": Ibid., 71.
"something that ought to": Freud, "The 'Uncanny,'" 148.
"the part she had": *FWBT*, 354.
"To understand is to": Ibid., 355.
"his mind, that was": Ibid., 380.
"The orders on this": Ibid., 335.
"Too very clear": JK/EH 83/14, 676–698.
"climbed out on a": *FWBT*, 337.
"that business that my": Ibid., 469.
"the good juice": Ibid., 338.
"if he wasn't a": Ibid., 339.
"I wonder what I": Ibid., 229.
"Then, as he thought": Ibid., 338.
"He understood his father": Ibid., 340.
"Who forgives . . . since we": Ibid., 41.
"his moustache had been": Ibid., 405–06.
"now, at this parting": Ibid., 406.
"Maybe the bully in": Ibid., 339.
"the crime of death": Yeats, *Collected Poems*, 231.
"Let me see thy": *FWBT*, 33.
"looking into the future": Ibid., 27.
"If you are wounded": Ibid., 21.
"despise whatever bad ending": Ibid., 393.
"a man seeing ahead": Ibid., 250.
"that thing . . . gypsy nonsense": Ibid., 387.
"death-to-come": Ibid., 256.
"definitely horrifying": Berg, *Max Perkins*, 379.
"make an ugly noise": *SL*, 513.
"the smell of death": Ibid., 508–09.
"In this sack will": JK/EH, 451–475.
"I will do it": *FWBT*, 469.
"Farewell is about the": *SL*, 378.
"Good-by *guapa*, I": *FWBT*, 405.
"felt as I felt": *SAR*, 192.
"anxiety . . . can be shown": Freud, "The 'Uncanny,'" 148.
"knowing as he spoke": *FWBT*, 212.

"Good-by, *guapa*": Ibid., 405.
"It was only now": Ibid., 406.
"the way all men": Ibid., 14.
"Keep it accurate": Ibid., 466.
"Listen, if I do": Ibid., 469.
"I go with thee": Ibid., 463.
"He was a fascist": Ibid., 117–18.
"'Guillermo,' she cried. 'Guillermo'": Ibid., 118.
"After Don Guillermo, I": Ibid., 119.
"Go, stand up and": Ibid., 464.
"What you have with": Ibid., 305.
"That we have had": Ibid., 393.
"I hate to leave": Ibid., 467.
"*Have, you mean. All*": JK/EH 83, Chapter 43, 101–125.

CHAPTER 11: BEFRIENDING

"His best": Quoted in Bloom, *Modern Critical Interpretations*: The Old Man and the Sea, 5.
"It made a good": *IOT*, 142.
"lucky": *OMS*, 125.
"very long": *SL*, 479.
"novel – not war book": Ibid., 574.
"sea book": Baker, *Hemingway: A Life Story*, 493.
"horrendous scream": Hawkins, 271.
"a rare and unusual": Reynolds, *Hemingway: The Final Years*, 243.
"a sudden stressful incident": Kert, 464.
"if anything happened to": Baker, *Hemingway: A Life Story*, 494.
"I was very happy": *SL*, 720.
"The wave of remembering": Ibid., 737.
"attacking each thing that": *GOE*, 123.
"Let us take the": *OMS*, 15.
"relics of his wife": Ibid., 16.
"too far": Ibid., 120.
"the glow of Havana": Ibid., 115.
"knew where he was": Ibid., 120.
"how pleasant it was": Ibid., 124.
"fiction": Ibid., 16.
"If you . . . But you": Ibid., 13.
"papa": Ibid., 10.
"He is almost blind": Ibid., 14.
"I do not like": Ibid., 24.
"He never . . . years old": Ibid., 27.
"the love of a": Baker, *Hemingway: The Writer as Artist*, 305.
"I am a strange": *OMS*, 14.
"I told the boy": Ibid., 66.
"If you're not tired": Ibid., 67.
"motionless in the sky": Ibid., 98.
"strange in their love-making": Ibid., 36–37.
"the strange undulation of": Ibid., 60.
"the sail was patched": Ibid., 9.
"he knew that if": Ibid., 43.
"the hand game": Ibid., 69.
"Now he said his": Ibid., 39.
"that neither in his": Quoted in Nagel, *Critical Essays on Ernest Hemingway's* The Sun Also Rises, 4.
"any circumlocutions . . . would be": Berg, *Max Perkins*, 143.
"our old ruin": *IOT*, 32.
"isn't fun anymore": Ibid., 34.
"They sprinkled the surface": Ibid., 32.

"as erosions in a": *OMS*, 10.
"like mountains": Ibid., 35.
"like friendly piles of": Ibid., 61.
"a great island of": Ibid., 72.
"the fish's eye looked": Ibid., 96.
"They were shaped like": Ibid., 100–01.
"a writer who is": Young, *Ernest Hemingway: A Reconsideration*, 132.
"May I take the": *OMS*, 16.
"to think about all": Ibid., 105.
"antithetically": Brenner, *Concealments in Hemingway's Works*, 177.
"why *brother* dominates Santiago's": Ibid., 178.
"There are three things": *OMS*, 64.
"Santiago's wishes for Manolin": Brenner, 178.
"halo": Ibid., 177.
"An antithetical reading of": Ibid., 179.
"men loved him, women": Donaldson, 55.
"Wasn't his lifelong subject": Price, 140.
"*a might-have-been*": Faulkner, *Faulkner: Novels 1936–1940*, 118.
"sorry for the birds": *OMS*, 29.
"brothers": Ibid., 48.
"the wind is our": Ibid., 120.
"distant friends": Ibid., 75.
"You are killing me": Ibid., 92.
"a small bird came": Ibid., 54.
"The bird looked at": Ibid., 55.
"several different groups of": Strychacz, 240.
"Once the reader has": Baker, *Hemingway: The Writer as Artist*, 117.
"there isn't any symbolysm": *SL*, 780.
"Nick watched his father's": *IOT*., 17.
"withered": *SS*, 268.
"A man must not": Ibid., 271.
"I would not be": Ibid., 272.
"thing of the hand": *FWBT*, 387.
"Can you read in": Ibid., 27.
"Do you believe in": Ibid., 250.
"In regard to that": Ibid., 387.
"holding the gun": Ibid., 337.
"to do that business": Ibid., 469.
"the palm of his": Ibid., 471.
"glad at last to": Ibid., 35.
"for Christ sake have": *SL*, 707.
"big, long, strong, spatular": *ARIT*, 55.
"The wind was very": Ibid., 152–53.
"Go ahead . . . Go ahead": *THHN*, 114.
"There is very much": *ARIT*, 85.
"last week, every night": Ibid., 84.
"But you got your": Ibid., 135.
"There is nothing broken": Ibid., 287.
"He reached into his": Ibid., 306.
"treachery": *OAS*, 61.
"If he cramps again": Ibid., 85.
"the working part of": Ibid., 57.
"There are three things": Ibid., 64.
"How do you feel": Ibid., 58–59.
"They had gone one": Ibid., 69–70.
"I'll stay with you": Ibid., 52.
"He'll stay with me": Ibid., 53.
"Stay with them": Ibid., 10.
"you can stay with": Ibid., 58.
"stays down . . . then I": Ibid., 60.
"all the time the": Ibid., 49.
"He had . . . had stayed": Ibid., 49–50.
"I will bring you": Ibid., 125.

"The wind is our": Ibid., 120.

"Why did I never": JK/EH 190, 98–112.

"But I must think": *OAS*, 103–04.

"be worthy of the": Ibid., 68.

"If I could have": Ibid., 114.

"The line rose slowly": Ibid., 62.

CHAPTER 12: REPLACEMENT AND REMORSE

"unfinished novels": Burwell, 1.

"Whenever any Individual Rejects": Blake, 551.

"sexual experimentation": Burwell, 95.

"The first of the": Ibid., 97–98.

"anticipating that he might": Ibid., 98.

"an internal series of": Leonard in del Gizzo, 60.

"her conclusion seems based": Ibid., 70.

"during the late fifties": Kennedy in del Gizzo, 168.

"I have . . . Poverty in": JK/EH 123, unnumbered page.

"They were living at": *GOE*, 3.

"interesting adjectives": Ibid., 134.

"handsome": Ibid., 9.

"wonderful": Ibid., 10.

"They were always hungry": Ibid., 4.

"What are you thinking?": Ibid., 5.

"in it": Ibid., 128.

"I'm getting hungry already": Ibid., 5.

"With mee / I see": Milton, *Paradise Lost*, Book VIII, lines 363–64.

"living creatures": Ibid., Book VIII, line 370.

"conversation": Ibid., Book VIII, line 418.

"He poured her another": *GOE*, 11.

"actions . . . provide the": Willingham in del Gizzo, 235.

"a brilliant woman trapped": Doctorow in del Gizzo, 19.

"jealousy of the work": *GOE*, 204.

"the conversational artist Catherine": Spilka, 12.

"The Serpent me beguil'd": Milton, *Paradise Lost*, Book X, line 162.

"I did it and": *GOE*, 237.

"Devil": Ibid., 45.

"the happiness of the": Baker, *Hemingway: A Life Story*, 460.

"Should God create another": *Paradise Lost*, Book IX, lines 911–13.

"Tennessee as I remember": *LEH*, Vol. 2, 205.

"If it had not": *SS*, 60.

"I wondered about how": *UK*, 382.

"unfair . . . Then I had": Brenner, *A Comprehensive Companion to Hemingway's* A Moveable Feast, volume 1, 4.

"I'm going to be": *GOE*, 12.

"It was . . . as a": Ibid., 14-15.

"He had shut his": Ibid., 17.

"beyond a very small": Ibid., Publisher's Note.

"*lower . . . inside*": See 422.1/1, 20.

"At the end they": *GOE*, 17.

"Goodbye Catherine goodbye my": Ibid., 18.

"I did not want": *SAR*, 55.

"What can there be": *GOE*, 21.

"destructive . . . inventive": Ibid., 5.

"The posthumous novels return": Burwell, 14.

"distrust of women's entry": Ibid., 29.

"Burned the clippings": *GOE*, 216.

"time was all simple": Ibid., 37.

"I can't paint at": Ibid., 53.

"a text . . . not with": Willingham in del Gizzo, 222.

"Is Madame . . . No, Madame": *GOE*, 24.

"to work in the": Ibid., 37.

"the story which he": Ibid., 93.

"So make you own": Ibid., 39.

"fat with clippings": Ibid., 23.

"frightened by them . . . How": Ibid., 24.

"Please let's not fight": Ibid., 25.

"being the only one": Ibid., 40.

"a yearning that women": Friedan, 15.

"We were partners but": JK/EH 422.1/34, 23.

"unmarried young woman": *MF*, 209.

"She has the best": *TOTTC*, 297.

"whose word I take": Hawkins, 211.

"where Pauline and I": *MR-RE*, 55.

"where we saw": *MF*, 65.

"There is no mention": JK/EH 124, *A Moveable Feast.* Endings. Version Two, 3.

"I left out when": *MF-RE*, 234.

"That part, the part": Ibid., 235.

"a much finer man": Ibid., 219.

"Then I was happy": JK/EH 126, *A Moveable Feast.* Chapter 20. Schruns. Version Three. Typescript, 8.

"one good and lasting": *MF-RE*, 123.

"the destruction of two": JK/EH 123, *A Moveable Feast.* Chapter 20. Schruns. Version Two, unnumbered page.

"the part . . . It could": *MF-RE*, 235.

"*and the story of*": JK/EH 124, *A Moveable Feast.* Endings. Version Two, 2.

"unbelievable wrenching, kicking happiness": *MF-RE*, 218.

"All I can think": *SL*, 220.

"It wasn't that the": *MF-RE*, 219.

"Remorse is impotence": Balzac, *Séraphita*, 80.

CHAPTER 13: HOW TO END IT

"*start of all he*": *SS*, 70.

"I was writing about": *MF*, 5.

"not want to leave": Ibid., 76.

"went so well you": Ibid., 91.

"He did not think": *GOE*, 179.

"He did not sleep": Ibid., 159.

"whoever read it . . . would": Ibid., 129.

"he had found the elephant": Ibid., 173.

"that he had never": Ibid., 174.

"I did not know": *FTA*, 14.

"getting something . . . only delayed": *SAR*, 148.

"That was morality; things": Ibid., 149.

"think that he could": *GOE*, 179.

"he did not have": Ibid., 182.

"you have to put": *MF-RE*, 224.

"The distances did not": *GOE*, 182.

"He did not know": *MF-RE*, 214.

"I do not know": Ibid., 220.

"They were getting close": *GOE*, 197.

"The hardest to make": Ibid., 174.

"anchored, in such suffering": Ibid., 199.
"Well we got him": Ibid., 200.
"That was all he": Ibid., 201.
"I'm sorry you got": Ibid., 202.
"How long do you": Ibid., 180.
"I care, David thought": Ibid., 181.
"only to remember accurately": Ibid., 211.
"to write by the": *MF-RE*, 234.
"I cut ruthlessly and": Ibid., 243.
"Finishing is . . . If you": *GOE*, 108.
"the *remises* or storage": *MF-RE*, 225.
"There is nothing cut": *OMS*, 111.
"a man of big": *IIS*, 294.
"He could feel it": Ibid., 263.
"a boy": *GOE*, 56.
"high plateau air": Ibid., 57.
"*felt no remorse*": JK/EH 422.1/8, 5.
"*Don't get remorse even*": JK/EH 422.1/11, 25.
"*I had true remorse*": JK/EH 422.1/15, 22–23.
"*He really wanted to*": JK/EH 422.1/19, 22.
"like in the old days": *GOE*, 168.
"*I loved Madrid too*": JK/EH 422.1/23, 20.
"*I had remorse too*": JK/EH 422.1/36, 26–27.
"The new and strange": *MF-RE*, 217.
"undervalued the power of": Ibid., 218.
"to move steadily and": Ibid., 217.
"a necessary step": Ibid., 218.
"Remorse was a fine": Ibid., 218–19.
"If you deceive and": Ibid., 219.
"without a final chapter": *MF-RE*, 10.
"tried as many as": Burwell, 184.
"many rewrites": Tavernier-Courbin, 36.
"a typed manuscript with": *MF-RE*, 3.
"switching about some chapters": Mary Hemingway, 520.
"I had died before": *MF*, 210.
"perfectly fine": *MF-RE*, 162.
"tormented by . . . truths that": Burwell, 162.
"I failed . . . unfair . . . wonderful but": Brenner, *A Comprehensive Companion to Hemingway's* A Moveable Feast, vol. 1, photograph of letter follows page 215.
"making her out to": Ibid., 4.
"to write an ending": *MF-RE*, 10.
"Still work on it": Tavernier-Courbin, 167.
"betrayal of Hadley with": *MF-RE*, 9.
"(1) 'A Good Café'": Burwell, 161–62, and JK/EH 188.
"all references to Hemingway's": Trogdon in Moddelmog and del Gizzo, 146.
"disturbed . . . excited": *MF*, 5.
"I think it would": Ibid., 7.
"in his home where": *IOT*, 139.
"The story was writing": *MF*, 6.
"plenty of days coming": *IOT*, 156.
"Then I went back": *MF*, 6.
"The girl I was": Ibid., 210.
"The only one, Hadley": *MF-RE*, 123.
"When there were the": Ibid., 197.
"becomes the temporary best": Ibid., 209–10.
"He looked down into": *GOE*, 132.
"The husband has two": *MF*, 210.
"When spring came, even": Ibid., 49.
"nightmare winter": Ibid., 207.
"fight against poverty": Ibid., 51.

"Do you remember": Ibid., 53.
"We should live in": Ibid., 55.
"how much of what": Ibid., 56–57.
"It was a wonderful": Ibid., 57.
"beyond what they had": *GOE*, 14.
"the only thing that": *MF*, 49.
"During our last year": Ibid., 207.
"But Paris was a": Ibid., 58.
"In the spring mornings": Ibid., 49.
"back fast to climb": Ibid., 50.
"belong to me now": Ibid., 6.
"necessary with people as": Ibid., 5.
"I cut ruthlessly and": *MF-RE*, 234.
"the part with Pauline": Ibid., 235.
"Hemingway had decided against": Ibid., 3.
"the authority of editing": *SAR*, 5.
"it is not fair": *FTA-HLE*, 305.
"The bulldozing of three": *MF-RE*, 123.
"complete and entire": *GOE*, 247.

SCATTERED PAPERS

"There was always much": *SS*, 403.
"alone or in clumps": Ibid., 402.
"the letters, letters, letters": Ibid., 403.
"very lush and over-green": Ibid., 404.
"Outside of Fossalta there": Ibid., 408.
"unendingly": *OMS*, 62.

Works Cited

Ashley, Schulyer. "Hemingway Leads Young Ineffectuals Through Europe." The *Kansas City Star*, December 4, 1926, in Nagel, *Critical Essays on Ernest Hemingway's* The Sun Also Rises, 39–41.

Baker, Carlos. *Ernest Hemingway: A Life Story*: New York: Scribner's, 1969.

Baker, Carlos. *Hemingway: The Writer as Artist*. Princeton: Princeton University Press, 1972.

Balassi, William. "The Writing of *The Sun Also Rises*, with a Chart of Its Session-by-Session Development" in Nagel, *Critical Essays on Ernest Hemingway's* The Sun Also Rises, 106–125.

Balzac, Honore de. *Séraphina*. Trans. Clara Bell. New York: J. M. Dent and Company, 1997.

Barthes, Roland. *Mythologies*. New York: Farrar, Straus and Giroux, 1972.

Beegel, Susan F. *Hemingway's Craft of Omission: Four Manuscript Examples*. Ann Arbor: UMI Research Press, 1988.

Beegel, Susan F. *Hemingway's Neglected Short Fiction: New Perspectives*. Ann Arbor: UMI Research Press, 1989.

Bennett, Alan. *The Uncommon Reader*. New York: Farrar, Straus and Giroux, 2007.

Benson, Jackson J., Ed. *New Critical Approaches to the Short Stories of Ernest Hemingway*. Durham: Duke University Press, 1990. Reprints the essay "The Art of the Short Story."

Benson, Jackson J., Ed. *The Short Stories of Ernest Hemingway: Critical Essays*. Durham: Duke University Press, 1975.

Berg, A. Scott. "The Hunt for Hemingway." *Vanity Fair* 614 (October 2011), 282–295.

Berg, A. Scott. *Max Perkins: Editor of Genius*. New York: Dutton, 1978.

Bishop, Elizabeth. *One Art: The Letters of Elizabeth Bishop*. Ed. Robert Giroux. New York: Farrar, Straus and Giroux, 1995.

Blake, William. *The Poetry and Prose of William Blake*. Ed. David V. Erdman. Garden City, NY: Doubleday, 1970.

Bloom, Harold, Ed. *Ernest Hemingway: Bloom's Modern Critical Views*. Philadelphia: Chelsea House, 2005.

Bloom, Harold, Ed. *Modern Critical Interpretations: Ernest Hemingway's* The Old Man and the Sea. Philadelphia: Chelsea House, 1998.

Bouchard, Donald. *Hemingway: So Far from Simple*. Amherst, NY: Prometheus Books, 2010.

Brasch, James D. "Invention from Knowledge: The Hemingway-Cowley Correspondence" in *Ernest Hemingway: The Writer in Context.* Edited by James Nagel. Madison: University of Wisconsin Press, 1984, 201–236.

Brenner, Gerry. *A Comprehensive Companion to Hemingway's* A Moveable Feast: *Annotation to Interpretation.* Lewiston, NY: The Edwin Mellen Press, 2000.

Brenner, Gerry. *Concealments in Hemingway's Works*: Columbus: Ohio State University Press, 1983.

Broer, Lawrence R. *Hemingway's Spanish Tragedy.* University, Alabama: University of Alabama Press, 1973.

Bruccoli, Matthew J., Ed. *Conversations with Ernest Hemingway.* Jackson: University of Mississippi Press, 1986.

Burwell, Rose Marie. *Hemingway: The Postwar Years and The Posthumous Novels.* New York: Cambridge University Press, 1996.

Cirino, Mark. *Ernest Hemingway and the Geography of Memory.* Ed. Mark Cirino and Mark P. Ott. Kent, Ohio: Kent State University Press, 2010.

Cirino, Mark. "The Persistence of Memory and the Denial of Self in *A Farewell to Arms*" in Cirino and Ott, pp. 149–165.

Comley, Nancy R., and Robert Scholes. *Hemingway's Genders: Rereading the Hemingway Text.* New Haven: Yale University Press, 1994.

Cowley, Malcolm. *A Second Flowering: Works and Days of the Lost Generation.* New York: Viking, 1973.

Cowley, Malcolm. "Hemingway's Wound – And Its Consequences for American Literature" in *The Georgia Review* 38.2 (Spring 1984), 223–239.

Cowley, Malcolm. *The Portable Hemingway.* New York: Viking, 1944.

Del Gizzo, Suzanne, and Frederic J. Svoboda, Eds. *Hemingway's* The Garden of Eden: *Twenty-Five Years of Criticism.* Kent, Ohio: Kent State University Press, 2012.

Didion, Joan. *Slouching Towards Bethlehem.* Farrar, Straus and Giroux, 1968.

Doctorow, E. L. *Billy Bathgate.* New York: Random House, 1989.

Donaldson, Scott. *Hemingway vs. Fitzgerald: The Rise and Fall of a Literary Friendship.* New York: Overlook Press, 2000.

Eliot, T. S. "Tradition and the Individual Talent" in *Selected Prose of T. S. Eliot.* Edited by Frank Kermode. New York: Harvest Books, 1975.

Ellison, Ralph. *Shadow and Act.* New York: Random House, 1964.

Evans, Robert. "Hemingway and the Pale Cast of Thought" in Waldhorn, pp. 112–126.

Faulkner, William. *Faulkner: Novels 1926–1929.* New York: Library of America, 2006.

Faulkner, William. *Faulkner: Novels 1936–1940.* New York: Library of America, 1990.

Faulkner, William. *Faulkner: Novels 1942–1954.* New York: Library of America, 1994.

Fiedler, Leslie. *Love and Death in the American Novel* (1960). Urbana: Dalkey Archive Press, 1998.

Fitzgerald, F. Scott. *F. Scott Fitzgerald: A Life in Letters.* Edited by Matthew J. Bruccoli. New York: Scribner's, 1994.

Fitzgerald, F. Scott. *The Great Gatsby* (1925). The Authorized Text. Edited by Matthew J. Bruccoli. New York: Simon & Schuster, 1995.

Fitzgerald, F. Scott. *The Letters of F. Scott Fitzgerald.* Edited by Andrew Turnbull. New York: Scribner's. 1963.

Fleming, Robert E. *The Face in the Mirror: Hemingway's Writers.* Tuscaloosa: University of Alabama Press, 1994.

Fleming, Robert E. "Second Thoughts: Hemingway's Postscript to *The Sun Also Rises*" in Nagel, *Critical Essays on Ernest Hemingway's* The Sun Also Rises, 163–69.

Freud, Sigmund. "Mourning and Melancholia" *in The Freud Reader.* Edited by Peter Gay. New York: Norton, 1989.

Freud, Sigmund. "The 'Uncanny'" (1919). *On Creativity and the Unconscious.* New York: Harper & Row, 1958.

Frye, Northrop. *Anatomy of Criticism.* Princeton: Princeton University Press, 1957.

Gellens, Jay, Ed. *Twentieth Century Interpretations of* A Farewell to Arms: *A Collection of Critical Essays.* Englewood Cliffs, NJ: Prentice Hall, 1970.

Gordimer, Nadine. "Hemingway's Expatriates" in *Telling Times: Writing and Living.* Madison: University of Wisconsin Press, 2012.

Gould, Thomas E. "'A Tiny Operation with Great Effect': Authorial Revision and Editorial Emasculation in the Manuscript of Hemingway's *For Whom the Bell Tolls,*" in Sanderson, 67–81.

Grebstein, Sheldon Norman. *Hemingway's Craft.* Carbondale: Southern Illinois University Press, 1973.

Griffin, Peter. *Along with Youth: Hemingway: The Early Years.* New York: Oxford University Press, 1985.

Hawkins, Ruth A. *Unbelievable Happiness and Final Sorrow: The Hemingway-Pfeiffer Marriage.* Fayetteville: University of Arkansas Press, 2012.

Hemingway, Ernest. Abbreviations and titles follow the format adopted in the Cambridge edition of *The Letters of Ernest Hemingway* (*LEH*).

ARIT Across the River and into the Trees. New York: Scribner's, 1950.

BL By-line Ernest Hemingway: Selected Articles and Dispatches of Four Decades. Edited by William White. New York: Scribner's, 1967.

CSS The Complete Short Stories of Ernest Hemingway: The Finca Vigía Edition. New York: Scribner's, 1987.

DLT Dateline: Toronto: The Complete "Toronto Star" Dispatches, 1920–1924. Edited by William White. New York: Scribner's, 1985.

DIA Death in the Afternoon. New York: Scribner's, 1932.

DS The Dangerous Summer. New York: Scribner's, 1985.

FC The Fifth Column and the First Forty-nine Stories. New York: Scribner's, 1938.

FTA A Farewell to Arms. New York: Scribner's, 1929.

FTA-HLE A Farewell to Arms: The Hemingway Library Edition. New York: Scribner's, 2012.

FWBT For Whom the Bell Tolls. New York: Scribner's, 1940.

GOE The Garden of Eden. New York: Scribner's, 1986.

GHOA Green Hills of Africa. New York: Scribner's, 1935.

IOT In Our Time. Paris: Three Mountains Press, 1924.

IOT In Our Time. New York: Boni and Liveright, 1925. Rev. edn. New York: Scribner's, 1930.
IIS Islands in the Stream. New York: Scribner's, 1970.
LEH The Letters of Ernest Hemingway. Volume 1. Edited by Sandra Spanier and Robert W. Trogdon. New York: Cambridge University Press, 2011.
The Letters of Ernest Hemingway. Volume 2. Edited by Sandra Spanier, Albert J. DeFazio III, and Robert W. Trogdon. New York: Cambridge University Press, 2013.
MAW Men at War. New York: Crown Publisher's, 1942.
MF A Moveable Feast. New York: Scribner's, 1964.
MF-RE A Moveable Feast: The Restored Edition. Edited by Seàn Hemingway. New York: Scribner's, 2009.
MWW Men Without Women. New York: Scribner's, 1927.
NAS The Nick Adams Stories. New York: Scribner's, 1972.
OMS The Old Man and the Sea. New York: Scribner's, 1952.
Poems Complete Poems. Edited, with an Introduction and Notes by Nicholas Gerogiannis. Rev. edn. Lincoln: University of Nebraska Press, 1972.
SAR The Sun Also Rises. New York: Scribner's, 1926.
SAR-HLE The Sun Also Rises: The Hemingway Library Edition. New York: Scribner's, 2014.
SL Ernest Hemingway: Selected Letters, 1917–1961. Edited by Carlos Baker. New York: Scribner's, 1981.
SS The Short Stories of Ernest Hemingway. New York: Scribner's, 1954.
TAFL True at First Light. Edited by Patrick Hemingway. New York: Scribner's, 1999.
THHN To Have and Have Not. New York: Scribner's, 1937.
TOS The Torrents of Spring. New York: Scribner's, 1926.
TOTTC The Only Thing That Counts: The Ernest Hemingway-Maxwell Perkins Correspondence, 1925–1947. Edited by Matthew J. Bruccoli with Robert W. Trogdon. New York: Scribner's, 1996.
TSTP Three Stories and Ten Poems. Paris: Contact Editions, 1923.
UK Under Kilimanjaro. Edited by Robert W. Lewis and Robert E. Fleming. Kent, Ohio: Kent State University Press, 2005.
WTN Winner Take Nothing. New York: Scribner's. 1933.
Hemingway, Ernest. "The Art of the Short Story" (1981) in Benson.
Hemingway, Ernest. First Installment of *Green Hills of Africa* in *Scribner's Magazine*, May 1935, Volume XCVII, No. 5.
Hemingway, Mary. *How It Was*. New York: Knopf, 1976.
Hoffman, Frederick J. "The Secret Wound" in Gellens.
Hoffman, Frederick J. *The Twenties*. New York: Viking, 1955.
Hovey, Richard. *Hemingway: The Inward Terrain*. Seattle: University of Washington Press, 1968.
James, Henry. "Henry James's First Interview" in *The New York Times*, March 21, 1915.

James, Henry. *Literary Criticism, Volume Two: European Works, Prefaces to the New York Edition*. New York: Library of America, 1984.

James, Henry. *Notes of a Son and Brother*. New York: Scribner's, 1914.

James, Henry. *Selected Letters*. Ed. Leon Edel. Boston: Harvard University Press, 1987.

James, William. *William James: Writings 1902–1910*. New York: Library of America, 1987.

Jenks, Tom. "Editing Hemingway: The Garden of Eden." *Hemingway Review* 7.1 (1987) 30–33.

Jenks, Tom. "An Interview with Tom Jenks." *Dictionary of Literary Biography Yearbook*. Ed. J. M. Brook. Detroit: BCL / Gale, 1987, 82–87.

Jobes, Katharine T. *Twentieth Century Interpretations of* The Old Man and the Sea. Englewood Cliffs, NJ: Prentice Hall, 1968.

Keats, John. *Selected Letters of John Keats*. Ed. Grant F. Scott. Cambridge: Harvard University Press, 2002.

Kempton, Daniel. "Sexual Transgression and Artistic Creativity in *The Garden of Eden*" in del Gizzo, 291–297.

Kennedy, J. Gerald. "Hemingway's Gender Trouble" in del Gizzo, 167–184.

Kert, Bernice. *The Hemingway Women*. New York: Norton, 1983.

Lamb, Robert Paul. *Art Matters: Hemingway, Craft, and the Creation of the Modern Short Story*. Baton Rouge: Louisiana State University Press, 2010.

Lamb, Robert Paul. "The Currents of Memory: Hemingway's 'Big Two-Hearted River' as Metafiction" in Cirino and Ott, 166–185.

Lawrence, D. H. *The Works of D. H. Lawrence: Introductions and Reviews*. Cambridge: Cambridge University Press, 2005.

Leonard, John. "*The Garden of Eden*: A Question of Dates" in del Gizzo, 58–74.

Lewis, Robert E. "Hemingway in Italy: Making It Up" in *Journal of Modern Literature*. Vol. 9, No. 2 (May 1982), 209–236.

Lewis, Robert W. "The Making of *Death in the Afternoon*" in Nagel, *Ernest Hemingway: The Writer in Context*, 31–52.

Lewis, Wyndham. "The Dumb Ox: A Study of Ernest Hemingway" in *Life and Letters*, April, 1934.

Lowell, Robert. *Collected Poems*. New York: Farrar, Straus and Giroux, 2003.

Lynn, Kenneth S. *Hemingway*. New York: Simon & Schuster, 1987.

Mann, Charles, and Philip Young, Eds. *Catalogue of the Ernest Hemingway Collection*.

Mellow, James R. *Hemingway: A Life Without Consequences*. Boston: Houghton Mifflin, 1992.

Milton, John. *Complete Poems and Major Prose*. Ed. Merritt Y. Hughes. New York: Odyssey Press, 1957.

Moddelmog, Debra A., and Suzanne del Gizzo, Eds. *Ernest Hemingway in Context*. New York: Cambridge University Press, 2013.

Moddelmog, Debra A., *Reading Desire: In Pursuit of Ernest Hemingway*. Ithaca: Cornell University Press, 1999.

Nabokov, Vladimir. *Strong Opinions*. New York: Vintage, 1990.

Nagel, James, Ed. *Critical Essays on Ernest Hemingway's* The Sun Also Rises. New York: Simon & Schuster, 1995.

Nagel, James, Ed. *Ernest Hemingway: The Writer in Context*. Madison: University of Wisconsin Press, 1984.

Nesmith, Chris L. "The Law of an Ancient God and the Editing of Hemingway's *Garden of Eden*: The Final Corrected Typescript and Galleys" in *The Hemingway Review*. Vol. 2. No. 2, Spring 2001, 16–36.

Oldsey, Bernard. *Ernest Hemingway: The Papers of a Writer*. New York: Garland Publishing, 1981.

Oldsey, Bernard. *Hemingway's Hidden Craft: The Writing of* A Farewell to Arms. University Park: Pennsylvania State University Press, 1979.

Peterson, Richard K. *Hemingway: Direct and Oblique*. The Hague: Mouton, 1969.

Price, Reynolds. *A Common Room: Essays 1954–1987*. New York: Atheneum, 1987.

Reynolds, Michael. *Hemingway: The 1930s*. New York: Norton, 1997.

Reynolds, Michael. *Hemingway: The American Homecoming*. Oxford: Basil Blackwell, 1992.

Reynolds, Michael. *Hemingway: The Final Years*. New York: Norton, 1999.

Reynolds, Michael. *Hemingway: The Paris Years*. Oxford: Basil Blackwell, 1989.

Reynolds, Michael. *Hemingway's First War: The Making of* A Farewell to Arms. Princeton: Princeton University Press, 1976.

Reynolds, Michael. *Hemingway's Reading. 1910–1940: An Inventory*. Princeton: Princeton University Press, 1981.

Reynolds, Michael. *The Young Hemingway*. Oxford: Basil Blackwell, 1986.

Ross, Lillian. *Reporting*. New York: Simon & Schuster, 1964.

Rovit, Earl, and Gerry Brenner. *Ernest Hemingway*. Revised Edition. Boston: Twayne, 1968.

Sanderson, Rena, Ed. *Blowing the Bridge: Essays on Hemingway and* For Whom the Bell Tolls. New York: Greenwood Press, 1992.

Sartre, Jean Paul. "An Explication of *The Stranger*" in *Camus: A Collection of Critical Essays*. Edited by Germaine Brée. Englewood Cliffs, NJ: Prentice Hall, 1962, 108–119.

Smith, Paul. *A Reader's Guide to the Short Stories of Ernest Hemingway*. Boston: G. K. Hall, 1989.

Spilka, Mark. *Hemingway's Quarrel with Androgyny*. Lincoln: University of Nebraska Press, 1990.

Stanton, Edward F. *Hemingway and Spain: A Pursuit*. Seattle: University of Washington Press, 1989.

Stein, Gertrude. *Stein: Writings, 1903–1932*. New York: Library of America, 1998.

Stoneback, H. R. "The Priest Did Not Answer: Hemingway, the Church, the Party, and *For Whom the Bell Tolls*" in Sanderson, 99–112.

Strychacz, Thomas. *Hemingway's Theaters of Masculinity*. Baton Rouge: Louisiana State University Press, 2003.

Svoboda, Frederic Joseph. *Hemingway and* The Sun Also Rises: *The Crafting of a Style*. Lawrence: University Press of Kansas, 1983.

Tavernier-Courbin, Jacqueline. *Ernest Hemingway's* A Moveable Feast: *The Making of A Myth*. Boston: Northeastern University Press, 1991.

Trogdon, Robert W. "Posthumous Publications" in Moddlemog and del Gizzo, 141–150.

Waldhorn, Arthur, ed. *Ernest Hemingway: A Collection of Criticism*. New York: McGraw-Hill, 1973.

Warren, Robert Penn. *All the King's Men*. New York: Harcourt Brace Jovanovich, 1946.

Warren, Robert Penn. *Talking with Robert Penn Warren*. Eds. Floyd C. Watkins, John T. Hiers, and Mary Louise Weeks. Athens: University of Georgia Press, 1990.

Wilde, Oscar. "The Critic as Artist" in *The Artist as Critic: Critical Writings of Oscar Wilde*. Edited by Richard Ellmann. Chicago: University of Chicago Press, 1982.

Williams, Bernard. *Shame and Necessity*. Berkeley: University of California Press, 1994.

Willingham, Kathy. "Hemingway's *The Garden of Eden*: Writing with the Body" in del Gizzo, 221–236.

Wilson, Edmund. "Hemingway: Gauge of Morale" (1939) in Bloom, *Ernest Hemingway: Bloom's Modern Critical Views*, 7–24.

Wilson, Edmund. *The Wound and the Bow: Seven Studies in Literature*. (1941). New York: Oxford University Press, 1965.

Wilson, Jane E. "Good Old Harris in *The Sun Also Rises*" in Nagel, *Critical Essays on Ernest Hemingway's* The Sun Also Rises, 185–90.

Woolf, Tobias. *Old School*. New York: Knopf, 2003.

Wordsworth, William. *Wordsworth: Poetical Works*. London: Oxford University Press, 1974.

Wyatt, David. "Hemingway's Uncanny Beginnings." *The Georgia Review*. Vol. 31 (Summer 1977), 476–501.

Yeats, W. B. *The Collected Poems of W. B. Yeats*. New York: Macmillan, 1956.

Young, Philip. *Ernest Hemingway*. New York: Rinehart & Company, 1952.

Young, Philip. *Ernest Hemingway: A Reconsideration*. University Park: Pennsylvania State University Press, 1966.

Index

Anderson, Sherwood, 203

Baker, Carlos, 27, 84–86, 182, 187, 198
  Ernest Hemingway: A Life Story, 84–86
Balassi, William, 154
Balzac, Honoré de, 211
Barthes, Roland, 115
Battlefields of the World War, 83
Beegel, Susan F., 114, 125
Bennett, Alan, 95
  The Uncommon Reader, 95
Berenson, Bernard, 187
Berg, A. Scott, 160
Bird, William, 102
Bishop, Elizabeth, 2, 63
Blake, William, 23, 198, 201–202
Boni and Liveright, 29, 33
Bordeaux, 83
Borges, Jorge Luis, 18
Bouchard, Donald, 114, 119–120
Brague, Harry, 203, 220, 222
Brenner, Gerry, 6, 185
  Concealments in Hemingway's Works, 185
Burwell, Rose Marie, 5–6, 8, 64, 197–199, 205, 223–224
  Hemingway: The Postwar Years and the Posthumous Novels, 5, 197

Caporetto, 70, 83
Castro, Fidel, 1
Cezanne, Paul, 44–45
Cirino, Mark, 164
Codroipo, 63
Comley, Nancy, 16, 126
Conrad, Joseph, 2
Copenhaver, Eleanor, 203
Cowley, Malcolm, 5, 85–86, 88, 93
  "Hemingway's Wound—And Its Consequences for American Literature," 88
  The Portable Hemingway, 88
  A Second Flowering: Works and Days of the Lost Generation, 5

DeVoto, Bernard, 119
Didion, Joan, 128
DiMaggio, Joe, 183, 192
Doctorow, E. L., 150–151, 201
  Billy Bathgate, 150–151
Dorman-Smith, E. E. "Chink," 99–100

Eliot, T. S., 113
  "Tradition and the Individual Talent," 113
Ellison, Ralph, 165–166
  Shadow and Act, 165
Emerson, Ralph Waldo, 164
Esquire, 115, 180
Evans, Robert, 164
  "Hemingway and the Pale Cast of Thought," 164

Faulkner, William, 148, 162–163, 170, 179, 186
  Requiem for a Nun, 162–163, 170
Fiedler, Leslie, 16
Fitzgerald, F. Scott, 50, 56–62, 64–65, 185, 223–224
  The Great Gatsby, 58
Fitzgerald, Zelda, 60
Flaubert, Gustave, 112
Fleming, Robert E., 61
Florence, 85
Ford, Ford Madox, 28
Fossalta, 76, 83, 87, 233
Freud, Sigmund, 17–18, 22, 41–42, 89, 104
  "Mourning and Melancholia," 104
  "The 'Uncanny'", 17–18
Friedan, Betty, 207
Frisch, Max, 2
Frye, Northrop, 127–128, 156
  Anatomy of Criticism, 156

Ganivet, Angel, 111
  Idearium Espanol, 111
Gellhorn, Martha, 204, 207
Gingrich, Arnold, 175
Gordimer, Nadine, 117–118
Gould, Thomas. E., 151
Gradisca d'Isonzo, 63
Grebstein, Sheldon, 74
Guthrie, Pat, 61

Havana, 1
Heap, Jane, 27
Hemingway, Ernest
Books:
  Across the River and into the Trees, 4, 46, 65, 107, 112, 188–190
  The Dangerous Summer, 49
  Dateline: Toronto: The Complete "Toronto Star" Dispatches, 1920–1924, 4
  Death in the Afternoon, 5, 23, 42, 45, 49, 83, 99–116, 118, 208, 232
  A Farewell to Arms, 4, 7, 24, 34, 41, 63–95, 110, 157–158, 166–167, 173, 175–176, 183, 187, 207, 214, 234
  A Farewell to Arms: The Hemingway Library Edition, 8, 74–75, 78–80
  The First Forty-Nine Stories, 33
  For Whom the Bell Tolls, 2–5, 23, 46, 111, 122, 125, 147–188, 207, 230, 232
  The Garden of Eden, 3–4, 6, 8, 25, 27, 90–91, 181, 197–232
  Green Hills of Africa, 41, 50, 117–133, 135, 139, 151
  in our time, 27–46
  In Our Time, 13–46, 76, 87–88, 110–112, 130, 172–174, 183, 225–226, 230
  Islands in the Stream, 5, 8, 77, 198, 220
  The Letters of Ernest Hemingway (Cambridge), 36, 235
  Men at War, 4, 24
  Men Without Women, 35, 150
  A Moveable Feast, 4–5, 8, 15, 23, 30–31, 39, 43–45, 52, 56, 59, 61, 106–107, 112, 181, 197–232
  A Moveable Feast: The Restored Edition, 8, 94, 208–211, 220–226, 228, 230–232
  The Nick Adams Stories, 21–22, 24, 28, 32, 35, 44–46
  The Old Man and the Sea, 4, 179–193, 220, 234
  The Short Stories of Ernest Hemingway, 4
  The Sun Also Rises, 4, 8, 16, 19, 49–62, 72, 92, 94, 110, 130, 166, 175–176, 183, 204–205, 214
  The Sun Also Rises: The Hemingway Library Edition, 4
  Three Stories and Ten Poems, 28
  To Have and Have Not, 189
  The Torrents of Spring, 33, 207
  True at First Light, 8, 198
  Under Kilimanjaro, 8, 198, 203
  Winner Take Nothing, 35
Stories and Sketches:
  Another Country, 187
  The Battler, 29–30
  Big Two-Hearted River, 17, 21, 28, 32, 34–35, 37–46, 90, 92, 111, 164–167, 179, 219, 226, 230
  Birth of a New School, 61, 95, 225
  Cat in the Rain, 29, 34
  Cross-Country Snow, 29, 34
  The Doctor and the Doctor's Wife, 29
  The End of Something, 29, 35, 179, 183
  A False Spring, 228–229
  Fathers and Sons, 35, 42
  A Good Café in the Place St.-Michel, 230
  Hunger Was Good Discipline, 40
  Indian Camp, 5, 13–26, 28–33, 40–46, 89, 110–111, 130, 172–174, 183, 187, 213, 230
  The Last Good Country, 154
  L'Envoi, 32, 111
  Mr. and Mrs. Elliot, 29
  My Old Man, 27–29, 37
  Now I Lay Me, 41, 84, 89–92
  On the Quai at Smyrna, 16, 32–33, 111
  On Writing, 21, 44–46, 49, 165
  On Writing in the First Person, 94
  Out of Season, 28
  The Pilot Fish and the Rich, 210, 221
  The Revolutionist, 29
  The Short Happy Life of Francis Macomber, 104, 127–129, 132, 133–143, 155, 163
  The Snows of Kilimanjaro, 9, 127–129, 132, 203
  Soldier's Home, 29, 83, 87, 105
  The Strange Country, 41, 81
  There Is Never Any End to Paris, 221–222, 224, 231
  The Three-Day Blow, 29–30, 35, 42
  Three Shots, 24, 32
  The Undefeated, 139
  Up in Michigan, 27–30
  A Very Short Story, 29
  A Way You'll Never Be, 40, 233–234
  Winters in Shruns, 226, 231
Hemingway, Grace, 180, 197
Hemingway, Gregory, 180
Hemingway, Hadley Richardson, 27–28, 36, 90, 107, 185, 204–205, 207–232
Hemingway, Mary Welsh, 1–2, 6, 160, 198, 203, 220, 222–225
  How It Was, 223
Hemingway, Pauline Pfeiffer, 147, 180–181, 197, 202–204, 207–211, 219–232

Hemingway, Seán, 8, 74–75, 78–80, 208, 223–224, 231
Hoffman, Frederick J., 88
"The Secret Wound," 88
The Twenties, 88
Hovey, Richard, 42, 164
Hemingway: The Inward Terrain, 164

James, Henry, 82, 92–93, 112, 207
James, William, 157
Jenks, Tom, 25, 93, 204, 220–221
Joyce, James, 131
Finnegans Wake, 29

Keats, John, 122
John F. Kennedy Library, 1–2, 6, 30, 32, 37, 44, 58, 73–75, 79, 149, 160, 165, 223, 233–234, 235
Kennedy, J. Gerald, 199
Kennedy, Jacqueline Bouvier, 2
Kennedy, John Fitzgerald, 2
Ketchum, Idaho, 1
Key West, 209, 234

Lamb, Robert Paul, 106, 142
Lane, Cornelia, 203
Lawrence, D. H., 35, 39
Leonard, John, 198–199
Lewis, Robert W., 85
"Hemingway in Italy: Making It Up," 85
Lewis, Wyndham, 164
Life Magazine, 179
The Little Review, 27, 44
Liveright, Horace, 30, 115
Loeb, Harold, 61
Lowell, Robert, 81
Lynn, Kenneth, 88–89

McAlmon, Robert, 28, 102
MacLeish, Archibald, 81
Mann, Charles, 60
Mann, Thomas, 123
Marvell, Andrew, 48
Milan, 73, 83–84
Milton, John, 65–66, 201–203
"Lycidas," 65
Paradise Lost, 201–203
Mitchell, Tennessee, 203
Moddelmog, Debra, 89
Mowrer, Paul, 223

Nabokov, Vladimir, 48
Nairobi, 130
New York *Sun*, 84, 86–87
New York *Times*, 82, 119
The New Yorker Magazine, 55

O'Brien, Edward J., 29
Oldsey, Bernard, 7, 32, 64, 73–75, 85

Pamplona, 99, 75
Paris, 27–28, 197, 210, 219, 222, 225
Paris Review, 56, 107
Perkins, Margaret "Peggy," 160–161
Perkins, Maxwell, 33, 36, 56, 59–60, 92–93, 149, 159–161, 174, 180, 183, 207, 231
Peterson, Richard, 151
Petosky, 234
Pfeiffer, Gustavus Adolphus, 207
Pfeiffer, Virginia, 180
Phillips, Jenny, 160
Piggott, Arkansas, 210
Plimpton, George, 107, 151
Pound, Ezra, 27–29, 36, 100
Prall, Elizabeth, 203
Price, Reynolds, 47, 67, 77, 124, 185–186

Querschnitt, 119

Reynolds, Michael, 6–7, 24, 63, 74, 78–80, 82, 85–87, 114, 119, 126, 197
Hemingway's First War, 74, 78–80, 82, 85–87
The Young Hemingway, 86
Rovit, Earl, 6

Sartre, Jean-Paul, 41
Sassoon, Siegfried, 2
Scholes, Robert, 16, 126
Scribner, Charles Jr., 180–181, 188
Scribner, Charles IV, 203, 222
Scribner's, 33, 59, 117, 203, 223
Scribner's Magazine, 126
Shakespeare, William, 18, 201
Shenandoah, 179
Smith, William, 99, 203
Smith, Paul, 30, 32, 91, 138, 142–143
Spilka, Mark, 56, 68–69, 88, 201
Hemingway's Quarrel with Androgyny, 88
Stanton, Edward F., 108–109
Stein, Gertrude, 29, 44, 61
Stendhal, 123
Stevens, Wallace, 63
Stewart, Donald Ogden, 45
Stoneback, H. R., 152
The Story of the Red Cross in Italy, 83
Strychacz, Thomas, 38, 187
Svoboda, Frederic, 50, 55, 60, 87
Hemingway and The Sun Also Rises, 60

Time Magazine, 55
Toklas, Alice B., 44

Tolstoy, Leo, 123
Sevastopol Sketches, 124
Toronto, 28
Toronto *Star*, 102
Transatlantic Review, 29, 31
Trogdon, Robert, 225
Turgenev, Ivan, 123
Turnbull, Andrew, 60
The Letters of F. Scott Fitzgerald, 60
Twysden, Duff, 61

Udine, 61

Valencia, 152
Venice, 83
University of Virginia Special Collections, 57, 117, 235

Walsh, Ernest, 35, 70
Walton, William, 1
War and Peace, 24
Warren, Robert Penn, 5, 165
Wilde, Oscar, 100–101
The Critic as Artist, 100–101
Williams, Bernard, 133–134, 142
Shame and Necessity, 134
Willingham, Kathy, 201
Wister, Owen, 14, 73
With British Guns in Italy, 83
Wolff, Tobias, 126
Woolf, Virginia, 150
Wordsworth, William, 34

Yeats, William Butler, 172
Young, Philip, 21, 28, 32, 35, 38, 60, 81, 88, 93, 165, 184
Ernest Hemingway, 88
Ernest Hemingway: A Reconsideration, 81, 88, 184

Lightning Source UK Ltd.
Milton Keynes UK
UKOW04f0823010218
317193UK00001B/236/P

9 781107 525290